Warwickshire County Council

MOBILE LIBRARY SERVICE

7/12
Stegga...

D0589986

5/4/18
1 1 DEC 2012   26/4
                     17/5
                      6/6

2 8 MAR 2013

This item is to be returned or renewed before the latest date above. It may be borrowed for a further period if not in demand. **To renew your books:**

- **Phone the 24/7 Renewal Line 01926 499273 or**
- **Visit www.warwickshire.gov.uk/libraries**

Discover • Imagine • Learn • *with libraries*

Warwickshire County Council

Working for Warwickshire

ℂONTENTS

ACKNOWLEDGMENTS

I should like to thank all those who have helped in the preparation of this book, either by providing material or in other ways. In particular, my thanks are due to the Master and Fellows of Trinity College, Cambridge, for permission to quote from the Munby diaries and to the staff at the libraries and record offices in which I have worked. These include the Bodleian Library, Oxford, the British Library, Reading University Library, the British Library of Political and Economic Science at the London School of Economics, the Museum of English Rural Life, Reading, the National Archives, London, and county record offices for Berkshire, Buckinghamshire, Dorset, Essex, Gloucestershire, Hampshire, Northamptonshire, Oxfordshire, Warwickshire and Worcestershire. I am indebted to them for much efficient assistance.

I am equally indebted to the editors of the *Land Worker*, the *Western Morning News* and the *Oxford Times* who inserted appeals for reminiscences and photographs of Victorian country life on my behalf, and to all those who so kindly answered these appeals. Some of the material they sent has been incorporated in the book and is acknowledged in the reference notes.

Finally, I owe a debt of gratitude to my family for help in the preparation of the book. My mother, indeed, knew at first hand something of village life in the early years of the last century, while my brother-in-law gave much help on conditions in Buckinghamshire. But as always I owe a particular debt to my late husband, who helped in so many different ways. Without his assistance neither this nor any of my books could have been written.

Pamela Horn

1

THE RURAL COMMUNITY: A BACKGROUND SURVEY

From 1800 and up to about 1918 ... communities (and the poorer or working classes in them) passed through an era of authority. They were dominated by those who owned the land. This system of domination was expressed through the squire's personality, in his family circle and estate, in institutions and parish government ... Inside the boundaries of the country estate (and in country rectories) there was affluence, leisure and conviviality. Outside it small farmers, craftsmen and village labourers eked out a bare living ... Everyone accepted the fact that the axis of rural life was the country house and the estate. When squires served as magistrates or guardians they did so with full knowledge of their role. No one opposed them openly unless reckless enough to court social disaster ... If a labourer poached pheasants or partridges, hares or rabbits, the squire would judge him in his office of magistrate; if a farmer was behind with his rent the squire chided him as landlord, and if a family failed to attend church regularly the squire, as parish leader, would question the head of that household.

E. W. Martin, *The Shearers and the Shorn* (1965)

In the closed or estate village there was at least the appearance of a well-ordered existence which was symbolised by the neat cottages, the well-kept gardens and allotments, the excellent repair of the farmhouses and farm buildings, the well-kept hedges and the overall appearance of thoughtful planning of the village landscape.

George Ewart Evans, *Where Beards Wag All* (1970)

When Queen Victoria came to the throne in 1837 the majority of her subjects were countrymen, dependent for their livelihood upon agriculture and upon the vagaries of the seasons and of harvest yields. Despite the spreading influence of northern industrialism, rural life and the village community still dominated English society. The ploughman and his horses tilled the soil, the seeds were sown, and in due time the crops were gathered. Other members of the rural community, such as the country craftsmen – carpenters, wheelwrights, blacksmiths, millers and saddlers served the needs of the farmers and were reliant upon agricultural prosperity for their own well-being. Together they formed a tightly knit group, integrated for the carrying out of a particular task – the cultivation of the soil and the raising of stock – and for them mutual dependence and co-operation were essential. Farming was still a labour-intensive industry and at harvest time the whole village would turn out to bring in the crops safely.

Sometimes this self-sufficiency led to narrowness of outlook and parochialism, with people from even the next village regarded as strangers. Although ordinary commerce made contacts between parishes for business purposes inevitable, 'any intimacy was frowned upon: to be married to [anyone from] one of them was almost a crime'. Even at the close of the nineteenth century, when transport improvements and increased mobility of labour had broken down many barriers, a girl from Needham Market in East Anglia who was walking out with a man from the next parish was told by her father: 'You must not do it! I can't have a daughter of mine a-courting one o'those owd Creeting *jackdaws*.' Creeting was less than half a mile away, on the other side of the river.[1]

In the commercial sphere, however, farms were linked to one another and to their customers by a network of markets, ranging from ancient fairs to the new Corn Exchanges which were springing up in many country towns by the middle of the century. Most of the towns and even the bigger villages had their weekly market, to which farmers' wives and daughters brought their poultry and eggs, their butter, cheese, honey and fruit for direct sale to the householder. They rode in gigs and pony carts, or by side-saddle on a quiet pony. Some travelled by carrier's cart, while others came on foot, bringing their baskets of goods with them. The carrier on his own account also collected produce from local farms to sell in nearby markets or in town shops on behalf of the farmer. Even at the end of the nineteenth century one old Leicestershire carrier remembered collecting thousands of eggs and a large quantity of poultry each week for sale in the county town. At Christmas time rods or poles were fixed to the top and sides of the cart and hundreds of birds were suspended from them, for eventual disposal to a shopkeeper with whom prior arrangements had been made. Dairy produce, fruit and vegetables would likewise be despatched by carrier's cart, while on his return the carrier would bring the tea, medicaments and other small items required by his fellow villagers. Mr D. Thomas, member of a family of carriers from Leckhampstead in Berkshire, who visited Newbury each week, likewise recalls that items of drapery or clothing were sent out to villagers 'on approval' by way of the carrier. He had to undertake to return them safely to the shops if they were not sold. And for the 'weekly Newbury papers we used to have a standing order of about 9 or 10 dozen, and return what was unsold. We used to bring brewer's yeast to help make the bread of the local bakers.' Passengers also travelled into Newbury with the carrier – at a fare of 1*d* a mile.[2]

Alongside these smaller retail arrangements, many towns would have a day set aside for cattle sales, when the butchers and dealers would haggle over pigs and sheep, calves and cattle, and when the main street became a 'pandemonium of bargaining men, bleating sheep, frightened bullocks and pathetically muzzled calves unable to suckle their unmilked dams'. Such markets, designed to satisfy local needs, were supplemented by sales made on the farms to the agents of wholesalers, so that the larger farmers did not always need to carry their corn or drive their cattle to market.

The coming of the railways to some degree disturbed the old pattern of trading, bringing certain centres into greater prominence at the expense of those still reliant upon the footpaths and drove-roads of an earlier era. But to the end of the century local markets continued to play an important role, both as outlets for farm produce and as places where the labourer and the rural craftsman and their families could make their modest weekly purchases.

In spite of the hurry and bustle of market days and the movement of the herds of cattle along the drove-roads, the early Victorian countryside remained largely unaffected by events in the outside world. Newspapers were expensive and, in any case, few men were able to read well enough to search for information from that source. Such news of wider events as did reach farm and cottage came by way of the pedlar, the carrier and the traveller at the village inn.

Yet, at least in southern and central England, this rural calm was shattered for a time in 1830 by rioting, as gangs of men moved through the countryside, burning stacks and destroying the threshing machines which threatened their already scanty winter employment. It was a spontaneous reaction by workers made desperate by low wages and unemployment. The riots started near Canterbury at the end of August 1830, with the destruction of a threshing machine, but by November had spread to many other counties, including Sussex, Hampshire, Wiltshire, Berkshire, Oxfordshire and East Anglia. In West Sussex, for example, the men of Ringmer took a leading role, demanding higher wages, a dismantling of all threshing machines and the dismissal of unpopular poor law overseers, as well as of the governor of Ringmer poor house. At Overton in nearby Hampshire, several hundred labourers paraded the streets demanding money and food and higher wages, 'saying that they had been starving too long on a diet of potatoes and bread'.[3]

Although the disturbances caused considerable alarm among better-off members of rural society, they were quickly suppressed. In the end nineteen men were executed for their part in the riots, nearly five hundred were sentenced to transportation to Australia and over six hundred more were imprisoned.[4] In the years that followed, other isolated upsurges of discontent occurred, as, for example, after the passage of the 1834 Poor Law Amendment Act which sought to tighten up the distribution of poor relief to able-bodied labourers. But these uprisings were easily brushed aside by the authorities, as was the incendiarism in the Eastern Counties during the difficult years of 1843 and 1844, when men were dismissed by farmers hit by falling grain prices. Numbers of men and boys were charged with arson at the assizes and convicted. But these rumblings of discontent never flared into mass violence, and in 1837 when the Queen ascended the throne, the events of seven years earlier seemed little more than a bad dream. Not until the agricultural trade union movement of the 1870s was there another large-scale and effective expression of discontent on the part of land workers.

Despite this darker side, therefore, to many contemporaries it was the peaceful character of village life in the early Victorian years which was worthy of emphasis. Men such as William Howitt wrote in optimistic vein of 'cottages half buried in their garden and orchard trees' in southern and midland England. Howitt saw 'home-crofts, with their old, tall hedges ... rows of bee-hives beneath their little thatched, southern sheds ... rich fields and farm houses, surrounded with wealth of corn-ricks, and herds and flocks ... hedgers and ditchers, ploughmen and substantial farmers, who seem to keep through life the 'peaceful tenor of their way,' in old-English fullness and content'.[5]

But others, like Alfred Austin, an Assistant Poor Law Commissioner, saw a much harsher reality beneath the picturesque exterior in less fortunate parishes. When he reported on the cottages of the west of England in 1843 Austin declared:

It is impossible not to be struck, in visiting the dwellings of the agricultural labourers, with the general want of new cottages, notwithstanding the universal increase of population. Everywhere the cottages are old, and frequently in a state of decay, and are consequently ill adapted for their increased number of inmates of late years. The floor of the room in which the family live during the day is always of stone in these counties, and wet or damp through the winter months, being frequently lower than the soil outside ... In the village of Stourpain, in Dorsetshire, there is a row of several labourers' cottages, mostly joining each other, and fronting the street, in the middle of which is an open gutter. There are two or three narrow passages leading from the street, between the houses, to the back of them. Behind the cottages the ground rises rather abruptly; and about three yards up the elevation are placed the pigsties and privies of the cottages ... The matter constantly escaping from the pigsties, privies, &c, is allowed to find its way through the passage between the cottages into the gutter in the street, so that the cottages are nearly surrounded by streams of filth ... This is perhaps an extreme case; but I hardly visited a cottage where were any attempts at draining.[6] (See also Appendix B)

Although the passage of sanitary legislation from the late 1840s (particularly the relevant sections of the 1890 Housing Act) helped to raise standards by the end of the nineteenth. century, serious weaknesses persisted. Even in 1915 the Medical Officer of Health for Somerset could write:

The idea of every country cottage standing in its own grounds with its well-filled kitchen garden kept in order by the labourer in his spare time is one which we could wish realised, but which is very far from being the reality. Every variation is met with from the cottage with an acre or more of land attached, to half-a-dozen or more houses crowded together on a little piece of land without back entrances or even space for the provision of proper sanitary conveniences.[7]

Another critic, in an article in the *Land Magazine* of 1900, declared that the public health acts were 'treated in country districts as so much waste paper'.

Certainly the attractions of village life were insufficient to prevent the heavy migration of country folk to the towns in the second half of the nineteenth century, and in the year of Queen Victoria's death less than one-quarter of the total population was living in rural areas. The townsman was now the typical Englishman and cries of 'rural depopulation' were heard throughout the land. The appeal of urban trades, offering better wages, a higher social status and more free time, had become too strong for villagers, and fears were widely expressed that this would mean the disappearance of those who had provided 'the power and permanent strength' of the country. Politicians responded by passing legislation in the 1880s and 1890s designed to increase the number of allotments and smallholdings available, but the benefits derived from having a small 'stake in the soil' were more than outweighed by the growing opportunities for employment in the towns or overseas in Australasia and North America. The flood of men leaving the countryside continued, with the loss of the younger men a particular cause for concern. As one Wiltshire agriculturist declared in 1901: 'Young men ... are now seldom to be seen upon the land, while hedgers, ditchers and thatchers are all over fifty years of age.' In that year more than one-fifth of all the men engaged in agriculture were over the age of fifty-five – the only occupational grouping at that date with such a high proportion of older men. At the same time the aggregate number of male farm labourers, shepherds and farm servants employed at all ages in England and Wales had fallen from over 920,000 in 1871 to just over 600,000 thirty years later.

However, the drift from the land was partly a response also to the falling demand for labour on the part of farmers faced with growing competition from cheap imported grain, dairy produce and refrigerated meat. From the late 1870s hard-hit arable producers moved over to less labour-intensive pastoral farming or cut corners in the tilling of their soil. Cornelius Stovin of Binbrook, Lincolnshire, was not the only substantial tenant farmer who responded to the bleakness of the 1880s and 1890s by reducing his labour force to a minimum, and expecting all the children in the family to help with the work before and after school. It was an uncomfortable existence but 'they kept going, making a bare living until the first years of the present century when conditions slowly improved and farming began to show some profit again'.[8] Machinery became a substitute for labour on many farms, especially at the busy hay and corn harvests, when mowers, reapers and self-binding reapers greatly reduced the demand for casual work.

Nor was it only the agricultural labourers who were leaving the countryside. Although the number of farmers remained steady, country craftsmen found their skills undermined by the cheaper products of the factory, and gradually the village shoemaker, the tailor and even the baker disappeared from the scene. From the 1870s some of the isolation and self-sufficiency of the village community was breaking down, so that ploughs and agricultural implements were made in the towns, rather than by the village blacksmith. Farm carts, ladders, milking stools, buckets, hayrakes and countless other tools – the work of the carpenter and wheelwright – were also mass-produced. Village life itself changed, for the decline in the number of tradesmen and artisans meant the loss of men who had always formed the nucleus of village associations. They had fostered independence of thought – the radicalism of the village shoemaker was proverbial – and had provided the social leadership which was so clearly lacking among the rural labouring classes in the last years of the century, once the agricultural trade union movement of the 1870s had faded away.

Yet, despite these changes and the migration of population from country districts, for those who remained behind the basic hierarchical structure of village society survived. In its stereotype of the 'closed' parish, where land ownership was concentrated in the hands of one or two proprietors only, the stratification was at its clearest. At the head of affairs stood the principal landowner, followed by other gentry living in the parish, and then by the parson, the substantial farmers, the rural craftsmen, the shopkeepers and the smallholders. At the bottom of the scale came the agricultural labourers and their families. In a number of counties, including Norfolk and Leicester, between one-third and one-half of all the villages were 'closed'. But where there was no resident proprietor, notably in 'open' parishes where land ownership was widely dispersed, the parson was perhaps the only 'gentleman' in the community, and the social divisions were less marked.

The leadership of the squire in village affairs was rarely challenged. It extended, in some parishes, not only to employment and the maintenance of cottage accommodation but to a wider sphere as well. Some men, like Lord Tollemache at Helmingham in Suffolk, insisted that farm workers attend church on Sunday, while if a tenant's daughter had a baby before marriage 'she had to leave the village; and her parents had little say in the matter'. The cultivation of allotments was also regulated; the land must be dug and not ploughed, with one half then planted with wheat and the other half with peas, beans, potatoes or other vegetables. The produce was to be consumed by the family or by the pigs they might have, and not sold, while 'all the rows had to be pointed inwards from the road so the Lord could see the rows were straight and properly weeded'. Even the style of dress was controlled, although this had its positive and negative sides:

> If a family was in need the Tollemaches helped them with the provision of boots and clothes. But it would not do for an estate tenant to have his own ideas about dress. 'You had to dress according to your station. If you didn't they soon let you know about it. 'This strict sumptuary law is confirmed in other parts of Suffolk. Farm-workers had to go to church and had to shine up their working-boots, the only pair they possessed, on a Saturday night; and they went in corduroys. If they wore anything but cords they were considered to be getting above their station and there was trouble.[9]

Of course, many landowners had neither the time nor the inclination to be as restrictive as this. Yet their importance within society was none the less recognised – and not merely by the labouring classes. In 1876, Mr John Lane, a farmer from Broom Court, Bidford, Warwickshire, wrote to the Marquis of Hertford on the subject of educational provisions in his area in the following vein:

My Lord,

I am sure that your lordship's innate benevolence will excuse my troubling your lordship on the matter of the form of the resolution supported by your lordship at Quarter Sessions on Tuesday last; the more so because I have already heard a conversation that it will have a tendency to promote expensive School Boards which mean an additional burden upon occupiers which they can ill afford and which I am sure is not the object of your lordship... I am sorry to trouble your lordship and I will never take undue advantage of your lordship's kindly condescension, but this is a public matter of great importance to the farming interest and I cannot sit down quietly ...

I am Your Lordship's

Obdt. Humble Servt.[10]

Mr Lane's servile tones continued in later correspondence between the two.

Similarly, the power of a landowner to wield petty patronage – in such matters as the appointment of a local postmastership – is confirmed in the Fremantle family papers in Buckinghamshire. In 1877 the position of postmaster at Winslow was to be filled, and on 7 May in that year the Hon. T. F. Fremantle was invited to nominate someone for the position: 'The salary is £70 a year with an allowance of £25 a year for assistance ... In the event of your not wishing to recommend any Person, the nomination will be left to the Post Office Authorities.' However, even before this date local candidates had been lobbying for Fremantle's support. On 11 April, for example, the man who eventually obtained the position wrote to say that his premises were 'well adapted for a post office ... I trust I may receive your kind patronage'. Eventually on 8 May, Fremantle gave the nomination to him on the grounds that he was 'a Conservative'. Fremantle himself was a Conservative Member of Parliament at this time.[11] But such policies were followed by landowners of all political persuasions.

If landed gentry and clergy stood at the top of the social hierarchy in most villages, the larger farmers, on the next rung of the ladder, also exerted a considerable influence over affairs; particularly in the arable areas, they controlled a big labour force and some were well enough off to be able to afford to leave much of the routine running of their farms to a bailiff or foreman – as at Chesterton Farm on the Bathurst estate in Gloucestershire. Here the rules of service prepared in 1850 included the specific regulation: 'The servants are required to attend to all directions given by the Bailiff, whether as to work to be done, or the mode of doing it', and any fines imposed for breaking the rules were 'to be stopped by the Bailiff out of the wages of the servant'. A similar state of affairs existed at Juniper Hill in North Oxfordshire, in the 1880s. The bailiff was irreverently nicknamed 'Old Monday', and as soon as he was sighted the men would warn one another by whistles. As he rode across the furrows on his little long-tailed grey pony, he would swish an ash stick and shout: 'Hi, men! Ho, men! What do you reckon you're doing!' Although he had a sharp tongue and found fault, he was just in his dealings with them. But he had one great fault in their eyes. Because he was always in a hurry himself, he tried to hurry them, and that was, a thing they detested.[12] Men like 'Old Monday' were employed by the farmer to carry out any 'dirty work' required, including the issuing of notices of dismissal and the giving of reprimands. Their presence also left their master free to attend meetings of the local Chamber of Agriculture or farming club, or to go hunting, shooting and racing. And even when the agricultural depression of the 1880s and 1800s caused a number of such farmers to cut back on personal expenditure, their standard of life remained comfortable – certainly well above that of the craftsmen and smallholders who stood below them on the social scale.

Rural craftsmen, shopkeepers and smallholders had, indeed, far more in common with one another than had the peasant cultivator with the big farmer. Each of these smaller men ran his own business and valued the independence which it bestowed. Each played his part in the smooth running of the village economy. The carpenters repaired farmhouses and cottages, mended barns and put up new stalls for the cows. The wheelwrights built wagons and carts, while the main task of the blacksmith was to shoe horses and to make or repair the iron implements used on the farms.

But of these small proprietors none worked harder than the peasant farmer. He above all had to possess physical toughness to endure prolonged labour, and the determination and ability to tackle a variety of jobs. Habits of frugality and early rising were essential and many of these small men were 'more hardly worked and less well fed and housed' than the hired labourer.[13] George Stuart saw the tail-end of this peasant system towards the close of the nineteenth century at Bourne End, near Farnham in Surrey, where a few old people carried on with their own cottage, a little land, and their pigs, donkey and a few cows. 'They kept bees, too; they made wine; they often paid in kind for any services that neighbours did for them; and with the food they could grow, and the firing they could still obtain from the woods and heath, their living was half provided for.'[14]

In some counties small farmers were sufficiently numerous to influence the whole character of village society. This was true of the dairy farms of South Lancashire, the tenant farms of much of Wales and the peasant holdings in the Lincolnshire fenlands, where landownership was widely dispersed. A return of land distribution for 1870, for instance, showed that between a half and three-quarters of all holdings in the Lincolnshire fen country were of twenty acres or less. Not all of them were owner-occupied, but many were, the men often borrowing money to start their farming operations, and then adding to their properties bit by bit. One small Epworth farmer described how he had acquired his first piece of land by marrying a wife with three or four acres. Later, in piecemeal fashion, he had saved enough to buy an additional seven or eight acres. Others saved money by working for a time on the railways, or as policemen or shop assistants in the towns. Many turned to market gardening, especially when traditional arable farming was hit by the importation of cheap wheat from the United States of America and Russia, and when harvest yields were ruined in the late 1870s by a run of wet seasons. On the Isle of Axholme potato growing held pride of place, but carrots, cauliflowers and, from the 1890s, celery, also provided cash crops. In Holland, too, vegetables, bulbs and flowers became well-established in the smallholder's crop rotations.[15] A number of men, in order to make ends meet, took casual work whenever they could spare the time from the cultivation of their own holding. Ploughing allotments, carting coal and gravel, and in some parts timber hauling, were all noted as work which the smallholders of the Holbeach area of Lincolnshire undertook in the early 1890s.

The effects of this dominance of smallholders on population structure can be seen in the parish of Epworth, which had a population of nearly 2,300 at the 1871 Census. There were no large households in the parish, and the rector was the only inhabitant with any pretensions to gentility. In all, there were about 123 farmers in the parish, of whom three-fifths were stated by the census enumerator to hold 50 acres or less, and many others were merely classed as 'farmer' without the size of holding being stated. In other words, more than one in five of all the families in Epworth were farmers. They were supported by the customary range of craftsmen and tradesmen, including plumbers, saddlers, carpenters, wheelwrights, and blacksmiths, as well as by a number of hawkers and shopkeepers. Nonconformity was well represented, as might be expected in the parish of Wesley's birth. In addition to a Methodist minister, a Baptist and a Primitive Methodist minister were also recorded.[16]

In Wales, too, the existence of large numbers of small tenant farmers working alongside their labourers led to an absence of the pronounced class divisions that existed over much of England. Labourers frequently achieved their ambition of becoming tenant farmers themselves, since the small Welsh holdings could be taken with only a little capital. 'Often the first stage in this process was for the labourer, while working as an agricultural wage earner, to acquire a small holding. Thus, farmers and labourers shaded imperceptibly into one another. Close contact on the social plane arose from their worshipping together in nonconformist chapels and their mixing in the farm houses at meal times.'[17]

Yet if smallholders provided one variant on the village theme, another was supplied by the communities of the downland and fell country, where sheep grazed on huge holdings or on common land. Such a one was the township of Kidland in Northumberland, where the entire community consisted of eight farms. All were tenanted by shepherds, who had been born or bred locally. A similar state of affairs existed in nearby Linbridge, which had a total population of sixty-four. Included among them were a farmer of 4,000 acres employing six shepherds and another of 3,000 acres also employing six shepherds.[18] In the Glendale area of Northumberland even in the 1890s the population was so sparse that shops and public houses were rare. Families were dependent for their purchases on hawkers with their travelling carts or upon shopkeepers from nearby towns sending out groceries by van. In such circumstances it is scarcely surprising that the small Glendale town of Wooler (population 1,237) had at least ten hawkers among its inhabitants in the early 1870s. Travelling tailors also visited the lonely communities and would make up a suit from provided cloth for as little as 3s 6d.

In the solitary uplands of Northumberland the distinctions between 'open' and 'closed' parishes had little relevance. But this was not true of more heavily settled areas elsewhere. Normally the closed parish would have a smaller population perhaps fifty to 300 persons only—whereas the typical open village could contain between 300 and 1,000 and sometimes more, depending on conditions in a particular area. One of the reasons for this disparity in population size was that prior to the passage of the Union Chargeability Act of 1865 each parish was responsible for supporting its own paupers only. Consequently it was in the interests of the landowner, who was the principal ratepayer in his own estate village, to keep the number of people down to as few as possible, so as to reduce the level of poor rate expenditure and to maintain the 'select' nature of the neighbourhood. Many labourers who worked in estate villages could not obtain cottages in them but were obliged to walk to work each day from homes in neighbouring open villages. Even tradesmen were excluded from the 'closed' parish where possible, since they employed journeymen and apprentices who might fall on the rates. Open parishes thus became sadly overcrowded, acting as dumping grounds for the unwanted inhabitants of estate villages. For a man of doubtful character could always be excluded by the proprietor simply by refusing him a cottage. One such open parish, Castleacre in Norfolk, was described as 'the coop of all the scrapings in the county', while in another, Steeple Aston in Oxfordshire, there were complaints in 1846 because the neighbouring villages each belonged to a single proprietor 'and it [had] been the policy for some years past of such single proprietors to destroy existing cottages and to prevent the erection of new ones'. As a result Steeple Aston ratepayers were having to support poor persons who had moved away from estate villages where new housing was not encouraged. These complaints were borne out by the comments of Grenvil Pigott, a poor law inspector, who noted in 1849 that over the previous ten years 'in eighty-six open parishes in Oxfordshire there had been a net increase of 1,352 new cottages; [but] in thirty-four closed ones, only seven' new dwellings had appeared.[19]

In 1865 this system of maintaining the poor was changed. Instead the cost was spread equally throughout the area of the whole poor law union. The incentive to the landowner to keep down expenditure in his own parish was thus lost, since he was equally responsible for paying his share of the costs of nearby 'open' parishes. As a result of the passage of the Union Chargeability Act, therefore, the number of new cottages built on estates in the 1860s increased. Nevertheless, throughout the nineteenth century cottages in estate villages remained limited in quantity if superior in quality.

There were, of course, some labourers who preferred to live away from the estate in any case, despite the inconvenience in getting to work that this might entail or the fact that housing in the closed parish was better and charitable help more often available. For these benefits were all too frequently counterbalanced by interference from the proprietor or his agent in the cottager's daily life, along the lines already discussed. In one 'model' parish a labourer declared sourly that you mustn't sneeze in the village without the permission of his lordship's agent, while in another, an agreement had to be signed by which the landlord reserved for himself and his agent the right to enter and inspect the whole of the cottage without notice at any hour between 6 a.m. and 6 p.m., and to say 'what portion, if any, of the garden shall be used for the cultivation of flowers'. In tied cottages there was also insecurity of tenure to contend with. As one critic put it bitterly in the 1890s, 'The tenant is liable to eviction at a week or a fortnight's notice, and is often subject to the most vexatious restrictions. He may not work for any other farmer save the one from whom he holds his cottage. Sometimes he is forbidden to keep a pig or to take in a lodger, or is bound to worship at a certain place. He is liable to eviction if he … commits an offence against the Game Laws; or if his grown-up sons refuse to work on the farm on the same conditions as their forebears.'[20] Not all landlords and farmers imposed such stiff conditions as these, but where they did exist they clearly interfered with a tenant's freedom of action.

By contrast, the larger 'open' villages were both more independent and more turbulent in character than the 'closed' communities already considered – Tetsworth in Oxfordshire was known as 'Botany Bay' for this reason. The conflict between farmer and farm-worker was 'softened by no mediator; malnutrition among the children was usually worse than in the closed villages', and resentment at what was felt to be exploitation by employers ran more deeply and more bitterly.[21] Housing in such villages was often jerry-built and was let at comparatively high rents by small tradesmen, builders and other speculators, anxious to make a profit. Yet despite the disadvantages, social life was freer and the population 'mix' wider. Thus at Kingham in Oxfordshire, an open village with a population of 613 in 1871, there was a whole range of tradesmen, in addition to the minor gentry, clergyman and large farmers who headed the social hierarchy. They included, for example, six carpenters, five stonemasons, four bootmakers, four grocers, an earthenware dealer, a butcher, a tailor, a hawker, two carriers, and, among the women, six dressmakers, two laundresses and a charwoman. At the bottom of the scale came the farm labourers, a railway signalman, two porters and twelve railway labourers, plus several grooms and gardeners. The village also had two public houses and a school with an attendant schoolmaster and mistress.[22] This diversity was mirrored in the experience of larger villages elsewhere.

In open parishes, too, Nonconformist chapels were common, whereas on estates they were often frowned upon. Even the well intentioned Lord Wantage would allow no chapel to be built in his model villages of Ardington and Lockinge (then in Berkshire); at the 1851 Census of Religion it was shown that, for example, in Kent and Lincolnshire less than one in five of estate villages had chapels. 'Indeed, in parishes where all the land was controlled by a single magnate, Dissent hardly ever established a foothold.'[23] Yet by running their own chapel and seizing the opportunities for preaching and public speaking which this offered, labourers could gain in self-confidence and in powers of expression. It is significant that many of the leaders of the agricultural trade union movement of the early 1870s were Primitive Methodist local preachers.

In most communities, however, it was the inn which acted as the social centre of the village. In its clubroom members of the local friendly society would meet to discuss common problems and interests. Its taproom acted as an impromptu debating chamber, and in the skittles yard adjoining there was more vigorous fun for those who sought it.

On a wider front, village social life included penny readings, usually held in the schoolroom, flower shows and the annual feast day, which usually coincided with the celebrations of the village friendly society. Communal parties were organised during the winter, while the harvest suppers held by farmers for their workers provided additional entertainment. Clothing, shoe and coal clubs were to be found in many parishes, while some had penny banks, particularly in Yorkshire, where the Yorkshire Penny Bank was said to be 'a popular institution'. On Lord Wantage's estate at Ardington and Lockinge a small savings bank was established for the two villages in addition to a sub-agency for the Berkshire Friendly Society.

Charity also played a role, especially at Christmas time, when landlords and farmers would present meat, clothing or coal to the labourers and their families. Arthur Wilkinson, who was born in 1884 at Bladon near Woodstock in Oxfordshire, remembers the Duchess of Marlborough visiting his village each Christmas. She 'went from house to house and took a big parcel in almost every house in the village and the Duchess would sit and talk to the people'. Similarly, a girl born at Takeley in Essex at around the same time recalls each winter visiting the kitchens of Easton Lodge, on the estate of the Countess of Warwick, for the soup which was regularly provided for the poor. 'We would look in awe at the Housekeeper climbing up steps to dip out the soup from the great copper.'[24] At Ardington and Lockinge, Lady Wantage not only sent soup and milk puddings to anyone who was ill, but sold dripping from the great joints which were eaten at house parties for 4d a pound. Such aids were, of course, more characteristic of the 'closed' parishes than 'open' ones, but in the latter the clergyman or the larger farmers might step in to provide help, especially during the winter months or when a member of the family was ill.

During the long winter evenings socials were organised from time to time. They were usually held in the schoolroom or a barn, with ham, beef 'and all good things to eat, cider and beer and lemonade and tea and coffee, quite a good feast ... Then after it were all cleared away they had a sing-song, and the country dancing – used to keep it up till perhaps one o'clock in the morning.' An old Cotswold man who attended some of these gatherings remembered the barns, lit with candles and hurricane lamps: 'We had one country dance which was *very familiar*. Cushion Dance. A gentleman walks round with this cushion and when the music stops he drops it down before a lady, and she's got to kneel on it and kiss the young man ... If she didn't she had to pay a penny. That went to the fiddler. He got a lot of pennies; girls was very shy in them days.'[25]

But it was at the time of the annual feast that villagers enjoyed themselves most of all. On the morning of the great day stalls would be set up in the main street, displaying every kind of delicacy for sale – sausages, gingerbreads, oranges, cakes and sweets. Swingboats and roundabouts (the latter often pushed by lads who would take their reward in the form of an occasional free ride) would provide the entertainment, along with Aunt Sallies, visiting clowns and perhaps a dancing booth. In Cumberland and Westmorland these amusements were combined with rather rougher ones, especially at the half-yearly hiring fairs, where prizes for wrestling, racing, leaping, shooting at a mark and similar events were among the attractions held out by innkeepers in order to draw customers to their public houses. However, in this part of the world the most powerful attraction was considered to be the 'ball', which was organised in the evening and 'without which no entertainment would be considered complete'. According to a contemporary, the accomplishment of dancing was universal in mid-Victorian Cumbria:

> A day labourer with a large family may declare that he is too poor to pay the weekly pence for his children's schooling, but he seldom fails to find money enough to pay for the lessons of the itinerant dancing master. A passion for dress among the women is universal, and no inconsiderable part of the wages of a farm servant girl is expended on her person ... and a girl whose ordinary costume is a coarse petticoat, pinned close round her body, and wooden clogs, will appear at a dance in a white muslin dress, white kid boots and gloves, and with a wreath of artificial flowers on her head.[26]

Most village feasts were less ambitious than this, being merely occasions for heavy drinking and jollification. But they represented a welcome break in the monotony of the daily routine and for this reason were eagerly looked forward to by all members of the rural community. At Haddenham in Buckinghamshire the feast day fell in the third week in September and as the village carpenter, Walter Rose, later recalled, it was a day when sons and daughters, hired out as servants on neighbouring farms, returned home to meet their family: 'Each cottage home was ready for them; the gleaned corn had been ground, the pie of pears had been made from its flour, and a joint of fresh meat had been cooked ... Winter's pinch had not yet begun; autumn still smiled with benevolent cheer; it was the hour not to worry about past or future, but to enjoy the delights of the present.'[27]

2

HOME LIFE

In the eighteen-eighties the hamlet consisted of about thirty cottages and an inn, not built in rows, but dotted down anywhere within a more or less circular group ... A few of the houses had thatched roofs, whitewashed outer walls and diamond-paned windows, but the majority were just stone or brick boxes with blue-slated roofs ... Some of the cottages had two bedrooms, others only one, in which case it had to be divided by a screen or curtain to accommodate parents and children. Often the big boys of the family slept downstairs, or were put out to sleep in the second bedroom of an elderly couple whose own children were out in the world ... The inhabitants lived an open-air life; the cottages were kept clean by much scrubbing with soap and water, and doors and windows stood wide open when the weather permitted. When the wind cut across the flat land to the east, or came roaring down from the north, doors and windows had to be closed; but then, as the hamlet people said, they got more than enough fresh air through the keyhole.

Flora Thompson, *Lark Rise to Candleford* (1963 ed.)
(The hamlet referred to is Juniper Hill in North Oxfordshire.)

For most country families in Victorian England one of the major factors affecting their comfort was the condition of the house in which they lived. For cottages varied enormously in both quality and quantity, ranging from one-room mud-and-thatch hovels to four- or five-roomed dwellings built of substantial brick with well-repaired slate roofs – like those at Helmingham in Suffolk on the Tollemache estate. Here the labourers' tenements were laid out with a pair of cottages to an acre of ground; each cottage had a half-acre garden with a pig-sty in one corner. Similarly in the estate villages of Chilton and Worminghall in Buckinghamshire and Waterstock in Oxfordshire the best cottages had 'three bedrooms, a sitting room, kitchen or scullery, a good size garden, with an outhouse and pigsty, the charge for which [varied] from 1s to 1s 6d a week only.'

   Unfortunately these favourable examples catered for a minority
of families only. In the more densely populated open parishes, where
cottages were frequently owned by local tradesmen and small farmers
for speculative purposes, the situation could be very different. Among
these countless minor landlords were men like Thomas Oakley of
Oxsett, Essex, a blacksmith who owned nine cottages and insured
them in the early 1860s with the Sun Insurance Company for a mere
£20 to £30 each. Or there was Francis Horn, a grazier from Ivinghoe
Aston in Buckinghamshire, who also owned nine cottages and valued
each of them at around £33 for insurance purposes. In other cases-
as at Connington, Cambridgeshire – a thatched carthouse cum stable
and a labourer's cottage were both insured for £30 by their owner.
Such examples were not uncommon. And although the properties
may have been undervalued, in order to keep down the premiums, it
is unlikely that their true quality was high. This is especially so when
one remembers the view of contemporaries that it was impossible 'to
erect and complete an improved cottage, with three sleeping rooms
of sufficient size ... under £110 in any district of England'[1] (see also
Appendix B). Even in 1894 the Final Report of the Royal Commission
on Labour pointed out that all too often there was a 'painful feeling'
that agricultural labourers were living 'under conditions which [were],
both physically and morally, unwholesome and offensive'.
   Despite sanitary legislation, therefore, and the effects of rural
depopulation, which had led to the abandonment of some of the worst
property, cramped conditions were common in many households up to
the end of the century. A report on housing in certain villages in Dorset,
Essex, Kent, Somerset, Surrey, Wiltshire and Worcestershire in the early
1890s noted than in 'an ordinary two-storied cottage, downstairs there
is usually a living room, in size about 12ft by 12ft by 6ft, and a small
back kitchen, scullery, or pantry. Upstairs, in an old cottage there will be
one good sized bedroom and one smaller one, into which the staircase
often leads.' This latter was frequently little more than a ladder and it
was common practice for both bedrooms to be without a fireplace – so
that anyone ill in bed could have no heat in the room. Ceilings were
often not underdrawn, and if the bedroom floor had holes in it, one
could see into the room below. It was impossible to scrub such floors
because the water would drip through to the room beneath. In certain
cases, too, the windows were so constructed that they could not be
opened, and in hot weather the small upper rooms, little more than
lofts, became unbearably stuffy.[2]
   Many of the other amenities of the house were equally unsatisfactory.
Privy accommodation was inadequate, 'there being only one closet to
two or even three houses' in many instances, while a number of the

older cottages had been erected at a time when 'such conveniences as ovens, coppers, or sinks were considered luxuries which the poor man could very well dispense with'.[3] In some villages communal bakehouses were supplied for a group of cottages, or else, as at Helmingham, the landlord provided a brick-oven to share between two families in the semi-detached dwellings.

A few cottagers had their own wall ovens by the side of the fireplace, and these were heated by burning faggots of wood in them. When the oven was hot enough, the glowing embers were raked out, and the bread, pies and cakes slipped in. Normally there would be a family baking once a week, and, as one Warwickshire labourer remembered, 'if the oven was hot enough, and the bread taken out at just the right time, all was well, and very thankful we were … If the oven was not hot enough the bread would be heavy, or "sad"; but we had to make the best of it. My mother was relieved when the local baker, seeing his trade diminishing … offered to bake for us at a ha'penny a loaf.'[4]

However, for women without these culinary refinements everything had to be cooked over the living-room fire. Into a large iron pot would be dropped the small square of bacon or stewing meat, the vegetables, and perhaps dumplings or a rolypoly pudding wrapped in a net. Such families had no means of roasting meat for themselves, and from time to time at the weekend the children would be sent off with a joint to the local baker. He would roast it in his large oven, along with pies and cakes, for the small charge of a penny.

Fuel for both fire and oven was itself a problem, especially in areas like East Anglia, where wood was scarce. Not until the coming of the railways did coal become readily available in this part of the country at prices labouring families could afford, and even then it was a major item in the family budget. In Shropshire, for example, close to the coalfields, it was reckoned that the average annual coal bill for labourers in the 1890s was £3 – usually paid for out of the extra earnings secured at harvest time.[5] But in more distant counties in southern England the cost would be still greater, and where possible other forms of firing would be used. In Cornwall, for example, one old lady remembers that gorse and heather were cut to provide fuel for the fire.[6]

But if poor cooking facilities created difficulties for many country women, the shortage of water was an even more pressing problem. In all too many parishes there would be only one or two pumps or wells to cater for the needs of the whole community, and the pails of water had to be carried long distances. At Shotesham in Norfolk, on the Fellowes estate, even in 1900 water was brought to the cottages 'twice a week by horse and cart in milk churns and it was stored in large earthenware pots in the pantry'.[7] Some people relied upon the contents of their rainwater butts (fouled though the water might be with dust, moss and insects), while the lazier or more desperate families would turn to nearby streams and ponds, where the danger of pollution from cesspools was an ever-present hazard. In the Atcham area of Shropshire it was noted in the early 1890s that at the parish of Bicton, the village pump was always out of order. 'The principal owner will not spend any money upon it, and his cottages suffer, but nobody has the pluck to stand up about it.' Other householders on the nearby Sandford estate had to fetch their water 'from a distance of three-quarters of a mile to a mile, and have to get over one or two gates on the road to and fro'. At Bourne End in Surrey, too, George Sturt noted than in at least one cottage 'the people were saving up the cooking water of one day to be used over again on the day following' in order to ease the water shortage.[8]

In such circumstances even washing was difficult. Members of the family would usually have a quick dip in a bowl by the back door, and in summer, if water were particularly short, all would use the same supply. The laundering of clothes was a still greater problem. Water had to be heated in small quantities over the living-room fire, unless the house were fitted with a copper, and then carried out to a tub in the back yard. Here the clothes were scrubbed with hard yellow soap before being hung out to dry. It was exhausting work for a wife, especially where families were large and pregnancies frequent. One Norfolk girl remembered going with her mother in the 1880s to mangle the linen in a room at the back of the local public house: 'The mangle consisted of a huge box of large stones collected from the beach, and was worked with a large handle which, fastened to a large roller, propelled the box of stones back and forth. A charge of twopence was paid to the owner.' At Davenham and Shavington in Cheshire communal mangles provided a means of support for widows who would wring out the freshly washed clothes for a penny or so a bundle.[9] But the majority of wives had to manage without such aids.

Given the small size of cottage rooms and the large number of people occupying them – six to ten inhabitants being by no means uncommon – furniture was usually kept to a minimum; a fact which family poverty was in any case likely to enforce. A few wooden chairs, a table and perhaps a dresser on which were displayed the family's pots and pans – these were the sum total of furnishings in the living room of most houses. Some women would display a few plants on the windowsill, or there would be pictures (often with a religious theme) on the walls. Rag rugs covered the bare flagstone or earth floors found in many cottages, while gaily coloured cushions brightened the rooms of the more house-proud women. Books were rare, but bright brass candlesticks or pieces of Staffordshire crockery would adorn the chimney piece. However, where families were large and the women too poor or too disheartened to provide such extras, the room was bare and depressing, with a few cheap and battered sticks of furniture and a superannuated potato sack doing service for a rug. 'Interiors varied according. to the number of mouths to be fed and the thrift and skill of the housewife, or the lack of those qualities.'

Upstairs the furnishings were equally scanty. In large families where several members slept in a single room, beds were shared, or if no beds existed, there would be straw pallets on the floor, with perhaps little more than rags to act as bed coverings. The family's scanty belongings would be kept in a large wooden box, and where a number of older children shared the room with their parents, counterpanes or old gowns would be cut and sewn to form a curtain across the room, in order to provide a little privacy. But this had the disadvantage of preventing the circulation of air in a room already too small for the number of occupants.

Many of the poorest families lacked even these limited amenities. Francis G. Heath, reporting on cottages in Somerset in 1872, wrote:

> It was really a pitiable sight to see the bedrooms of several of the Montacute cottages which I visited. An old table, and perhaps a broken chair in addition, would constitute in most cases the only articles of what could scarcely be called furniture. Seldom a vestige of carpet on the floors. A few bedclothes, perhaps, huddled down in one corner. At night these had to be distributed amongst the several members of the family, who, lying about on different parts of the floor, could not possibly in cold weather get a reasonable amount of warmth.[10]

It was in such circumstances that village blanket charities provided much-needed help – as at Steeple Claydon in Buckinghamshire.

At mealtimes it was difficult for families living in these crowded conditions to sit round the table together. Either the children were fed in relays or they sat down in a corner of the room or on the step, with their food in their hands or on a plate in their lap. One Essex lad, member of a family if eight children, even recalled that in his home 'the younger children had to eat their meals under the table'.[11]

Nor when the day's work was over was there much opportunity for relaxation and leisure: the space was too limited for the children to be allowed to play inside, and so they were sent off to work in the garden or allotment, or to fetch water for the following day, or to amuse themselves as best they could. When it grew dark they would come in and be sent straight to bed. Very often the man would spend his evening at the public house, while the wife continued her chores at home, airing and ironing clothes, washing the children, mending and making. But some of the bolder women went along with their husband to the local inn or beer shop, like Mrs Durbeyfield in Thomas Hardy's novel, *Tess of the D'Urbervilles*. In the early Victorian period, indeed, when lighting depended on rushlights and candles, all who did not go out went to bed as soon as it grew dark, so as to conserve their lights. But with the coming of oil lamps not only was the standard of illumination improved but economies became less essential. Now husband, wife and the older children had some opportunity for discussion and gossip when the younger members of the family were in bed. As George Sturt declared, 'Cheap lamps and cheap paraffin have given the villagers their winter evenings. At a cost of a few halfpence earned in the course of the day's work a cottage family may prolong their winter's day as far into the night as they please; and that, without feeling that they are wasting their store of light.' In Dorset, Thomas Hardy even claimed to know of a shepherd, not many miles from the county town, who had 'brass rods and carpeting to the staircase, and ... a piano strumming within', and whose 'large paraffin lamp throws out a perfect blaze of light upon the passer-by'.[12] But few labourers attained such a comfortable standard as this.

Money for rent, to provide a roof over the heads of the family, was the first charge upon the wage of any countryman – unless he lived in rent-free accommodation. But food was equally important. Bread, lard and weak tea were the principal items in the diet of the women and children, especially in the early Victorian period. As one observer, the rector of Bexwell in Norfolk, declared: 'The best and most careful labourers have bacon, or other meat, twice or perhaps three times a week; but I have no hesitation in saying that no independent labourer can obtain the diet which is given in the Union workhouse.'[13] In the western counties the loaves were often made of dry and unpalatable barley or, as in Dorset, from a grist of second-class tail wheat, purchased from an employer at 6s or 7s a bushel. This latter, in the words of the Reverend S. Godolphin Osborne, rector of Bryanston-cum-Durweston, was only 'refuse wheat – chicken food'. Yet as he indignantly declared in a letter to *The Times* of 9 July 1846, although the men were so provided for they were 'expected not to poach or to open their lips to tell the truth of their condition... Fed like fowls, sheltered like beasts, they are expected to hallow the Sabbath, reverence the Game Laws, and hold their tongues.'

In the north of England, too, barley bread was common but here it was supplemented with oat cake and porridge – the latter eaten unsweetened with milk. Bread soaked in broth or spread with dripping might provide a slight variety for the main meal of the day, while potatoes were eaten with melted butter or other fat. But in some counties nearly half a man's weekly wages were spent on bread alone, and in 1863 it was noted that 'in nearly two-thirds of the counties' in England and Wales, adults consumed between 11 and 13 pounds of bread a week.

Bacon, salt pork and cheese were also eaten in small quantities at the main meal of the day, supplemented by vegetables from the garden or allotment, but usually such 'strengthening' food would be reserved for the wage earner, while the women and children managed on bread and vegetables. As Dr Smith, a government medical officer, reported in 1863: 'the labourer eats meat or bacon almost daily whilst his wife and children may eat it once a week'. In the worst-off families there were perhaps two days in the week when the children ate dry bread alone.[14] Fresh beef or mutton was seldom consumed, except in some of the higher-wage northern and north midland counties, where it was eaten on Sundays. Elsewhere an occasional meat meal was provided, 'very lean and poor, the product of a sick sheep killed on the farm and taken by the labourers as part of their wages'.

But in the southern counties during the earlier Victorian years even the families of the smaller farmers fared little better. John Boaden, a small farmer's son from Cury in Cornwall, recalled that in his home the midday dinner each day followed an unvarying routine, and 'the Bill of Fare would be the same in all well regulated farmhouses in this district'.

> On Saturdays and Mondays it would be fish and potatoes, two days potato pie with rind or crust around it with a piece of salt pork roasted on the top. On Sundays there would be a piece of fresh meat instead, another day it would be broth with apple dumplings in season and hard 'do' otherwise, this was either salt or dried pork. Fridays was a sort of an odd day about which there was some uncertainty, sometimes peas, at other times fry, when a pig was killed it would be pig's fry. For breakfast and supper there was usually milk and bread; the bread used for both meals was barley bread except on Sunday evenings when it would be extra white bread or cake.[15]

This diet may be compared with that of another youngster – a farm servant – in Yorkshire at around the same time, in the 1840s. Both day labourers and indoor servants were better off in the north of England than their compatriots farther south, thanks to the influence of competing urban industries on the labour market, and this certainly applied to their food. The day began with a breakfast of bread, milk, beef and bacon. On Sundays a mug of tea was also allowed. For the midday dinner on three days a week there was beef and bacon, plus hot rice and apple dumplings and on the other days there were meat pies. 'For tea there would be a basin of boiled milk, with bread, beef and bacon. Cups and saucers were never used; instead they had wooden basins for milk, mugs for tea, and wooden trenchers at dinner for meat.'[16]

But in less fortunate areas weak tea remained the great standby, especially for women – even though in the early 1860s Dr Smith calculated that the 'average' purchase of tea in labouring families was a mere '½ oz per adult weekly'. Where families could not afford that small quantity, 'toast water' made from a burnt crust was the unpalatable alternative. Milk was in surprisingly short supply in many counties, even at the end of the century. As one critic noted in the early 1890s: 'Farmers want the skimmed milk for their calves and pigs, and they do not care for the trouble of selling it to labourers in detail.' Village shops rarely stocked it, there was seldom a village dairy, and it was only in areas where smallholders were numerous that a ready supply was obtainable. In a few counties, such as the north of Derbyshire and Cheshire, labourers hired or purchased a cow of their own and grazed it on pastureland they had rented. A minority might be granted free grazing by their employers, while in other cases a local philanthropist might keep a cow or two especially for villagers' children. Thomas Hare, the barrister and political reformer, who died in 1891, was one such. On his small estate of under a hundred acres at Hook near Surbiton he kept a cow specially to supply villagers 'who came up daily with jugs'. Mr Hare began his scheme when a large dairy started to collect milk for London in the parish.[17] But most labouring families were without such aid and as 'An Old Country Clergyman' from Wiltshire declared in a letter to *The Times* of 30 August 1864, in his area he had 'heard mothers complain that they could not procure a drop for their pining infants, though pigs were fattening upon it'. More than thirty years later, similar complaints were still heard, and there were claims that babies had to be fed on nutritionally inferior tinned milk because fresh was not available.

However, even if milk supplies had not improved very much by 1900, for many other items in the labourer's diet the last quarter of the nineteenth century saw a welcome advance. Thanks to the growing importation of cheaper foreign foodstuffs, meals became both more varied and more plentiful. Contemporaries pointed out that wheaten bread was now 'universally eaten', while 'fresh meat – beef or mutton – is now generally within the reach of all', at least for Sunday dinner. Butchers' carts visited villages once a week, and at the local shops there was an increasing demand for tinned meats of all kinds. Other articles of food 'now partaken of, some of which were practically unknown in the "fifties" and "sixties", but which are now brought round in carts to the labourer's door, are ... fish, jam, pickles, tea, butter, sugar, fruit, eggs, coffee, cocoa, currants and cake'.[18]

Yet despite the improvement, most country housewives still had to husband their scanty financial resources carefully. A girl who was born in Essex at the close of the Victorian era remembers that the family relied on her father's large garden to grow all the vegetables they needed, 'including parsnips for home made wine'. But other items had to be purchased:

> Mother used to send us to Mr Cooper the Butcher for 1s worth of pig's fry about once a week. This lasted our family of nine for several days. 6d worth of pieces was our regular Sunday dinner. Our diet consisted chiefly of a basin of porridge for tea, dripping toast for breakfast, plus a midday meal. We only had butter once a week on Sundays for tea, also home-made seed cake. We used to fetch our milk from the Dairy ... for which we paid 1d a pint (for skimmed milk). We also fetched my mother 2 pounds of dripping a week at 4d a pound from the cook at a place called Down Hall. My mother used to bake her own bread, and we children also used to fetch her flour from ... the mill. An approximate amount was an 8 pound bag for 6d and the yeast was 2d ...
>
> Every Sunday morning my brother paid a visit to the lady next door and purchased eggs at a penny each for our breakfast.
>
> They were hard boiled and we were given half an egg each. A man came round to our door with a basket of fish, we could purchase kippers for twopence a pair, herrings for 1d each and most Saturdays for our midday meal we had a piece of fried fish in batter which cost the large amount of twopence. Butter cost 1s a pound, mixed nuts 2d a lb, sugar 1½ d a lb, quaker oats 2d a lb, tea (medium price) 1s. per pound, and a large loaf cost 2d. We could also buy a small packet of tea for 2d ... stewing steak 4½ d a pound, pork 6d a pound, sausages 4d a pound and wild rabbits 8d each.
>
> Other foods we could not afford.[19]

In some families food was obtained as a gift or perquisite from the father's employer, so that stockmen in Lincolnshire in 1901 were said to receive 'thirty stone of bacon, fifty pecks of potatoes, threescore kids' (i.e. faggots) in addition to their money wages and a rent-free cottage. Other men purchased foodstuffs from their employers and would then have this set off against their wages – like the employees of a Dorset farmer, Mr John Butler. During the 1860s he normally paid his workers once a month only, but in the interim several of them bought wood, bacon, eggs and butter from him, and then had the relevant sums deducted from their earnings at the end of the month.[20] A similar policy was adopted in the 1880s and 1890s by workers employed by Mr Hyatt at Snowshill House Farm in Gloucestershire. Among the items purchased here were bacon, mutton (sold at 6*d* and 8*d* per lb), hops, coal (at 15*s* a ton), eggs for 1*s* 3*d* a score and cheese at 7*d* a lb. Pigs, with the barley to feed them, were also paid for on an instalment plan. Like the men employed by Mr Butler, these labourers, too, were paid only once every four weeks. And as a result of these purchases of food, the cash they received was often very little. Thus in January 1880, William Ireland, a labourer ostensibly earning 12*s* a week, 'left £1 for pig, four bushels barley 14*s*.' and as a consequence secured only 14*s* in cash. During the next month he bought four more bushels of barley and was able to work only three weeks and two days at 2*s* a day – so his money earnings on that occasion amounted to £1 6*s* Despite the possible advantages of bulk buying from an employer, the tight budgeting this system must have imposed on the wife is easy to appreciate.[21]

Another difficulty for the women was the custom of many employers of paying their workers late in the evening of Saturday, so that a wife had little time to make weekend purchases to feed her family. George Swinford of Filkins in Oxfordshire recalled that in the 1890s John Garns of the Manor Farm 'used to pay the men on Saturday nights from 6 to 8 p.m. I remember seeing the men's wives standing by the little shop waiting for their husbands to come out, so that they could go and shop and buy the groceries for the week.' The wages here were small enough anyway. According to Swinford, the day labours received '10*s* per week and cottage. The shepherd, cowman and carter had 3*s* per week extra and boys 3*s* per week'.

In laying their money out to best advantage these country housewives fared far worse, of course, than their urban counterparts, since the towns had many more shops and hence, usually, a wider choice of food. Keen competition between grocers and bakers kept food prices down below those in most village shops, while specialist outlets like the pork butcher or the tripe shop made available cheap regional delicacies like faggots, black puddings and brawn. But against this were serious disadvantages, including a shortage of fresh vegetables, the widespread adulteration of food – even common items of diet like bread and tea – and a grossly inadequate water supply. A lack of suitable cooking equipment in overcrowded urban slums also made preparation of food difficult. Nor could town dwellers take advantage of the small harvest offered by hedgerows and fields. The more prudent villagers gathered elderberries and cowslips for wine, while blackberries could be eaten raw or made into jams and pies. As a Norfolk child remembered, her family would go out to gather 'all the food that was for free: watercress from running streams, rabbits, pigeons, wild raspberries, wild plums and blackberries, crab apples, hazel nuts, chestnuts, walnuts. No squirrels hoarded these more carefully than we did ... A god-mother who kept bees had all the children in to help scrape out the sections.'[22] Similarly, in mid-Victorian Warwickshire a labourer recalled that during his childhood his mother would send him and his brother into the fields to gather 'cowslip-pips for her on the second Monday in May, for cowslips are best and sweetest then. Before this we gathered coltsfoot flowers ... On market days, mother used to take the butter to sell for the mistress, and then she sold the cowslips and coltsfoots. The druggist wanted violets and roseleaves, and hips which we gathered in their seasons for him.'[23]

However, for many cottagers the most valued addition to their diet came from the killing of the family pig. Often one half of the animal only would be kept by the householder, and the other half sold to a butcher to pay off debts run up earlier, including those with the mealman who had supplied the barley needed for the final fattening process. The animal was fed on potato parings and other vegetable trimmings, mixed with the pot-liquor in which the food had been boiled. 'The children, on their way home from school, would fill their arms with sow thistle, dandelion, and choice long grass, or roam along the hedgerows on wet evenings collecting snails in a pail for the pig's supper.'

The day the pig was killed was always one of special celebration. A professional pig-killer, either a butcher or a skilled fellow villager, would usually be hired for about 2s 6d to carry out the task. He arrived trundling a sort of wooden stretcher with handles at each end, supported on an iron wheel. On top was a big wooden tub, called a 'killer', in which were the tools of his trade. To those of a sensitive turn of mind the pig's frantic squeals as it met its end were an ordeal, but most country people took the commonsense view that unless it was slaughtered there would be no bacon or pork to form a staple item in their diet for several weeks to come.

As a Norfolk woman recalled, when the pig had been killed, there 'came the task of removing all the hair from his hide by means of hot (not boiling) water, and sharp scrapers. He was then cut open and hung up till the next day. Then our man returned to cut him up. Mother salted the hams and later sent them to be cured. She also made pork pies and chitterlings and pork cheeses, till one got rather tired of pig at last.'[24] Part of the pig's fry would be sent round to neighbours as a gift, so that all could share in the unaccustomed plenty. Later, when someone else killed a pig, the gesture would be reciprocated. In this way families could help one another.

But the enrichment of the diet which occurred at pig-killing time was only a short break in the monotony of the daily fare. Soon the usual routine of bread, fat bacon and potatoes would be restored.

Anything left over from a father's weekly wage packet when rent and food had been paid for was set aside to cover purchases of boots, clothing, candles or oil, friendly society contributions, and the thousand and one other items in any family budget (see Appendix A). But usually there was little to spare, and these extras were normally paid for out of the additional money earned by the family at harvest tune. Charity and the handing-down of items of clothing from one member of the family to another also helped.

By the end of the century most men and boys were wearing clothes made of serviceable corduroy or tweed. Smock frocks were now out of favour and at Waterstock in Oxfordshire the trustees of a charity complained in the early 1890s that they could not even give away smocks provided for boys and young men under the terms of a local bequest. For the smaller children, clothes were usually cut down or altered versions of those worn by their older brothers and sisters. In the case of some unfortunate lads this might mean wearing a dress which had belonged to a sister, if nothing else were available. A photograph of school children from Sheldon in Derbyshire at the end of the century shows three small and rather sheepish boys dressed in this fashion.

The men wore flannelette or cotton shirts, without collars, corduroy trousers and a corduroy or tweed jacket – although some favoured a long-sleeved waistcoat instead of the jacket. This was made from fustian and was so long that it reached down almost to the knees. It was normally worn fastened up to the neck, leaving just enough space for a red-spotted muffler to be seen underneath. And as a Stowmarket tailor remembered nearly all of these waistcoats had a 'hare-pocket on the inside on the left. If you were wearing one of these weskits you could double up an owd hare and place it inside and button up; and no one knew anything about it'.[25] A hat – a wideawake, bowler, billy-cock or cap with ear flaps, according to individual preference – was also worn, and for horsemen, thatchers and hedgers there would be leather buskins or gaiters. In the early 1890s a working suit consisting of trousers, waistcoat and linen jacket would cost on average between 14s and 15s, although a better quality 'Sunday' suit would amount to about £1 14s or £1 15s. It was perhaps a sign of growing affluence, too, that in the early 1890s in the North Witchford area of Cambridgeshire it was reported that 'nearly everybody after the age of twenty carries a watch'. A similar comment was applicable to most labourers elsewhere.

Among the women and girls there was a natural desire to wear fashionable and attractive clothes. Although this ambition was often thwarted by poverty, a little ingenuity could help. At Juniper Hill in Oxfordshire cottagers' wives and daughters fitted themselves out with bustles by rolling a piece of old cloth into a cushion which they could then wear under any frock. But where women worked in the fields – as they did in Northumberland, for example – clothing had to take a practical turn. In the Glendale Union of Northumberland during the 1890s the dress of the female labourers consisted of: 'a short skirt of thick material, stout boots, a large picturesque straw bonnet, over a bright coloured handkerchief which covers the neck and lower part of the face. A shawl is worn over the shoulders, and oversleeves are tied on while at work. In the summer a slip or pinafore is put on over the whole dress, and in the winter a wrapper or apron of stouter make.' Younger girls, on the other hand, wore pinafores over long linsey or print dresses, while their underwear was made of calico or flannelette and their stockings of wool. At Juniper Hill Flora Thompson remembered that the material for the underwear was provided by the rectory and was made up at school. There were 'roomy chemises and wide-legged drawers made of unbleached calico … harsh but strong flannel petticoats and worsted stockings that would almost stand up with no legs in them'.[26] Yet despite their unattractive appearance they were welcomed by mothers because they eased the ever-present problems of clothing a family. In villages without this kind of charitable help, underwear often deteriorated into a very ragged condition, as the efforts of a mother were devoted to securing a good outer show.

All but the poorest families would also have a 'best' Sunday outfit which they would wear to attend church and for a sedate afternoon walk round the village. The materials for this were often obtained from parcels of clothes which were sent by relatives who were away in service. These were worn and altered and dyed and turned for as long as the shreds would hang together. Women had to be skilled with the needle if they were successfully to make do and mend. Some even made their husbands' shirts by hand, as well as dresses and jackets for themselves and their children.

However, if clothing presented one major headache for a hard-pressed family, an even greater difficulty was buying boots. To be 'dry-a-foot' was a wise maxim, and villagers would place an order with their favourite shoemaker well in advance of need, so as to give the leather time to harden before the winter set in. But boots were expensive – perhaps as much as 14s a pair for men and 8s 6d for boys. They were made of tough leather with steel tips, plates and hobnails all over the sole. On rough roads they would strike sparks from the flints, and they were very uncomfortable to wear, especially when they were

being broken in. Most members of a family would have only one pair
of weatherproof boots or shoes in use at a time, and so if these got wet
they had to be dried in front of the fire during the evening in readiness
for wear on the following day. This made them still more unpleasant
to wear, despite the judicious administering of oil and grease to soften
the leather and to help keep them waterproof. It was small wonder
that during the winter months many children suffered so badly with
chilblains and 'bad feet' that they had to stay away from school.

Where the cost of keeping a family well shod and clothed proved too
much for weekly earnings, purchase on an instalment system might be
adopted – although sadly the boots and clothes were all too often worn
out before the bill was paid. A few men borrowed the necessary sum
from their employer and then paid back at the rate of a shilling or two
a month, as entries in farm wages books make clear. Others joined local
thrift clubs, paying a small amount each week and then sharing in the
annual distribution of the money thus saved; usually the local clergyman
and the gentry would boost the funds at the time of the distribution. The
village schoolmaster, too, would sometimes organise a coal and clothing
club for the parents of his pupils, while even public houses ran thrift
clubs as a sideline – somewhat inappropriately.

In a minority of cases families obtained clothing as a perquisite from
the father's employer. For example, in 1892, a Herefordshire farm
labourer interviewed in connection with the Royal Commission on
Labour stated that he received a coat, a pair of trousers, a blanket and
some flannel from his employer every other Christmas, while another
labourer in the same county obtained, in addition to these perquisites,
'help for children's clothes' (see also Appendix A).

Day-to-day shopping was normally carried out in the village, but
most families would try to visit the local market town at least once a
week in order to stock up on major items, since in the more competitive
atmosphere of a town, goods were cheaper. The local market day was
especially favoured for bargains. Women and their children would walk
into town or else the mother would travel by carrier's cart. Indeed, an
Essex girl from Hatfield Heath remembered her mother occasionally
hiring a local pony and trap for 6d to take the whole family into Harlow
if particular purchases had to be made.[17]

Nevertheless for many households indebtedness to the local
shopkeepers was a perennial worry, and one which some of the more
desperate tried to overcome by resorting to a system of barter as a
supplement to their cash repayments. In one Devon village shop, for
example, a local family had by 1898 run up the considerable debt of
£4 16s 10d Later in that year goods to the value of £2 2s 10d were
purchased (including 3s 6½d for a hat, 8s 6d for a cradle and over 12s

for meal – presumably to feed the pig). In September a repayment of
10s was made but almost immediately a bucket was bought for 1s,
a pair of boots for 5s 11d and a pair of shoes for 3s 11d. A second
repayment of 5s followed, coupled with the depositing of four fowls,
which the shopkeeper accepted and for which a credit of 9s was given.
In the following year 'there was a cash payment of 9s plus a fowl.
valued at half-a-crown. Potatoes were sold to the store, but by the end
of the year £5 5s 10½d was still owing, although no [further] purchases
had been made.'[28] The family was eventually brought before the county
court and was ordered to pay off the debt in small instalments but the
hardship that this decision must have caused in a low-wage household
is easy to imagine.

Nor was it just farm workers who resorted to the barter system.
Smallholders, too, relied heavily upon it. One such, who owed £9 10s to
a Devon village store in September 1895, managed to reduce the debt a
little by selling his entire potato crop to the shopkeeper. Another man in
a similar plight sold fowls, ducks and turkeys, bushels of oats, bundles of
straw and most of his potato crop in order to try to get out of debt.

Because of the dragging burden which these debts could represent
some reformers advocated the setting up of co-operative stores in
the villages, where the members had to pay for their goods as they
bought them and where the profits were distributed to them in the
form of dividends. One enthusiast in this cause was Lord Wantage,
who established a co-operative store in his estate village of Ardington
in 1885. The society baked its own bread and sold meat, groceries and
coal. By the early 1890s it was not only selling goods more cheaply than
those in neighbouring shops (bread was 4½d for a quartern loaf instead
of 5d elsewhere), but a dividend had been paid to the customers equal to
about 10 per cent of the weekly receipts. The manager was paid a salary
so that he should have no incentive to sell inferior articles.

In other parishes, such as the shoemaking centre of Long Buckby
in Northamptonshire, the initiative came from the villagers themselves
rather than from an outside philanthropist. In 1867, nine years after
the Long Buckby Society had been established, it had a membership of
283 – over one in ten of the total population – and an annual turnover
of nearly £9,000. Through its dividend system it provided members
with a painless way to save money – committee minute books show
that sums of £1 or more were regularly accumulated – and purchases
could be made on terms more favourable than in the ordinary village
shops. A surprisingly wide range of items was stocked. For example,
in the six weeks ending mid-February 1866 the committee authorised
the purchase of 105 sacks of flour, nine firkins of butter, eight sides of
bacon, a chest of green tea, coffee, sugar, treacle, pepper, ground ginger,

bacon pigs, beef, pork, lamb, five cwt of soap, ipecacuana wine (used as a purgative), six dozen broom heads, three dozen zinc buckets, nails, slippers, soda, notepaper and envelopes, snuff, tobacco, cough drops, blacking, flax and hemp for the shoemakers, paper bags and ten gallons of hair oil! Later in the year other items were ordered, including figs, currants and nuts, plus garden forks, shovels and spades. Together they provide an indication of the sort of goods in demand among Victorian country folk.[29]

However, despite the success of the Long Buckby enterprise and of similar societies in Northamptonshire, in most rural areas co-operative stores made a limited impact only. It was the little private shop which was the usual resort of labouring families.

Small purchases could also be made at the door from the pedlars and hawkers who periodically toured the villages, bringing with them a ripple of excitement to otherwise quiet communities. In the pedlar's pack were cotton reels, lace, shoe laces, pins and needles, lengths of material, aprons, pinafores, coloured scarves and ribbons for Sunday wear. Hawkers, with their little carts or vans, brought with them heavier items like garden tools, baskets and oil for the lamps. At Wood Norton in Norfolk an old man with a donkey cart regularly brought clean silver sea sand which he sold to housewives for scouring pots and doorsteps and for spreading on the brick floors.[30] Tinkers and knife and scissor grinders would also make periodic appearances to repair cottagers' few utensils, while another caller at Wood Norton among other villages – was 'the rabbit-skin man, bearing on his shoulder a long stick on which were skewered rabbit skins, purchased at the cottage doors for twopence apiece'. And at Filkins George Swinford remembered a traveller named Burrows who came to the village twice a year in spring and autumn, staying for about a month each time.

> He was agent for the cutlers named Brades from Sheffield. He had a large covered wagon where he kept his cutlery and every morning he would be off with his wagon and two large black horses round the countryside, selling his wares to the farmers. In the evening he would lay his goods on the village green for the villagers to come and buy a pocket knife, a hoe, a billhook, or some other tool they needed ... If we boys had one of Burrows' pocket knives, we thought a lot of it ... When he arrived, his ware was spread out near the Lamb and we boys received a few coppers for going round the village with a bell, and telling them that Mr Burrows had come again ... If you did get a bad tool, he would exchange it for a new one, next time he came.[31]

In the early years of the century, Filkins was also visited by a salt merchant from Lechlade who used to bring his salt round the villages 'for sale in a small cart drawn by a team of dogs'. When he reached the Lamb Inn he unharnessed the animals while he ate his midday meal and they ran round the village picking up scraps of food where they could. When he was ready to start once more, 'he blew his horn, his dogs came back to him, he harnessed them up and was soon on his way again'. (This use of dogs as draught animals was made illegal in 1854.)

Nevertheless, such breaks in the village routine were few and far between, and for most, day followed day in a pattern varied only by the differing demands of agriculture and of the seasons.

Of course, for some families a change in surroundings was secured periodically by moving house. When the father obtained a fresh situation in a distant village then he and his family must dig up their roots and move off. George Millin, a correspondent with the *Daily News,* described one such exodus in the autumn of 1891:

> You cannot go far along country roads just now without meeting waggons piled up with the goods and chattels of farm hands changing quarters ... They have been to some Michaelmas hiring fair, and have got fresh places, and here they are jogging about the country with their tables and chairs, and beds and boxes, and wives and children heaped up on the new master's wagon ... Some of these little family cavalcades, with their pots and kettles, and cradles and hen coops, have looked forlorn and desolate enough – more so, perhaps, than they really were. One unlucky wight in the neighbourhood I was in yesterday had had a dire disaster. He had stuffed the family wardrobe and all the bed linen into a sack, and as they had gone bumping and jolting along the country roads it had somehow tumbled off, and they had lost it all. Search and inquiries were alike fruitless, and he had been going all round the neighbourhood trying to buy postage stamps enough to send on for an advertisement in a local paper.[32]

In the later Victorian years such migrations were fairly common. But in the earlier part of the century, when village populations were more static, it was not uncommon for a husband and wife to stay in the same cottage all their married life, leaving only at death or perhaps, sadly, if they became destitute, to enter a workhouse in old age.

3
SCHOOL

In many cases it will be found that the attendance in summer is little more than half what it is in winter. In the former case, the children can find employment, in the latter they can not.

Revd H. W. Bellairs, HMI, Report on schools in the Western District, Minutes of the Committee of Council on Education, Parliamentary Papers, 1845, XXXV

Attendance very poor again this week several boys away beating for the shoot ...

Ordinary routine this week, but the attendance was poor, several children away fruit and pea picking.

Entries in Elmdon School Log Book, Warwickshire, 3 February and 21 July 1899

Throughout the nineteenth century a recurring problem for teachers and education authorities alike was the poor attendance at school of many country children. The difficulties persisted despite the passage of the Education Acts of 1876 and 1880, making it compulsory for all children to attend school to the age of ten, and thereafter to fourteen, unless they could pass a satisfactory leaving examination or gain exemption in some other way.[1] Parents and employers who allowed children to work illegally could be fined. But, in practice, the smallness of the fine – usually only 2s 6d for each offender – coupled with the expense and trouble of bringing culprits to court and the laxity of magistrates and school attendance officers in dealing with offenders, meant that prosecutions were few. As one of Her Majesty's Inspectors of Schools reported of the York district in 1898: 'So long as certain farming operations can be performed by children, and so long as we hear of agricultural depression, it appears that employers and parents will continue to break the law, magistrates will be slow to convict, school attendance committees will not press cases against employers and parents, managers will not furnish names of offenders for fear of losing subscriptions or making the school unpopular, and teachers will not make enemies by furnishing information.'

This situation was underlined by the poor pay normally given to attendance officers, for in country areas the post was always a very part-time one, carried out by poor law relieving officers, local shopkeepers and the like. At Ledbury, Herefordshire, during the 1880s, for example, relieving officers were appointed to school attendance positions with an addition to their salary of £2 per annum. And in 1881 Church Enstone School Board in Oxfordshire appointed an attendance officer at £3 a year. Such tiny sums were equally applicable elsewhere, and it was small wonder that a number of officers showed little enthusiasm for the 'educational' calling.

In certain areas, too, school attendance committees were prepared to set aside their own educational bye-laws if the needs of agriculture warranted it. In the Pershore area of Worcestershire as late as August 1886, the committee resolved that the restrictions on the use of child labour were to be suspended 'for a period of one month from 20 August inst. to the 20 September next'. Other entries in the minute book indicate that this was not an isolated case.[2]

The reasons behind these attendance difficulties had been pinpointed almost thirty years earlier by the Royal Commission on Popular Education (the Newcastle Commission) when it declared that whilst 'almost all the parents appreciate the importance of elementary education ... they are not prepared to sacrifice the earnings of their children for this purpose, and ... they accordingly remove them from school as soon as they have an opportunity of earning wages of an amount which adds in any considerable degree to the family income'.[3] Although it was agreed that the name of 'almost every child' appeared 'at some time or other on the books of some school', the continuity of education received was much less satisfactory. One Assistant Commissioner, the Reverend James Fraser, claimed, for example that in the rural districts of Devon, Dorset, Hereford, Somerset and Worcestershire which he had examined, there were 'more than one third' of the children aged between four and twelve, 'the reasonable educational limits', who received no regular instruction:

Two thirds of these, perhaps, are precariously employed on odds and ends of labour, to a certain extent remunerative; or, if girls, in either assisting or taking the place of their mothers in the domestic exigencies of large families. The other third, whose homes are mainly in the back lanes of the country towns, are to be found idling, or playing, or begging about the street, or else extemporising, considerably to its damage, various ingenious playthings of the hobby or rocking horse

kind, out of the furniture of the cottage, which the absent mother has
left entirely at their mercy.

Fraser attributed this situation to apathy on the part of parents towards
education and to family poverty. As regards the latter, it was pointed
out that lack of suitable clothing and shoes prevented some youngsters
from attending. The point was a valid one, for as late as the 1890s the
bad condition of boots was recorded in many school log books as a
reason for absence. Other youngsters were kept away because parents
could not afford to spend 1d or 2d per week in school fees, especially
where there were several children in the family. But in the majority of
cases the cause lay in what Fraser called the 'deep poverty' of those who
could not afford 'to dispense with the pittance, however scanty, which
the child's earnings add to the 8s or 9s a week, which is the ordinary
income, in this district, of the agricultural labourer. The peasant's wages
are *never* up to the mark that can allow of his sacrificing the earnings
of his child to higher considerations.'[4] The sons and daughters of the
smaller farmers were similarly placed. As a smallholder from Thornbury,
Devon, frankly admitted, he 'could not afford to pay a man 2s a day to
do work the boy could do'. The 'remote possibility of a 5s fine could not
weigh against an immediate 2s a day'.[5] And when in 1873 an attempt
was made with the passage of the Agricultural Children Act to prohibit
the employment of youngsters under the age of eight and to require them
to attend school either to the age of twelve, or until they had passed an
appropriate leaving certificate, the reaction of both parents and farmers
was hostile. The Act came into operation on 1 January 1875, but thanks
to this opposition and to the fact that there was no effective enforcement
agency, it quickly became a dead letter. The position was summarised
by HMI Du Port in respect of the Berkshire area in his annual report
for 1876: '[The] Act had not been in force more than three or four
months ... before it began to transpire that in this or that parish or
neighbourhood its provisions were being calmly ignored, and that with
full impunity. This proved a very contagious influence, and after the
expiration of the first six months of the Act's brief existence, I never
again saw or heard of a case in which the Agricultural Children Act
... was not a dead letter.' It was as a consequence of this situation that
the Act was rapidly superseded by the general education legislation of
1876 and 1880.

In the decades that followed the increase in labourers' cash earnings
over their 1870 position, coupled with the fall in the price of food,
gradually helped to raise rural living standards and at the same time
removed some of the economic pressures which had encouraged the
early employment of children. Nevertheless, as has been indicated by

the comments of those HMIs and school teachers quoted, even in 1900 some difficulties remained.

Furthermore, if economic pressure had been one factor influencing the standard of education achieved in country districts, it was not the only problem to be faced – especially in the earlier part of the nineteenth century. The scattered nature of school provision in some areas and the indifferent quality of the teaching were two additional weaknesses undermining support for education even among favourably disposed families. Thus in the late 1850s there were whole districts in the west of England without adequate facilities – like forty parishes in the Dorchester/Sherborne area of Dorset, where there were said to be only six schools which could be classed as 'efficient'. In Herefordshire the position was equally unsatisfactory, and here the difficulty was aggravated by the poor roads, with 'their deep retentive red-clay soil', which made it almost impossible for 'children under seven or eight years of age' to walk to school during the wet winter months. Even in Oxfordshire there were in 1854 about 8 per cent of the parishes without any day school at all, and a considerable number of the remainder were dependent on ineffective 'dame' schools rather than upon anything more worthwhile.[6] (Not that some of the larger towns were faring a good deal better. In 1870 it was calculated that about one-quarter of the children in Liverpool aged between five and thirteen attended no school at all, and a similar proportion in Manchester. Leeds was considered 'to be as bad as Liverpool; and so, also ... [was] Birmingham'.)

With the passage of the 1870 Education Act this situation slowly changed. Every child had now to be provided with an elementary school place, and to carry this into effect rate-aided school boards could be set up to supplement the Church of England and other denominational schools already in existence. Although the Act's provisions took more than a decade to come into operation in certain of the more backward rural counties, by the 1880s at least there was a school within reach of all but the most remotely situated children. Nevertheless, some of the distances to be covered were still considerable. One girl who started school in Upminster in 1897, at the age of three, remembers that some of her fellow pupils lived as far as four miles away. 'The elder children would "pick-a-back" their small brothers and sisters. A crippled boy who lived more than two miles from school was drawn by other boys in a truck made from a Tate's sugar box with perambulator wheels. His cart was always surrounded by boys who took turns at being the "horse" between the truck shafts, with a string on each arm for reins which the crippled boy held.'[7] She also recalls that the 'long distance children took their dinners to school. In cold or wet weather they ate in the classroom;

in warm fine weather they sat on the school steps or on the ground in the playground'. Most brought slices of bread and dripping or cheese with them. Sometimes there would be a pasty, but only rarely was meat provided; it was too expensive. Water or cold tea would be the usual drink, unless a kind-hearted schoolmaster or mistress agreed to provide hot cocoa or tea during the winter.

Where children had a long walk to school their attendance was very much affected by weather conditions, for few classrooms had facilities for drying damp clothes, and so the children had to sit all day in their wet things. At such times a common log book entry was: 'Wet day, few attended.'

Yet if the Education Act of 1870 brought about a much-needed advance in the number of schools provided in country districts during the last quarter of the nineteenth century, an equally necessary improvement secured over the same period was in the quality of teaching. From 1862 official regulations laid down that schools receiving state educational grants must be under the charge of a qualified teacher. Although a number of inefficient unaided 'dame' or private 'adventure' schools lingered on, by the 1890s they catered for a tiny minority of children only. But in the early Victorian period, the situation had been very different. Thus at Kniveton, Derbyshire, in the 1840s the master was described as 'utterly incompetent and unfit in every sense of the word for his post. The school in its present state is a positive injury to the parish.' Similarly at Danby in Yorkshire in the 1840s the new incumbent, the Reverend J. C. Atkinson, discovered to his surprise that the schoolmaster was an unsuccessful small farmer who had frittered away his patrimony. When Atkinson asked why he had been appointed to the school, he was told: 'Whea, he could dee nowght else. He had muddled away his land, and we put him in scheealmaster that he mou't get a bite o'bread.' Later Atkinson and a friend visited the school, and found the place in uproar, with the master 'fast asleep ... with his tall hat on, in a large high wooden-backed chair by the fireside'. But the unwonted stillness caused by the two men's entrance 'did for him what all the preceding hullabaloo had failed to do: it woke him. Rubbing his eyes with a half comprehending consciousness, he presently recognised the presence of strangers in his abode of the Muses'. As he 'staggered up to make a show of receiving his visitors', Atkinson and his friend beat a hasty retreat.[8]

John Boaden of Cury in Cornwall had similar memories of the school run by a former carpenter, named Hugh John, which he attended in the late 1830s. When gout prevented John from following his trade he tried to obtain a post as master at the local National School (i.e. the Church of England one) but 'failing, he started one independently in a room called the "Hall" in his own house ... In the middle of the room there stood a large tool chest and carpenter's bench which served for [a] desk, and around the room on one side were other desks. The school material was of the most inexpensive kind, quills alone were used for writing ... The slate pencils were found by the boys and taken out of the soil and scraped and pointed for use, for which purpose two knives were kept inside the schoolroom door.' Nor did Mr John confine his activities to teaching. Among other sidelines he killed pigs for local farmers, 'cleaned clocks, measured land, castrated cattle ... He was also a cattle doctor.' Unfortunately for his pupils he sometimes returned from these duties rather the worse for drink.[9]

It may be asked why parents paid to send their youngsters to such places. One can only assume that their own lack of education prevented them from assessing the quality of the instruction that the children were receiving or else they regarded the school as a mere child-minding institution, to which they sent the youngsters just to keep them from under their feet.

Needless to say the 'education' provided was minimal. Few children managed to acquire the most elementary skills and, as one critic observed, it was 'quite common to meet with boys engaged in farms who [could] not read or write. The unity of God ... the number of months in the year, are matters not universally known.'[10] This comment was made in 1843, but over twenty years later the Reverend James Fraser interviewed an eleven-year-old boy 'keeping sheep in Redenhall churchyard' in Norfolk, who declared that 'a sovereign is five shillings; (afterwards changed it to 10 shillings.) Asked how many pence there are in a shilling said "ten"; but questioned again, replied "twelve pennies more likely".'[11] Not surprisingly he was also unable to write, although he did claim to be able to read 'a little'.

And, as late as January 1884 a new mistress taking up appointment at the small school at Spelsbury, Oxfordshire, could complain: 'I find the school in a dreadfully backward state not one standard knowing their arithmetic although HMI will be here in two months ... Examined children in Grammar and Geography and finding them entirely ignorant of these subjects, resolved to devote the whole time to the "three Rs" till the Examination.'[12]

However, even without such gross inefficiency, concentration on reading, writing, arithmetic and religious knowledge – plus needlework for the girls – was common in country schools for most of the nineteenth century. Partly this was because parents considered these the only important subjects for their children and partly it was the result of government grant policy towards elementary education. The limited time children spent at school also had a role to play, particularly up to the 1860s. As a contemporary pointed out, the majority of country boys at that time left the day school by the age of eleven and so any really worthwhile achievement was out of the question. Ideally, if he had been 'properly looked after in the lower classes', the youngster, when he left, should

> be able to spell correctly the words that he will ordinarily have to use; he shall read a common narrative – the paragraph in the newspaper that he cares to read – with sufficient ease to be a pleasure to himself and to convey information to listeners; if gone to live at a distance from home, he shall write his mother a letter that shall be both legible and intelligible; he knows enough of ciphering to make out, or test the correctness of a common shop bill; if he hears talk of foreign countries he has some notions as to the part of the habitable globe in which they lie; and underlying all, and not without influence, I trust, upon his life and conversation, he has acquaintance enough with the Holy Scriptures to follow the allusions and the arguments of a plain Saxon sermon, and a sufficient recollection of the truths taught him in his catechism, to know what are the duties required of him towards his Maker and his fellow man. I have no brighter view of the future or the possibilities of an English elementary education than this.

Yet, as he sadly admitted, not a quarter of the children who left school could boast even that humble level of accomplishment.

Many of the school inspectors agreed with this judgment. In 1858, HMI Alderson complained that children 'often reach a comparatively high position in the school, reading inarticulately, spelling incorrectly, and with the vaguest notions of numeration'; while his colleague, HMI Brookfield, declared that he had posed the question: 'What do you mean by that state of life into which it shall please God to call you?'. Of 1,344 scholars whom he had addressed in the 'first classes' of fifty-three different schools, only eleven in every hundred had known what he meant. 'In two schools only out of the fifty-three were the answers satisfactory from every child in the first class'. In all too many cases he was answered in 'words the indiscriminate and utterly incoherent use of which is familiar to everybody accustomed to examine school children in religious instruction'.[13]

It was in an effort to counteract the neglect of what was seen as 'basic' education that in 1862 the Revised Code was drawn up by the Education Department in London. This linked governmental grants for elementary schools both to the attendance levels achieved by the pupils and to the results of an annual examination in the three 'Rs' (reading, writing and arithmetic) conducted by an HMI. Each infant under the age of seven was to attract a grant of 10s 6d provided that attendance was satisfactory, and each older child, 12s – 4s of which depended on satisfactory attendance and the remainder on the successful completion of the examination. The Code also laid down the level of achievement expected from each class – or standard – throughout the school:

Standard I
Reading   Narrative in monosyllables.
Writing   Form on blackboard or slate, from dictation, letters, capital and small manuscript.
Arithmetic   Form on blackboard or slate, from dictation, figures up to 20; name at sight figures up to 20; add and subtract figures up to 10, orally, from examples on blackboard.

Standard II
Reading   One of the Narratives next in order after monosyllables in an elementary reading book used in the school.
Writing   Copy in manuscript character a line of print.
Arithmetic   A sum in simple addition or subtraction, and the multiplication table.

Standard III
Reading   A short paragraph from an elementary reading book used in the school.
Writing   A sentence from the same paragraph, slowly read once, and then dictated in single words.
Arithmetic   A sum in any simple rule as far as short division (inclusive).

Standard IV
Reading   A short paragraph from a more advanced reading book used in the school.
Writing   A sentence slowly dictated once by a few words at a time from the same book, but not from the paragraph read.
Arithmetic   A sum in compound rules (money).

Standard V

Reading	A few lines of poetry from a reading book used in the first class of the school.
Writing	A sentence slowly dictated once, by a few words at a time, from a reading book used in the first class of school.
Arithmetic	A sum in compound rules (common weights and measures).

Standard VI

Reading	A short ordinary paragraph in a newspaper, or other modern narrative.
Writing	Another short ordinary paragraph in a newspaper, or other modern narrative, slowly dictated once by a few words at a time.
Arithmetic	A sum in practice bills of parcels.

Although changes were made in the Code during the course of the next thirty years, including an increase in the grant-earning subjects from 1867 to include grammar, history, geography, etc., the overall effect was to restrict the school curriculum to the three 'Rs', since these remained the basis of the grant up to 1890. The Code also gave great power to the HMIs who conducted the annual examination and upon whose findings the financial fate of a school rested. As the mistress of Hittisleigh School, Devon, wrote in her log book in 1893: 'One always feels that the fate of a whole year's work may hang on the humour or caprice, and absolutely on the stroke of a pen, of some Assistant Inspector.'[14] Although in her case the Inspector's charge of inefficiency seems to have been justified by the comments of her successor at the school, the sentiments she expressed were common to more conscientious and effective teachers. Needless to say, their anxiety as the date of the annual inspection drew near, transmitted itself to the children, and it is possible to trace a note of rising hysteria in the entries of many log books. Thus at Leckford Board School, Hampshire, in the middle of June 1880, the mistress wrote: 'Sent word to the parents to send the children as regularly as possible as Government exam. is drawing near', while at Cublington in Buckinghamshire, needlework was apparently the weak point. An entry for 29 January 1877 reads: 'Must give the Girls needlework all this afternoon instead of the usual lessons in order to be ready for the Inspector's visit.'

The HMIs recognised the ordeal that their visit represented. Some of the more insensitive seem even to have enjoyed the power they wielded over hapless school teachers and pupils alike.

Certainly one of their number – Mr Sneyd-Kynnersley – recalled in his autobiography that in many of the villages where he worked during the 1870s 'the annual inspection of the village school [was] the event of the year'. In ironical vein he then continued:

> To this people October is the first of months, because of the 'Xaminashun'. September is the long Vigil, during which, in spite of late harvest, truants are hunted up, cajoled, threatened, bribed to complete their tale of 250 attendances. Rising early, and so late taking rest, the teachers struggle with their little flock. The third week comes, and the post is watched with keenest anxiety. Has the day been fixed? Surely he won't come on the First! Surely he won't keep us in suspense till the last week! Suppose it rains! Suppose they get the measles! ... The children do not look so far ahead but when the actual day is fixed they catch the infection, and weary their mothers with speculations of probable success, possible failure. The eve of the awful day brings a half-holiday, on which the school floor has its annual wash: but the children hang about the playground and the school gate; for even blackberrying has lost its charm today.

The ambition of inspector, teacher and children on examination day was to finish by 12.30 p.m. at the latest. Consequently, the lowest standards, where the bulk of the children were to be found, were tackled first. The youngsters were lined up, together with their slates, pencils and a reading-book, and, standing back-to-back 'to prevent copying', they did dictation, arithmetic and reading. Very often the reading-book would have been learnt off by heart beforehand, so that even if the book fell to the ground whilst they were reading, they 'could go on equally well'. When the results of these tests had been marked on the Examination Schedule, the younger children were sent home. 'Then we proceeded to examine the rest, the aristocracy, who worked their sums on paper. As a rule, if we began about 10 we finished about 11.45. If the master was a good fellow, and trustworthy, we looked over the few papers in dictation and arithmetic, marked the Examination Schedule, and showed him the whole result before we left ... But if the man were cross-grained, and likely to complain that the exercises were too hard, the standard of marking too high, and so on, he would be left in merciful ignorance of details.'[15]

For the older children, above the age of ten, success in the Standard IV or Standard V examinations – the usual leaving certificate level – meant freedom to engage in full-time employment, and so for them the annual inspection had a special significance. Even as late as 1900 HMI Henderson noted that in rural areas very few children stayed on long enough 'to work in any Standard above the fifth'.[16]

But if the annual inspection provided a break in the daily routine – albeit not a very pleasant one – for the remainder of the school year, week followed week in monotonous succession, along lines laid down by the official timetable and approved by the HMI. For the timetable was sacrosanct and any deviation from its provisions had to be explained and justified in the log book. Even a failure to keep it hanging on the wall of the classroom could call down the wrath of the HMI and a threat that 'a repetition of this want of care might endanger the payment of the grant'.[17] Walter Rose, a carpenter's son from Haddenham, Buckinghamshire, remembered the irksome daily round that adherence to the timetable involved in his school during the 1870s. 'No one expected us to *like* school; indeed the adult idea was that it was good for us to be made to do what we didn't like. Not until I had passed my teens did the notion that school might be attractive ever enter my head.' Most of his fellows agreed with him:

Every morning at nine o'clock (after a run in the playground, where on cold days 'cockwarning' was a favourite game) we were rung into the school room by a bell on the roof. We sang the morning hymn ('Awake, my soul') led by a bronchial harmonium, which one of the monitors played. I do not remember ever singing another opening hymn; we never expected to, and the idea seems never to have occurred to those in control. When I was moved up from the infant room, I picked up the words as well as I could, from others who had picked them up before me. None of us knew the right wording, and most of the hymn was sung to an incredible jargon in which only a few lines were rendered fairly correctly. Outside we compared our versions, which were always different, except that all agreed in singing 'Shake off dolls' clothes' as the third line of the first verse.

An extempore prayer by the master followed; and then he mounted his platform desk and filled up the register, while we were given a lesson from the Old Testament by a monitor, who read aloud the vivid records out of the Books of Joshua, Judges, Samuel, and Kings. Those readings were anything but dull to us; we took the side of the Israelites, regretted their reverses and revelled in their slaughter of the Amalekites and the Jebusites, wicked tribes who deserved to he swept off the face of the land to make room for the chosen people of God. Now and then the monitor stopped and questioned us; those whose answers were wrong were called from their seats to stand in line at the front, along with any others who had otherwise misbehaved.

All through that scripture lesson the master was peaceably at his own duties – we noticed that he would spend much time every day in sharpening his pencil to a good point … When the scripture lesson was over he caned all the boys (and now and then a girl) who were standing out in line ... When the row of culprits was extra long, he began normally, but increased in zest as he proceeded, so that the poor unfortunates at the end could not keep back the tears. To be beaten without weeping was our ideal; we used to time how long the tingling lasted by the clock on the wall, and compare times later to know who had endured the most.[18]

This ready use of the cane was common in many other schools. At Launton in Oxfordshire, for example, the newly-appointed master noted in his log book for 15 November 1865: 'Obliged to use the stick very freely in school today, for without it I could in no way obtain anything like Discipline, as if I simply spoke to the children they would stand and laugh at me.' Certainly HMI Bellairs, as early as 1845, regarded this kind of situation with considerable misgivings, declaring:

One of the chief obstacles to success in the moral and religious condition of our parochial schools is the injudicious, if not unprincipled, way in which punishments are frequently administered ... On some occasions I have observed [the master] walking about the room, cane in hand, brandishing it over the heads of the children, who, trembling under the anticipated stroke, have lost all sense of the lesson in which they were engaged, and with eyes wandering from their book to the avenging rod, have brought upon themselves, as they caught the master's eye, the blow.[19]

At Haddenham, as in many schools, after the scripture lesson and its attendant beatings, came arithmetic, and then the children were allowed out to play. Writing and reading followed, with constant repetition and learning by rote the usual method of instruction. Textbooks varied in quality and quantity from school to school, but many were of an uninspiring character. In the case of arithmetic, questions often took the form of extremely long mechanical sums which would occupy a class for some time while the hard-pressed teacher moved round to look after another group. (For in most village schools there was only one trained teacher to cope with children of all ages and abilities, aided perhaps by a pupil teacher or monitor.) A typical example of this long-winded type, intended for Standard IV pupils, reads: 'Reduce 453 hogsheads (of wine), 45 gallons, 1 pint to gills; and divide your answer by 347.' Similarly, scholars were asked to 'bring 5 years 45 weeks, 5 days, 17 hours, 49 minutes to minutes. Write out your answer in words.' A page of workings was the result of what must have appeared to the pupils as a totally irrelevant and boring exercise.

Of course, there were always a few teachers who tried to make the work more interesting for their charges – despite the deadening influence of the daily routine. At Bromsberrow School, Gloucestershire, for example, the master noted in April 1900 that a 'circular [had] been received from the Education Dept. ordering the Managers to make the teaching in school more suitable to the environment of the scholars than has hitherto been the case. All the boys have witnessed the operation of grafting fruit trees while some have performed the operation themselves in the garden adjacent to the school. One of the parents of the scholars has promised to lend me a chain for the purpose of measuring land; and as the farm labourers find a difficulty in estimating the various areas of ground upon which their work has been done, both in spring and Harvest, they are very anxious that their boys should be taught land-measuring.' Nearly a month later came a further entry on the subject: 'This afternoon I took the boys belonging to St. IV and upward just across the road opposite the school for the purpose of measuring land with a chain. The result was quite satisfactory.'[20] Nor was it just in arithmetic that an original approach was tried. Somewhat sanctimoniously the master noted on 23 November that an 'object lesson in "charity" and "thoughtfulness for others"' had been given at the school. 'The practical work of Dr Barnardo's Homes for Waifs has been explained, and the children asked to contribute themselves, and visit the houses in the parish with Collecting Cards.' Whether his gesture was appreciated by hard-pressed cottagers in the parish is not mentioned.

The reading books used in most schools were just as uninspiring as were those provided for arithmetic. The widespread choice of collections of extracts was particularly condemned. As one of Her Majesty's Inspectors declared in 1879: 'I should like to see books like "Robinson Crusoe", "Tom Brown's School Days", "Alice in Wonderland" and a host of similar works used by the upper standards in our elementary schools in place of scissor-and-paste compilations wherein the disjecta membra of scientific technicality are interspersed with ill-concealed sermonettes and mendacious stories of anthropomorphised animals. Then there would be some chance that reading would be found a pleasure.' Even the books chosen for school prizes appear unsuitable, given the limited reading ability of many of the pupils. In the early 1870s at Whitchurch in Oxfordshire, for example, among the prizes selected were improving tracts like *Self-Knowledge* and *Peter's £ became a Penny* or works like White's *History of Selborne* and Joyce's *Scientific Dialogues*. Yet Her Majesty's Inspector had reported that the children's reading showed 'no sign of skill', while their 'intelligence was still imperfect'. Perhaps, however, the youngsters derived some consolation from the fact that the prize-giving was followed by a substantial tea and a magic lantern display, organised by the rector. For as in most Church of England schools, the Whitchurch incumbent took an active interest in all proceedings involving the pupils.

At a number of schools even in the 1870s one lesson a week was devoted to drawing, and from 1890 a change in the Government Code made this subject compulsory for all boys 'unless certified impracticable'. But for many pupils, including Walter Rose, it was grammar which proved the Achilles heel:

> I have a hazy memory of taking sentences in hand, and of tackling each word in turn, declaring parts of speech, person, number, gender, and case. I was always weak on cases; but as 'nominative' seemed to be most frequent, I got into the way of using it in all my answers, until the master found me out and saved up for me the words that were not in the nominative case. Only because I know now that children can learn anything am I able to understand how it was that we could gabble it off as we did; but how grammar was an aid to speaking or writing nobody had the faintest idea, then, and nobody has been able to advise me since. On leaving school I straightway forgot it all, as all the others did.[21]

Small wonder in these circumstances that on bright spring and summer days a few of the more daring boys and girls played truant – running off to fish or gather flowers or simply to play games and enjoy a few hours of unaccustomed freedom.

It was not surprising either that teachers also found the routine discouraging. At Spelsbury, Oxfordshire, the mistress noted in November 1885: 'Gave Standards III and IV an examination in Arithmetic. They seem to know the rules, but are quite unable to do the easiest problems without help.' Similarly, in May 1887, came the dispirited entry: 'Children's Reading is entirely devoid of expression. They hurry over their reading never even noticing "Full stops".' Nearly twenty years earlier, her colleague at Souldern in the same county had commented: 'The progress of the scholars is very slow ... the parents here do not appreciate learning and fill their children's heads with its uselessness, they send their children to school simply to be free from the care of them.'

Lack of equipment and of books were further handicaps. Parents were often too poor even to purchase slates and pencils for their offspring, and the provision of these and of the textbooks thus depended upon the school managers – egged on by adverse comments from HMIs. At Spelsbury, for example, the children were unable to write in their copy books for several weeks in the autumn of 1891 because there was no ink. 'The upper Standards do all their writing, etc. on slates,' reads the entry for 20 October. Spelsbury School was largely financed by the local landowner, Viscount Dillon, and on 24 October the mistress received a further blow when he announced that the monitress was to be dismissed 'as he thinks the School Expenses are much higher than formerly. As I cannot well manage with all the Standards without some slight assistance I have told her I will pay her for the present.' That seems to have remained the situation for several months, until the girl left in February 1892. A similarly parsimonious attitude was displayed by the managers of some of the rate-aided board schools – like that at Bledington in Gloucestershire; here the two teachers of about a hundred pupils had to share a single blackboard and a single chair for a long time in spite of urgent requests for a second.[22] And at Leckford in Hampshire the mistress commented in March 1876, 'Commenced home lessons with the children, find a great difficulty in getting them to buy a spelling or geography book.'

A few schools had other extras to add on to the children's basic weekly fees. At Wrawby National Schools, Lincolnshire, rules prepared in 1877 noted that as well as the usual charges, 'Every Scholar pays 1s a year for fuel; but no family is required to pay more than 2s 6d on the whole. This payment must be made in October. Every Scholar in the Upper School pays 3d per quarter for pens and ink.' At Redbourne National School in the same county, rules prepared in 1855 likewise required, 'Each child ... to pay three pence per quarter for the use of books: no family to pay for more than two.' Here the children of labourers were allowed to attend on the payment of 2s a quarter in fees, provided they did 'the needlework, clean the Schools, and such other work as is necessary to the comfort and cleanliness of the Schools and playground etc.' The sons and daughters of tradesmen and farmers, on the other hand, were expected to pay 5s a quarter but were exempt from the menial duties. Nevertheless it was by no means uncommon for elementary school pupils to perform such chores. Many contemporaries considered them good training for girls who would later earn their living as domestic servants, before settling down to become wives and mothers. Certainly the Reverend James Fraser, an Assistant Commissioner with the Newcastle Commission, suggested that while boys could play cricket and football, such games were unsuitable for the girls; so they could find 'a little wholesome physical exercise' by cleaning the school. He noted regretfully that he had 'often visited schools when this so-called cleaning was going on, either at the dinner hour or when the school was closed for the day. I do not remember an instance in which any one was present to overlook the children, or to see the work done properly. In most cases it was a mere scene of helter-skelter, dust, mess, and confusion, and, as it seemed to me, a valuable opportunity for giving a little industrial training was thus thrown away.'[23]

But as the century drew to a close, more and more parents objected to their children being employed in this manner, and so paid school cleaners began to take over the firelighting, scrubbing and polishing which had formerly fallen to the lot of the pupils. Financial pressure on parents was also eased in the final decade by a further government grant in 1891 which made it possible for schools to offer elementary education free to the vast majority of children. Some teachers, like the master at Pershore National Boys' School in Worcestershire, hoped that this would encourage the children to attend school more regularly; but in his case at least the hope was a vain one. On 11 December 1891, he sadly recorded, 'The improvement in the attendance which took place on the abolition of school fees here has not continued. This week 277 were present at all, but the average was only 248.' Two years later the minimum school leaving age was raised to eleven and in 1899 it rose again, to twelve – even though in rural areas many school authorities still seem to have permitted children to leave at eleven.[24]

Further problems were created in certain areas by the lack of amenities within the schools themselves, especially during the first half of the nineteenth century. In some villages classes were held in cottages, lofts, outhouses and even in churches rather than in purpose-built properties. But from the 1870s this situation began to be rectified, even though few rural schools consisted of more than one large room, plus perhaps a smaller one for the infants. Often, however, the smaller children were accommodated in a gallery, or raised platform, in the main room, where the teacher could keep his or her eye on them. Older pupils were seated at long desks, some of which would accommodate as many as six children at a time. As a Norfolk girl recalled, they were extremely uncomfortable: 'The lids could be raised, but the seats were fixed and this necessitated an entry with bent knees.' In her school, pencils and papers were scarce, and so the younger children wrote with wooden skewers in shallow trays of sand. 'Any mistakes could easily be obliterated in the shifting sand, and so could a whole morning's toil. If an unfortunate inmate dropped his skewer, crawled down to the floor to retrieve it and ascended with doubled back, he would invariably raise the lid of the long, long desk, jolt all the sand trays and a morning's work could be lost in oblivion.'

Heating was normally provided by an open fire at one end of the room, but the warmth thrown out was often inadequate in the winter months, and the children were almost too cold to work. At Weston-on-Avon Board School, Gloucestershire, the master reported on 9 December 1878: 'Extremely cold. Could scarcely keep the school warm enough to manage with the writing.' And on 20 January 1879 came the further complaint: 'Excessively cold. Hardly able to carry the school on properly, the children shivering frequently with cold.' At Finedon, Northamptonshire, the heating problem at the boys' school was aggravated by a badly smoking chimney, which filled the room with fumes. This meant that on very windy days fires were impossible – hence entries like that on 6 January 1864: 'Let the boys play a little longer in the morning recess to warm themselves.' Despite attempts to rebuild the chimney the master was still complaining almost twenty years later of the 'extreme cold' which made it difficult for the boys to write.[25] But perhaps one's greatest sympathy should be reserved for the pupils at Tedburn St Mary, Devon, where a new board school was opened in 1877: 'Heating was quite inadequate; in 1894 "The thermometer stands at 24½ deg. F, 10 o'clock, fires lighted 2½ hours"; and later on "children shake with cold". Nothing was done about it, and six years later "Children obliged to exercise to keep warm – thermometer at 9.30 a.m. registered only 24 deg." Temperatures of 25–26 degrees continued to be registered at times, throughout the rest of the board's existence.'[26] The perseverance of the headmaster here, Alfred Walters, is also worthy of admiration. He remained at Tedburn from 1878 until his retirement in 1919, despite the obvious discomforts.

Sanitary arrangements were in many cases as unsatisfactory as were the heating facilities and there were complaints from HMIs that the 'offices' were 'too commonly mere pits, cleaned out, say, once a year'. All too easily they became a 'festering mass of corruption' harmful to the children's health. The 'offices' at South Creake in Norfolk at the end of the nineteenth century would certainly have confirmed these fears. As one of the pupils recalled, they were 'discreetly screened behind maroon corrugated iron … Six bucket closets with wooden seats of ascending heights served the Infants and the Girls, whilst a latrine at the far end, for the Infant boys boasted a drain which dripped constantly into the Beck. This area was slightly noisome, but country children like their parents [were] supposed to be accustomed to strong smells.'[27]

Yet, however uncomfortable or frustrating school might be, as the fingers of the clock slowly moved round to four each day, hopes would rise as the hour of release came nearer. At Tysoe in Warwickshire the young Joseph Ashby remembered that 'joy would burgeon' and the small sorrows of the day would be forgotten as the last hymn was sung. Then came the careful regimentation which preceded the final dismissal: 'All the children in a class came out together – or rather in order – to a series of commands. One! and you stood in your desk. Two! and you put your left leg over the seat. Three! and the right joined it. Four! you faced the lane between the classes. Five! you marched on the spot. Six!

you stepped forward and the pupil-teacher chanted, "Left, right, left, right, left, right". It was agony – you were so longing to get outside. But if one boy pushed another you would have to go back and begin the rigmarole again.'[28]

Once outside the children could run and jump and shout, to celebrate their release. In dry weather marbles would be played along the sides of the roads, or there would be skipping or the bowling of hoops and the whipping of tops. Some of the braver souls would climb into the hedges after birds' nests in the spring time, or would pick blackberries and nuts in the autumn. In winter there would be icy puddles to slide on and snowballs to throw, while from time to time as they walked home, a cart or carriage would pass. If the squire or the clergyman drove past the children were expected to curtsy or bow with suitable respect. Failure to do so could lead to severe reprimands in school the next day. For both inside school and out country children were always exhorted to 'labour truly to get their own living and order themselves lowly and reverently to their betters ... the word "betters" was especially firmly underlined and annotated'.[29] And in 1877 HMI Palmer reported that in many schools 'the farmer will not let his daughter (nor his son except in earliest years) sit beside the children of his labourers'. But this concern to instil notions of deference and humility into the children was perhaps expressed, most clearly in 1867 by Robert Lowe, a former vice-president of the Education Department: 'The lower classes ought to be educated to discharge the duties cast upon them. They should also be educated that they may appreciate and defer to a higher cultivation when they meet it, and the higher classes ought to be educated in a very different manner, in order that they may exhibit to the lower classes that higher education to which, if it were shown to them, they would bow down and defer.'[30] It was against this social background that, for example, a log book entry at Holbeton, Devon, for 1867 reads: 'Spoke to the children about making obeisance to their Superiors.' Soon even the dullest or most defiant youngsters realised where their duty lay and outwardly conformed to the standard expected of them. But inwardly they may have shared the doubts of Arthur Tweedy of Kirby Fleetham in Yorkshire, who remembered asking his father why he should say 'Sir' to the squire 'or anyone else who thought himself a step above' the farm labourers. His father's reply was: '"Sir", my boy, is only the nickname for a fool.'[31]

4

WORKERS ON THE LAND

You can say labourin's the hardest graft as a man can have. When yo're used to it yo' don't feel it so much. But it's mostly work and bed, work and bed, and bein' out in all sorts o' weather, summer and winter. The way I look at it is that a man should be what yo'd call paid for his work. A lot of folk think there's nothin' in it, and they're a good deal mista'en. It takes years before yo' can be what yo' may call a first-rate man.

An old labourer quoted in J. W. Robertson Scott,
The Land Problem (n.d., *c.* 1914)

For much of the nineteenth century agriculture continued to employ more men and boys than any other single industry. Admittedly the last twenty-five years saw something of a decline in that position, thanks to the effects of bad harvests and cheap imports of grain from, North America, Russia and India and of refrigerated meat from Australasia and America. From employing around a quarter of occupied males in 1851, British farming accounted for about 17 per cent of the male labour force in the early 1880s and only about 12 per cent in 1901. Nevertheless it remained the linchpin of the rural economy. Not only did its workforce, even in 1900, stand at around one million but the supplying of its day-to-day needs formed the principal means of earning a living for countless village craftsmen as well.

In the first year of Victoria's reign the daily routine of labourers and farm servants – the most numerous of the rural workers – was described by William Howitt, a popular author and journalist anxious to take an optimistic view of village life. Yet even he was forced to admit the hardships and the lack of opportunity which were the lot of many. And much of what he wrote was still valid at the end of the century, despite mechanisation, the decline of importance of arable cultivation and other changes on the farming scene. Howitt noted that village boys were set to work as soon as they were old enough to look after themselves. Often their first job would be watching a gate

> that stands at the end of the lane or the common to stop cattle
> from straying, and there through long solitary days they pick up a
> few halfpennies by opening it for travellers. They are sent to scare
> birds from corn just sown, or just ripening ... They help to glean,
> to gather potatoes, to pop beans into holes in dibbling time, to pick
> hops, to gather up apples for the cider-mill, to gather mushrooms and
> blackberries for market, to herd flocks of geese or young turkeys, or
> lambs at weaning time; they even help to drive sheep to market or to
> the wash at shearing time ... and then, they are very useful to lift and
> carry about the farm-yard, to shred turnips, or beet-root – to hold a
> sack open – to bring in wood for the fire, or to rear turfs for drying
> on the moors, as the man cuts them with his paring shovel, or to rear
> peat bricks for drying. They are mighty useful animals in their day
> and generation, and as they get bigger, they successively learn to drive
> [a] plough, and then to hold it; to drive the team, and finally to do
> all the labours of a man.[1]

From then on the young workers were expected to perform a whole range of tasks, for upon their skills and energy the smooth running of British agriculture depended. The experienced man could be called upon to set seeds, to hoe, to weed, to mow, to make hurdles, to cut chaff, to spread dung, to thresh, to hedge and ditch and even to help maintain the farm roads. As a Yorkshire labourer, Arthur Tweedy, recalled, some of the hand tools used in these operations were themselves heavy and tiring. 'You had to be fit and strong to use most of [them].' There were the grain hoppers, for example, which were used to sow corn or spread artificial manure by hand. They were 'large tin containers shaped to fit the body and strapped over the shoulders and round the waist and held 3 or 4 stone of grain ... I have seen men sow 20 acres a day with this and so tired [they] had to be assisted home.' Then there was the fiddle drill, for sowing grass and clover seed. This, too, was strapped to the back and was 'pulled to and fro like a violin bow to the tune of the feet'. Although not as exhausting as the grain hopper, the worker had to 'keep walking quickly and no stopping except to refill and to move pegs or markers'.

Richard Hillyer, a Northamptonshire farm lad, shared many of Arthur's feelings. In his autobiography, *Country Boy,* he bitterly described his first days at work:

Every night I dropped asleep over my supper, and then woke up just enough to crawl upstairs, and fall into bed ... Sunday was the only break, and then the racked body cried out to be let alone for an hour or two, so that the muscles could loosen ...

A black depression spread over me. 'This is what it is going to be from now on,' I thought ... 'Lifting, hauling, shoving, trudging about from day to day, nothing else through all the years' ... There was no chance of a better job in Byfield, and no hope of getting out of it ... It was like settling down into a deep bed of mud, cold, gluey, isolating ...

But Hillyer was lucky. Thanks to coaching from the local rector and success in a scholarship to Durham University, he escaped from this much-disliked routine.

A number of the tasks required of the general labourer were paid for by the piece rather than by the day, particularly if the farmer wished to get the work done as quickly as possible. In such circumstances a company of labourers might agree to take on a job together – hoeing by the acre, hedgecutting by the chain, and so on. On Viscount Dillon's home farm at Ditchley, Oxfordshire, the labour book for 1857 shows payments in March to 'Biles and company for turning 17 acres of sanfoin in hop yard @ 5s per acre', and to Henry Cross and Elijah Tidcomb 'for hoeing 9½ acres of wheat @ 5s per acre'. Four 'Stonesfield men' were paid 6s an acre for 'setting 3 acres of beans'. There are many similar entries. Again, in the Swaffham area of Norfolk piecework contracts were offered for such varied tasks as mowing hay, hoeing turnips, setting swedes, cutting grass, drilling corn, thatching ricks and stacks, and shearing sheep, while in the Wantage area of Berkshire during the 1890s piecework was available for at least two months a year, in addition to the harvest season.[2] What made piecework earnings particularly profitable was the extended day that many of the workers were prepared to put in, so as to complete the job speedily. Sometimes a man would even volunteer for piecework hoeing or stonepicking after his ordinary day's work had been completed.

Yet if the trademark of the good general labourer was versatility, the stockman, by contrast, often required specialised skills. For he must not only be able to care for the animals when they were well – working and living with them 'twelve or fifteen hours a day' – but also be capable of doctoring them when they were sick. Many stockmen, indeed, prided themselves on having their own remedies to treat the various ills, such as celandine to clear worms or horehound to cure a cold, or perhaps they would prepare a special brew whose ingredients were known only to themselves.

Carters and horsemen were particularly concerned about the appearance of their animals and sometimes went to the trouble of stealing extra fodder or spending long hours in grooming so as to make sure that their team was as good as anyone else's in the parish. Often the horses' tails were neatly plaited and 'tied up with braid of various colours', while if a team were going away from home, it 'was not reckoned in first-class style unless furnished with bells. The bells were fixed in iron frames by leather hoops, and the frames were fixed to the two hames of the horse. The "fore'st" (foremost or first) horse and the "lash" (second) horse, had four bells each. The "body" (third) and the "thiller" (fourth) horses had three each. Each set of bells was tuned harmoniously.'[3] Among the many young stockmen who stole food from fellow workers in order to bring their horses to top condition was George Sadler, a Cambridgeshire farmer's son. He used to help himself to the linseed cake which was intended for the sheep. 'I'd give it to the horses early in the morning before anyone got about. They'd eat that first and nobody would know. There's nothing like linseed cake for putting a gloss on their coats.' When he was found out, he turned to stealing locust beans, which had been specially bought for the lambs. Once again he was caught: 'But I wasn't satisfied even then. One of my brothers used to look after cattle; and of course he had all the grub he could get hold of. And I used to go and start pinching the grub out of his tubs to feed to my team of horses ... Well, I started pinching this cattle-food, and he soon guessed what was going on, and he put a bloody rat-trap in one of his big barrels. And the next time I went to scrape out a pailful of this bullock's grub I got my hand in this trap ... But even after that I went on pinching food for my horses. I really couldn't help it.'[14]

For carters and ploughboys the working day began earlier than for most of their fellow labourers – usually at 4 a.m. or 5 a.m., since the horses had to be fed and made ready to start work at about 7 a.m. or 7.30 a.m. Once at the stables the horsemen had to clean out the stalls and feed and harness the horses in readiness for whatever tasks the day might bring forth. Work would then continue until about 11 a.m., when the labourer would stop for 'a bait – bread and cheese which he has brought with him' and a drink of beer, cider or cold tea, according to taste and local custom. The horses usually had nothing 'except perhaps some water in hot weather'. This break lasted half an hour and then work resumed until 4 p.m., with perhaps a brief rest of a quarter of an hour in the early afternoon. According to William Stephens, a fourteen-year-old ploughboy from Bromsberrow, Gloucestershire, who was interviewed in the later 1860s, he would plough in all 'about three-quarters of an acre of land in the day. When [he] arrives at stable [in the late afternoon, he], has his dinner; bread and cheese, or bacon, which he has brought with him. This takes half an hour. Dinner finished, goes to the stable, and helps the carter to unharness and dress his horses; makes their beds. He and his carter have to look after six horses ... Has done work by seven o'clock and gets [home] about half-past seven. Has his supper, garden stuff, and bread and meat ... Goes to bed about half-past eight, and sleeps pretty firm.' William had started full-time work on the farm when he was eleven, and among his additional chores was the collection of the day's cider allowance (five quarts) for himself and the carter, from the farm house. He had three pints of this and the carter the rest.[5] But he was fortunate in that, unlike many youngsters working with horses, he was not expected to return to the stable in the evening to 'supper up' the animals and settle them for the night. For in the view of at least one writer, this 'suppering up' was as important in the farmer's eyes as the men's own meals: 'The first business in the morning and the last at night ... was the horses.'[6]

The duties required of the horseman and his team naturally varied with the seasons. In the late autumn there would be the drilling of winter wheat, the carrying of mangolds and other root crops, and winter ploughing. During late December and January, when the weather was bad, the horses were often allowed a rest, while the stockmen busied themselves with fencing, cleaning out stackyards and repairing implements. If the weather in February was reasonable, the beans and peas would be drilled, and the spring tares or vetches sown. And so the round continued until in August came harvest – the climax of the farming year[7] (see Appendix D for a calendar of the year's work). Sometimes the carter would be sent out with stones to make up the farm roads or would go on a journey with a load of corn for sale, or perhaps to collect coal.

Harrowing, dung spreading and haymaking were other jobs which involved the horsemen, and the variety in their working week is shown by the following extracts for the seven days ending 15 March 1889 from the Labour Book at Audley End Park Farm, Essex, where there were three 'horsekeepers' employed:

	Saturday	Monday	Tuesday	Wednes-day	Thurs-day	Friday
G. Marshall	Carting timber	Plough-ing	Drilling oats	Carting	Drilling	Drilling
C. Claydon	[Odd] Jobbing	Plough-ing	Drilling oats	Carting	Drilling barley	Drilling
W. Finworth	Jobbing	Plough-ing	Carting luggage	Plough-ing	Harrow-ing	Harrow-ing

The cowman and the shepherd, by contrast, had a more regular routine. The stockman in the dairying areas, for example, was concerned with milking the cows and rearing the calves, and, according to one observer, by the 1890s his hours were usually arranged 'according to the time for the morning milking, which has to be finished in readiness for the early morning train to London; generally they would be from 4 a.m. or 5 a.m. to 5 p.m. or 6 p.m., but he would usually be allowed an hour for breakfast after the morning milking, besides the usual dinner hour, and on some farms he has half-an-hour for tea'.[8]

The walks with the cattle twice daily from pasture to cowhouse and back were slow and leisurely and in summer time if the cows were not milked in the field they were a not unpleasant chore. 'It was wise that the. man in charge should dawdle, [since] each cow carried its heavy bag of milk, and to have hastened the pace would have reduced the flow.' Milking, too, was an orderly ritual. Once the buckets had been collected the milker started on his task: 'Each cow knew that a feed of juicy pulped roots, mixed with chaff and meal, awaited her arrival at the cow-stall. It mattered little that for the time being her head was secured between two upright slats of wood, the enjoyment of food was a compensation that happened twice daily; all that was expected of her was a free yield of the milk that hung heavy and perhaps painfully in the bag.'[9]

But it was far less pleasant to rise at 5 a.m. on a dark winter's morning and to 'put on coarse nailed boots, weighing fully seven pounds, gaiters up above the knee, a short greatcoat of some heavy material, and to step out into the driving rain and trudge wearily over field after field of wet grass, with the furrows full of water, then to sit on a three-legged stool, with mud and manure halfway up the ankles, and milk cows with one's head leaning against their damp, smoking hides for two hours, with the rain coming steadily drip, drip, drip.'[10] Yet most of the men accepted it without complaint, seeing it as part of the inescapable round of their daily life.

In Dorset, however, the dairy system was rather different, since many farmers here, instead of managing their own cows, let them out on contract to a dairyman. The dairyman was also often allowed to keep pigs and poultry for his own profit. Typical of the kind of arrangement made was that involving John Butler, a farmer of Tarrant Launceston near Blandford, and his dairyman, A. H. Bonditch, in the mid-1890s. Bonditch was to manage 'twenty-eight cows' and for this was to be paid '£1 per week wages & 5 per cent at the end of the year on all clear profit made on Butter, Cheese & Pigs'. He was to be provided with a house and garden rent free, plus two tons of coal, '100 Furze faggots for the Dairy work – Straw for litter to be delivered at Dairy House'. His duties included feeding the cows and pigs, making the butter and cheese and keeping the pigsties clean (although in practice his wife would also be involved in the butter and cheese making). He was to look after the poultry as well and was to be paid '1d per dozen for Eggs – 3d per couple for chickens reared. 3d per head for geese reared'. The provision of part of the dairy utensils was also to be his responsibility.[11]

But a number of Dorset farmers adopted an even clearer subcontract system-like Walter Ross, from Ibberton, who concluded an agreement in 1874 with John and Henry Watts, dairymen, by which they paid him £400 for the management of thirty-two cows and heifers for one year.[12] Ross, for his part, provided them with grazing, 'a sufficient quantity of Hay and Straw for the ... cows and heifers', and potato ground. The dairymen's profit was to be made from the sale of the milk and dairy produce, and possibly the rearing of pigs. And as Henry Rew noted in 1895, when reporting on Dorset for the Royal Commission on Agriculture, the system, despite its cumbersome character, had the advantage of providing a stepping stone 'for men to rise from the position of stockmen to that of dairymen, and from thence to tenant farmer'.

Elsewhere, on holdings concerned with raising beef, there were store cattle and fatstock to be fed with heavy skeps of meal and turnips. As one young Yorkshire worker, Fred Kitchen, remembered, this too was testing work: 'I was too small to keep out of the muck, and waded through slop and cow-muck until I became absolutely lost. My breeches became so caked in pigswill, calf-porridge, and meal I believe they could have stood upright without me inside them ... After tea I fed the calves again, and, to my credit, never spilled the porridge in the straw at night-time. But it's a messy job feeding calves; the little beggars will come fussing round, sucking at your clothes with porridgy mouths, and that is how my clothes came to be so stuck up.'[13]

Later Kitchen moved to another farm which concentrated on raising sheep and barley, and 'where a full-time shepherd was employed, along with a day-lad to help in winter when the sheep were folded on the turnips. Hurdles and feeding troughs had to be moved around and large supplies of turnips cut. Fred recalled this work as one of the roughest jobs on a farm during the winter. With two or three hundred sheep (fattening hoggets) folded on the turnips,

> the shepherd, his lad – and not forgetting the dog – spent their days from daylight to dusk in the field feeding sheep and dressing turnips. Artists have drawn some pleasing pictures of the shepherd leading his flock on the grassy uplands, or gazing pensively at a setting sun, but we have no picture of the shepherd in the muddy turnip field; of him and his lad sliding about in the muddy sheep-pen with skeps of sliced turnips; or the lad, bending down to clean out the troughs, receiving

a gallant charge in the rear from a too-playful tup; or when snow
and sleet swirls round their ears they 'chop and throw' in defiance
of foul weather.

Lambing was an especially busy season, with the newborn lambs
protected in pens and behind hurdles, or, on the smaller farms, put with
their mother in the empty stalls in the cowsheds. It often involved an
all-night vigil for the shepherd, who would sleep out among his flock in
a wheeled hut. Warmth was provided by a small oil-stove which would
also heat milk to feed to the orphaned lambs, while lighting came from
a horn lantern which gave out a gentle glow and did not scare the
ewes when it was carried round the fold.[14] A successful lambing was
important for the shepherd, since he was normally paid extra cash for
each youngster successfully reared; in the 1860s and 1870s the Dorset
farmer, John Butler, paid his shepherds 1*d* per lamb, for example, and
this was a typical rate.[15]

Sheep washing and shearing formed another peak period, especially
where flocks were large. As Mr F. W. Brocklehurst of Sheldon in
Derbyshire remembered, on the day decided upon for washing the
flocks in his parish, 'the farmers highest up the village would start
with their sheep about 8 a.m., having first taken the lambs away, and
amid a tremendous amount of bleating gradually all the sheep in the
village would be collected until over a hundred would be on their
way to the ... wash'. The ewes were first put into pens and then let
out one at a time. They were driven into the water and the thick wool
was worked and rubbed and squeezed so as to get as much of the dirt
out as possible. The animal finally emerged bleating pitifully from
the other side of the wash-dyke, weighted down with the water with
which its thick fleece was saturated. When the job was finished, the
sheep stumbled up the road and, as Brocklehurst recalled, they 'needed
no telling to go home when ready, as all the ewes were eager to get
to their lambs. They also needed no division, for when they came to
their own farms, they turned in without any sorting out.' The shearing
followed 'about ten days later as it was said to be easier clipping if the
grease had risen again'. Where flocks were large specialist migratory
shearers might be employed for this work, but elsewhere local labour
sufficed, and often shepherds would co-operate to shear one another's
flocks. All of the wool from Sheldon was sold to one firm, and when
it was ready to be weighed and packed, the boys would rush from
school to the packing room 'to help tread [it] tight' in the sheets in
which it was to be sent away. 'There was great excitement over whose
wool would weigh heaviest. I know ours averaged 14 lbs a fleece for
many years.'[16]

In addition to the various male workers, most farmers would also employ some women – usually on a temporary or seasonal basis to help with weeding, stonepicking, haymaking, harvesting, potato picking and similar tasks. In some counties, indeed, such as Dorset and Northumberland, it was customary for male workers to provide extra labour from among their families when the farmer needed it. As late as the 1890s the *Dorset County Chronicle* contained advertisements for labourers 'with a working Family', while others indicated a preference for men with large families – no doubt with the same end in view. But in mid-Victorian times a number of women worked full-time in the fields on their own account. At the 1871 Census of Population there were over 58,000 female labourers and farm servants recorded in England and Wales; by the end of the century that total had dwindled to under 12,000.

However, it was in Northumberland and the border counties that permanent female labour on the land persisted the longest. In these counties, too, the employment of resident male farm servants was common – in Cumberland they outnumbered the outdoor men in 1871, while in Durham one worker in three was an 'indoor' servant. Yearly contracts were customary, with the unmarried men boarded on the farm or in 'bothies' and receiving a large part of their wages in kind. But from the women's point of view it was the 'bondager' system which was the most controversial. Under this married farm workers were often required to provide and house an extra female labourer for employment on the farm. It might be a wife, daughter or sister, but if there was no suitable relative available, then another woman would be hired. This led to charges of immorality and to complaints from the workers themselves, until by the end of the century the system had largely died out except where the girl involved was a member of the family. Typical of the agreements made between farmer and hind in the early 1890s was that concluded between Bartholomew Dunn and William Hindmarsh, a farmer of Ilderton in the Glendale area of Northumberland. It also demonstrates the mixture of payment in cash and in kind which was a characteristic of this part of the country: 'Bartholomew Dunn agrees to serve William Hindmarsh as hind at Ilderton, from 12 May 1891, to 12 May 1892, for 13s a week and the keep of a cow (Mr Hindmarsh to provide the cow), sixteen stones of cake, and forty stones of bran for winter food. One pig and 1,200 yards of potato drill. Agnes Cownes (step-daughter) to have 1s 6d a day for the whole year, and 3s a day for 20 days' harvest.'[17] In addition, a rent-free cottage was provided and coals were carted free of charge.

Physically the Northumbrian bondagers were considered to be 'a splendid race'. They were young women, normally under the age of thirty, and extremely strong, being capable of carrying out a whole range of different jobs, including weeding, turnip hoeing, haymaking, harvesting, filling dung carts, spreading dung, turnip cutting, driving carts and harrowing. Sometimes they also loaded hay or corn on the carts, 'though when such is the case two women are put to the work of one man'.[18] In fact, according to Arthur Munby, who met some of them during the summer of 1863, once afield they could be 'put to anything, except ploughing and ditching'. And he added significantly that the farmer liked to 'have his wenches under bondage, because then he can send them afield to hoe or dig in all weathers, and they can't shirk it' (see Appendix F).

In the nearby county of Yorkshire, Munby met other women labourers engaged in various farming activities. Thus in October 1862, he encountered 'a gang of twelve stout women and girls, all in white smocks and rustic bonnets and kerchiefs' picking potatoes, near the village of Brotherton. They moved 'slowly over the rough ploughlands, stooping or kneeling on the ground, and digging up the potatoes with their hands'. Munby went to speak to them and was told by one of their number that they were paid a shilling a day 'and work in the fields from 7 or 8 a.m. till dusk'. The girl to whom he spoke worked on the land all the year round: 'at hay and harvest, at pea picking in June, at osier-peeling in May, at tater gathering in October, and at turnip pulling, and so on. For these Brotherton girls are regular day labourers, and have no other occupation: and in winter, alack! we have to stop at home idle ... and do our bits of household work and sewing. Field work is our delight.'[19] In another field at Brotherton Munby also saw a woman working alone, 'raking and burning weeds; the slow blue smoke and pungent smell of which is perhaps the most autumnal of autumn things...' But these women, unlike their Northumberland colleagues, were ordinary day labourers and not bondagers.

In addition to the female land workers, however, most farmers employed a resident maidservant to assist in the house, help with the dairy and look after the poultry. Sometimes at the busiest seasons of the year she, too, would share in the outdoor work. John Boaden of Cury in Cornwall remembered that during the 1830s and 1840s on his family's small farm the servant girl was often in the fields, 'picking stones, weeding, hoeing, haymaking and harvesting, drawing potatoes'. In October 1862, Arthur Munby recorded his meeting with another servant girl at Upper Poppleton in Yorkshire.[20] Here a threshing machine was at work, with two women labourers upon it, and they were aided by the servant who, 'in her cotton bonnet, was doing her part manfully: was incessantly running to and fro – drawing water and carrying, it by two pails at a time, to the engine, and feeding the boiler; digging coals and wheeling them by barrowfuls to the stokehole'.

But, perhaps fortunately, few maidservants were expected to share in such exertions as these, even though their own daily life was no sinecure. Florence Stowe of Whichford, Warwickshire, was one of many thousand Victorian country girls who obtained work as a general farm servant, and each day, in addition to the usual chores of lighting fires, cleaning the house and preparing meals she had, before breakfast, to skim the milk and put it in a five gallon copper pan to heat over the fire for 'the Cowman to feed calves'. After breakfast she would 'clean all the Milk Pans and separator and strainer and milk buckets, swill the dairy'. Each utensil had to be put in a large bath and scalded with boiling water. 'I would then get all veg. and sundries for cooking, dinner was served at 12.30. Each day brought its own particular job, mostly done in the afternoons. One was set aside for churning and making the butter, a two-hour work and about 30 to 40 lb to pot up, weigh, mark ready for market … Another afternoon was taken up to clean all Brass, Copper, Silver and Meat Dish covers and brass kettles and press pans. These were the maid's pride of her kitchen for they were usually kept on the kitchen dresser and hung around. All the wood and coal to get in for all fires.'[21] Occasionally, too, as in Thomas Hardy's Dorset, women were employed to help with the daily milking, while in other cases they assisted in brewing the farm's supply of beer.

But for all who worked on the land, no matter what their normal daily routine might be, it was at haymaking and harvest that the greatest pressures occurred. During these hectic weeks, men, women and children worked from dawn to dusk for as long as the weather held, with the children making bands to bind the sheaves of corn or leading horses in the field, or perhaps carrying food and drink to the adult workers. On many holdings it was customary for a farmer to make a special contract with his men to 'take the harvest'. The man who treated with his employer about the terms of the contract was known as the 'Lord of the Harvest' and he would control the company of workers for the duration of the harvest. Negotiations between the two parties could be lengthy before a satisfactory settlement was reached, as Arthur Randell recalled: 'It was quite a business when the harvest men met the farmer each year to fix the price per acre for tying, shocking and carting. First of all they would inspect each field in turn, then the farmer would leave the men to talk the matter over for a while before coming back to hear their decision. Often they would all argue for as much as half a day but in the end they always came to some agreement and then the farmer would send for some beer to seal the bargain and a start could be made on the work.'[22] It was at this time, too, that extra men were recruited to help with the harvesting operations. Randell's own father, who was a mole catcher, always took part in the harvest, while in some cases

Irish labourers or migrants from other parts of the country would be employed. Some tried to maximise their earnings by taking part in more than one harvest. William Clift of Bramley in Hampshire describes how several of the local families would ask their employers to let them go 'to where corn ripened sooner than here (say at Chichester, or some such forward place); there they could get a fortnight's harvest work before our corn was ready. And after harvesting our corn, they would ask for another fortnight to go into more backward counties (say, Wiltshire, or elsewhere) and get another two or three weeks' work.'[23] Similarly, George Ewart Evans notes that men from Suffolk would go first to Essex and take a harvest there before returning to Suffolk to do a second one. But some stayed away from home still longer. They were usually casual labourers who had no permanent employer in their own village but relied on catchwork. George Swinford of Filkins in Oxfordshire remembers that a group went in this way from his own small community to London for haymaking and would then take extra harvest work:

> I have known six or eight men who used to go every year. Some of them walked, and others went by train, if they had the money to pay the fare. They mowed the park and fields with the scythe, then helped make the hay and put it into ricks ... The mowers slept in sheds and cooked their own meals, and done most of the mowing by contract ... When the haymaking was done, they worked their way back by doing hoeing for market gardeners. After working a week in one place, they walked on Sunday a few miles nearer home, and by the time they got to Wantage, the harvesting was ready, as it was earlier on the downs than it was here. This was the time they cut it by hand with a fagging hook, and they arranged it so that they got back to Filkins by the time the harvest was ready, so that they could finish it here and then go to Northleach where the harvest was later still. Some of these men who was careful with their money saved enough to keep them through the winter with a few days thrashing now and then, and a bit of poaching with a dog and gun and a few snares.[24]

Once a harvest contract had been formally concluded it detailed not only the crops to be carried but also the methods to be used in harvesting them, and often the allowances to be made – such as the provision of beer or food for the workers and of gloves (or money to buy them) to protect the men's hands against thistles whilst they cut the com. One typical harvest agreement was that made at Hall Farm, Great Wilbraham, Cambridgeshire in 1891:

AGREEMENT OF HARVEST ON HALL FARM

The Company of Harvesters is to consist of 15 men (without the men to attend to carthorses) and the binder will be used as much as possible within reason in the wheat only.

The Company of Harvestmen will have to do as follows:

1. Wheat that is cut with the binder to be set up in rows right across each field.
2. Wheat that is cut with the reapers to be tied and set up in rows right across each field.
3. All the wheat to be carted and stacked in a workmanlike manner.
4. The barley to be cut with scythes or reapers according to the Master's orders which entirely depends on the weather and layer.
5. All the barley to be gathered by the Company.
6. All the barley to be carted, stacked and drag raked behind each cart in a workmanlike manner.
7. All the first lot of wheat rakings to be carted with the sheaves if required.
8. All the laid places in each field where the machines are at work to be mown out if required.
9. To let the reapers in every field that is required.
10. To thresh corn 1, 2 or 3 days as required.
11. The machines to be driven by men in the Company.
12. To gather, cart, stack and drag rake behind each cart all the rakings.
13. All sheaves to be set up when fallen down if required.
14. To get all stack bottoms.
15. To turn barley as many times as is thought necessary by the Master.
16. To cover up stacks each night properly and put loads under cover.
17. The Master finds drivers, leaders and does the horseraking.
18. All work to be commenced and discontinued according to the Master's orders.
19. In case of one or more of the harvestmen being absent the remaining part of the Company will complete his or their work and agree to payment thereof.
20. The wages of the harvestmen will be eight Pounds (£8) per man to work as long as the harvest lasts.
21. It will be the option of the Master to give a horkey or not according to the behaviour and satisfaction of the Company during harvest. [A horkey was the East Anglian term for a harvest frolic or feast.][25]

On this particular farm the men provided their own beer and when the harvest started in August 1891 there was 'drawn on account' the sum of £15 from their earnings for that purpose, i.e. a payment of £1 per head for beer. They were also each paid between 16s and £1 a week as advances on their harvest money until the last of the corn was gathered at the end of September. They then received their final settlement. This policy of paying in advance of the final settlement was common practice, since the men needed their weekly wages to tide them over whilst they were getting in the crops.

Once the harvest had commenced the fields were a scene of bustle and activity, with mechanical reapers operating long, revolving arms like windmill sails or, in the less advanced areas, with gangs of men swinging their scythes rhythmically. Even in 1871 only one-quarter of the corn area was cut by machine, and in many areas improvements in productivity were achieved not through mechanisation but through the use of faster working hand-tools. The sickle and the reap-hook were replaced by 'the higher working capacity scythe and bagging hook'.[26] In the fields the children made bands from a handful of wheat straw to bind the corn, and if the weather were very dry, the men would often take armfuls of straw and lay them in a brook to soak, 'otherwise the bands, being too dry, would have broken as soon as they made them.' The women helped to bind the sheaves together, and then they were arranged in stooks by the men.

It was hard, hot work. Female labourers usually wore large cotton sunbonnets to protect their faces from the sun, but the men were exposed to the full glare, and became increasingly tanned and weather-beaten as the weeks progressed. After a morning's labour in such conditions, the midday rest was greeted 'like nature's own blessing'. As soon as the simple meal of bread, bacon and cold tea or beer had been consumed, there would be a brief and well-earned rest in the shadow of a hedgerow or tree before the afternoon stint began.

By the last decade of the century, however, opportunities for harvest work were being reduced in some areas, especially for women and children, by the employment of self-binders. Frank Wensley, who was born at Morchard Bishop near Crediton in 1887, recalls that in his area the self-binder was introduced about 1895: 'It caused much concern among farm workers as it did the work of tieing the corn sheaves which, hitherto had been their work to do. As a child I gazed with amazement to see the corn sheaves falling from this huge machine tied in neat bundles. Next those sheaves were placed in stooks so that the corn would ripen and the straw become dry. The line of stooks followed in the wheelmarks of the self-binder right around the field.'[27]

After the reaping and binding came the carrying the busiest time of all:

> Every man and boy put his best foot forward then for when the corn was cut and dried it was imperative to get it stacked and thatched before the weather broke. All day and far into the twilight the yellow-and-blue painted farm wagons passed and repassed along the roads between the field and the stackyard. Big cart-horses returning with an empty wagon were made to gallop like two-year-olds. Straws hung on the roadside hedges and many a gate post was knocked down through hasty driving. In the fields men pitchforked the sheaves to the one who was building the load on the wagon and the air resounded with Hold tights and Wert ups and Who-o-oas. The Hold tight! was no empty cry; sometimes, in the past, the man on top of the load had not held tight or not tight enough. There were tales of fathers and grandfathers whose necks or backs had been broken by a fall from a load, and of other fatal accidents afield, bad cuts from scythes, pitchforks passing through feet, to be followed by lockjaw, and of sunstroke.[28]

In Berkshire, indeed, one old labourer recalled working in the barns at harvest time until eleven or twelve o'clock at night by the light of lanterns. The farmer would send out food to the men from time to time – but with it came the message: I don't begrudge you men the food but I do grudge you the time to eat it.' Such were the pressures of harvest.[29]

Yet because all had played their part in gathering the crops, there was general rejoicing and satisfaction when the last load was brought safely in. Bad weather not only meant a loss to the farmer but to the labourers as well. Especially when they had taken the harvest on contract, they could not afford to have the work dragging on for many weeks. At James Gale's farm at Chilsworth, Oxfordshire, during the 1870s, for example, the 'man who brought the last sheaf up had a bottle of beer, "Old Tom", the best ale, the horses who drew the last wagon had "posies" on their heads, and the children rode on the top of it carrying posies, and singing "harvest home". There was cake and a drop of beer for [them], and plenty of beer for the men, and a rare good supper.' Other farmers celebrated the end of harvest in a similar manner.

Once the wheat had been gathered some of the women would seek permission to glean the stray ears for their own use. Farmers often tried to make sure that gleaning did not start until a field was completely cleared, for otherwise the temptation to rob the sheaves might be too great. 'In 1853 a Dorchester farmer printed a notice warning gleaners not to enter his fields until they were cleared of their crops, "because of the loss and annoyance to the farmers of the neighbourhood".' But the notice had little effect and the farmer himself was charged with assaulting a woman who had refused to give up the barley she had gleaned.

He was acquitted 'as he "had acted in defence of his right" but could obtain no redress for his "stolen" barley unless he was prepared to bring an action for trespass'.[30] Similarly, at Sutton Courtenay (then in Berkshire) troubles were encountered in 1890 when two boys had to pay a fine of 5s each for gleaning beans 'after they had been previously cautioned. The farmer explained "We allow them to glean wheat on sufferance ..." but "not beans or barley".'

Nevertheless most agriculturists took a more generous view and like Horace Head's employer at Five Ashes in Sussex, would tell 'the men who bound the sheaves to leave plenty ... for the poor to glean'.[31]

On the day agreed, therefore, women and their children would gather in the field, the babies arriving in perambulators in the charge of slightly older brothers and sisters. The eldest, with their mothers, would then hurry over the stubble, with backs bent, eyes on the ground, looking for the ears. These would be bound together in miniature sheaves or dropped into linen bags ready to be carried home at night. If gleanings were plentiful and a family numerous and active, the ears collected would soon mount up. They were carried home in sheets and stacked in a corner of the house ready for threshing. The men normally used a flail for this and also for threshing any wheat they might have grown on their allotments. The grain would then be sent to the miller for grinding into flour – although some families, who kept pigs or chickens, might prefer to use the gleanings to feed their livestock instead.

But if these tasks formed the broad outline of day-to-day work on the land in Victorian England, at local level the routine could be influenced considerably by seasonal and soil conditions, or perhaps by the proximity of a suitable market for produce. Certainly the daily round of land workers in the stock rearing and dairying areas of the north and west was very different from that of men and women employed in the corn growing and store cattle districts of the south and east. Variations could exist even within a single county. In Herefordshire, which was largely pastoral, there were at least seven different 'harvests' reported annually in the early 1860s, including bark peeling, haymaking, corn harvest, hop picking, potato gathering, apple picking and acorning. Similarly, in Wiltshire the corn and sheep farming of the chalklands was alternated with dairying and beef enterprises on the county's claylands, while in Kent market gardening, fruit picking and hop gathering were all important. In late July 1862, for example, Arthur Munby commented on the large number of women at work in the market gardens on the route between London and Dartford. They were 'hoeing or grubbing.

They were kneeling and standing in the furrows among the wet turnips and potatoes, the rain soaking through the sacks which they wear as cloaks.' And about two years later, near Wilmington in Kent, he came across a party of peapickers, 'a folk I had often heard of but not seen before ... Two or three men and an old woman, all quiet and respectable looking English Rustics ... sitting under a hedge boiling a piece of beef and potatoes (it was 4 p.m.) in a pot, a row of eight huts stood in the field. In these huts they said thirty-five people are living ... Peapicking begins in June and lasts six weeks ... We pick 'em three times over and earn 1s to 2s 6d a day.'[32]

Some of these workers also went hop picking, for the hop gardens were great employers of rural labour in Kent. Indeed, in the view of at least one observer, there was 'perhaps, no produce in the country that requires so much or such varied human labour as the hop at the different periods of its progress. The ground is at one time of the year a field, at another a garden ... Unlike corn ... it must be trained and tended from its first shoot to its ripening. Then it is not gathered like corn, and stored upon the stalk but is culled at once by the finger ... The soil is handled and subdued by the man; the plant is tended and trained by the women; in the gathering are united all, man, woman, and child.'[33] Each year large gangs of men, women and children were recruited from the East End of London to help in the hop harvest. They camped in overcrowded huts and barns, with minimal standards of hygiene. But local people shared in the work, too, and one young Kentish picker, who started at the age of seven, recalled the customary routine:

At that time our school holiday was three weeks in July for fruit picking, a month back to school, and a month especially for picking hops. A few weeks before we started I was sent to the farm to book a 'bin' and to be told the farmer's orders. I used to think the bins were like hammocks with two long handles that closed up like scissors, making them easy to carry. All pickers had to be at their bins by 7 a.m. and this meant my brother and I leaving home by 6 a.m. to walk across country to the hop garden ... At 7 a.m. sharp the horn would blow ready for us to start ... We were all sorted out with twelve bins to a set and a 'pole puller' in charge of each set. From then on we stayed with the same pole puller until hop picking was over ... His job was to help us to move up through the rows of hops, to make sure all the bines were picked clean and to see no hops were left on the ground.[34]

At 9 a.m. the pickers were allowed a break of fifteen minutes to drink tea and eat a snack, before their operations continued. At midday the measurer would go round to each bin and weigh the contents. The hops were then tipped into large sacks and taken by horse-drawn wagonettes to the farm oast house. 'Each bin had a hop book and the number of bushels picked was recorded every day. The payment was usually eight bushels a 1s and this was totalled up at the end of each week.' Normally work stopped for the day at about 6.30 p.m. when the pickers would set off, tired and stiff, on the journey home. Yet, to hard-pressed families with little money to spare, the wages even of child pickers were valuable, and as one girl remembered: 'with the money we had earned, mother fitted us out with new clothes for the winter, always a new tam-o'-shanter for me and button-up boots'.

In Worcestershire, too, market gardening, fruit picking and hop gathering provided much employment. In the Pershore area of the county intensive cultivation of cabbage, rhubarb and strawberries began from the middle of the century and of tomatoes from the 1880s. A pioneer in the large-scale production of fruit was Mr Richard Varden of Seaford Grange, and in 1852 he told a meeting of the Central Chamber of Agriculture that, at the height of the season he gave work to two or three hundred women and children on his 140 acres of gooseberries, currants and plums: 'I do not employ children, but pay the mothers for the quantity of fruit picked. Schools in the six or seven surrounding districts are closed for the time. The entire family is there, except men and lads. The babies are placed under the hedge in charge of the older children. The wages are looked upon as a clothing fund.'[35] Entries in Pershore National School Log book certainly confirm the adverse effect of this work on attendance levels. As late as 8 September 1893 the master was complaining that many of the children had been 'kept away all the week to pick hops or blackberries', while at nearby Pinvin fruit picking and pea gathering were both listed as reasons for poor attendance.[36]

A still greater difference in farming methods existed on the large arable holdings of the Eastern Counties, particularly in the newly settled fens, where there was insufficient cottage accommodation to cater for resident farm workers. Given the labour-intensive methods which predominated for much of the nineteenth century in the corn growing areas, the demand for workers could only be met by using public gangs of women, children and young people who moved round from farm to farm under the direction of an overseer. They would supplement the farmer's full-time workers and were recruited from larger villages or towns in the vicinity. Although the system was well established by the 1840s, it was in the next decade or so that it reached its height. The conditions under which the gangs worked were examined in 1866 by the Children's Employment Commission, and their findings revealed, in the view of at least one contemporary, that there was 'nothing more shocking ... than the sufferings incidental to the employment of young children in certain kinds of agricultural labour'.[37]

The gangs were concentrated in the six counties of Lincolnshire, Huntingdonshire, Cambridgeshire, Norfolk, Suffolk and Nottinghamshire, though they existed on a small scale in Northamptonshire, Bedfordshire and Rutland as well. A list of the duties carried out by their members in the three first-named counties gives both an idea of the varied nature of cultivation within the area and the multifarious tasks expected of the workers:

January. Women and children were engaged in sorting potatoes, particularly in the Isle of Axholme and the fen districts of Lincolnshire and Cambridgeshire. 'During mild weather children are employed in gangs picking stones in many parishes.'

February. The pattern was similar to that for January, although in general 'little work' was available for the gangs.

March. Towards the end of the month children and women were employed, either in gangs or individually, in picking 'twitch' (the roots of the couch grass), spreading dung, hoeing and setting potatoes.

April. A continuation of the March tasks, plus weeding the growing corn towards the end of the month.

May and June. Weeding and twitch picking engaged most of the workers, with haymaking at the end of the period.

July. 'Gangs are still employed at weeding and singling turnips. In some districts a great many children and women are employed in getting up hay'.

August and September. These were the harvest months, when the number of women and children employed reached a peak. Nevertheless at this time few were engaged in public gangs, most being recruited by individual farmers for the harvest. All who were not employed in harvesting were 'pulling flax, gathering woad' or gleaning. *October.* Potato picking, gathering mangold wurzel, picking twitch and dung spreading were the principal tasks.

November. Potato picking, plus the gathering of mangolds, turnips and carrots occupied 'a great number of children in many districts. Gangs are still employed at twitch picking. Stone picking begins in the highland districts; but in most parishes the employment of children is reduced to a minimum towards the end of this month.'

December. Women and children, when employed, were engaged in 'the same work as in November until stopped by frost.'[38]

However, the most disquieting aspects to emerge from the Commission's Report were the youth of many of the gang members and the adverse effect which long hours of labour could have upon their health, particularly during the winter or in wet weather. The welfare of the workers was very much in the hands of their gangmaster, who all too often made his own living by 'pressing his gang to the very utmost of their strength, his object being to extort the greatest possible quantity of labour for the smallest possible remuneration'. Whipping, kicking, knocking down, beating with hoes and 'dyking' or pushing the child into the water, were all resorted to by the more brutal men in order to keep the youngsters at full stretch. But, as a writer in the *Quarterly Review* of 1867 pointed out, equally disturbing was the early age at which children commenced work and the distances they had to walk, 'or rather to run,' before they began the labours of the day:

> Eight appears to be the ordinary age at which children of both sexes join the common gang, although seven is not unusual, and instances are mentioned in which children only six years of age were found regularly at work. One little girl only four years old was carried by her father to the fields, and put to work under a gangmaster, and it seems to be a common practice with parents to stipulate that if the elder children are hired the younger ones shall be so too. When the gangs are working at a considerable distance from home the children leave as early as five in the morning and do not return before eight at night, and the few who attend Sunday schools after the labours of the week are described as in a state of exhaustion which it is distressing to witness. A little boy only six years of age is stated to have regularly walked more than six miles out to work, and often to come home so tired that he could scarcely stand ... When the gang has a long distance to go the children become so exhausted, that the elder ones are seen dragging the younger ones home, sometimes carrying them on their backs. In winter, the children often return from the fields crying from cold.[39]

Much of the work was itself exhausting. Pulling turnips, for example, was described as 'perhaps the most pernicious employment to which a child can be set; it strains the spine, and often lays the foundation of chronic disease'. And if the children snatched a rest whilst engaged upon it they ran the risk of receiving an oath or a blow from the gangmaster. Then, too, the turnip leaves in the early morning were often full of ice, and so the backs of the hands became swollen and cracked by the wind and cold and wet, the palms blistered and the fingers bled 'from frequent laceration. If strong women thus suffer, how great must be the torture of children, whose frames are unknit, whose strength is undeveloped, and whose tender hands must smart and agonise at every pore.'[40]

These comments were confirmed in the interviews carried out by the Assistant Commissioners with individual workers. Thus Mary Ann Gallay of Wimbotsham, Norfolk, informed one of them that she worked in a gang of thirty-seven women and children, nearly all of them younger than she, 'down to eight or nine years old'. She reported their hours of work as from 8 a.m. until 6 p.m. in summer and until about 3 p.m. in winter, stopping then 'only about ten minutes for dinner'. Sometimes the gang had to walk as far as five or six miles in each direction to reach the farm on which they were working. 'For those distances to reach the ground by 8 a.m. we had to start at 6.30 a.m. or sometimes 6 a.m., and we did not leave till 6 p.m., getting home at 7.30 p.m. or towards 8 p.m. All went, little as well as big. I have walked home without my shoes, because we thought it tired us less.'

Other witnesses drew attention to the miserable working conditions – especially during wet weather, when the gang was weeding among growing corn. One young woman, who had been 'quite broken in health' as a result of her experience of field work, declared that frequently she had been so wet that she had

> taken off [her] clothes and wrung them out and put them up to dry on the top of the wheat ... Often when it came on to rain there was no shelter within reach, but, if there was any, sometimes [the gangmaster] would not let us go to it till we were drenched ... The man knocked us about and ill-used us dreadfully with hoes, spuds, and everything, he would not care what. He was an old man, white-haired, and used to go about with his 'dickey' (donkey), as he could not walk far enough else. He used to 'gibbet' some if they were idle i.e. come behind them, put his hands under their chin, and so lift them off the ground ... We dared not complain. One ought not to be glad to hear of anyone's death, but a good many children were glad when he died.[41]

The Assistant Commissioners pointed out that, in all, about half of the agricultural gangs comprised children 'from the age of six to that of eighteen'. And in some gangs, especially those of mixed sex, there were allegations of immorality and depravity.

> The youngest children swear habitually. The rate of illegitimacy, where the system prevails, is double that of the kingdom in general, and cases of seduction by the gangmasters of young girls in their employ are far from uncommon ... The behaviour and language of women and girls in gangs is such that a respectable man, of whatever age, if he meets them, cannot venture to speak to, scarcely even to look at them, without the risk of being shocked. A mixed gang composed of

women, boys and girls returning from their distant labour on a rainy evening, weary, wet and foot sore, but in spite of their wretchedness singing licentious or blasphemous songs, is a spectacle to excite at once pity, detestation and disgust.[42]

It was in the light of this evidence and of information on the adverse effects of the work on the education of the children that in 1867 an Agricultural Gangs Act was passed, prohibiting the employment of youngsters below the age of eight in public gangs. Gangs of mixed sex were also forbidden, and gangmasters had to be licensed by the local magistrate. In this way men of bad character could be prevented from taking on the job of overseer. However, if these regulations gradually eliminated the worst excesses of the gang system, they did not affect children employed in agriculture outside the ranks of the public gangs. As we saw in Chapter 3, their casual labour continued as before. As late as 1899, entries in the school log book for Elmdon in Warwickshire reveal the employment of children as beaters for shooting parties, as pickers in the local pea and currant harvests and as workers in the hay and corn fields. The absences persisted despite the existence of bye-laws prohibiting the use of child labour and despite periodic visits by the school attendance officer. Most other rural parishes shared this experience.

Sometimes, too, parents and children got round the regulations by restricting the youngsters' employment to before and after school hours and at the weekends. One lad who worked in this fashion whilst still at school in Essex remembers that he took his first job on a farm at the age of eleven, for a weekly wage of 2s. He was the eldest of a family of six children and started his day's labour at 6 a.m. when he had to hand milk five cows. He then had to separate the cream from the milk, so that the latter could be sold – at three pints a penny – to fellow villagers:

At 8 o'clock I had to deliver milk at the local J. P., schoolmaster's and the rector's on my way home. Then breakfast if we had any [and] clean the shoes for school. Many's the time I had the cane for not cleaning because they were too wet and the only pair I had. After coming out of school at 4 p.m. I had to get cows up from meadow, then milk the same five, separate cream from the milk, then deliver milk … on my way home. This would be about 6 o'clock. On Saturdays I had to work 6 a.m. to 6 p.m. In the summer I had to cut Lawns and look after flower beds between milking, on Sunday hours same as Monday to Friday … In the winter months on Saturdays I had to cut mangel [*sic*] and chaff for twenty cows to last the weekend.[43]

Arthur Tweedy of Kirby Fleetham, Yorkshire, was another part-time child worker. Every Saturday he and his brothers and sisters would go down to the farm where their father was employed. They were each given a broom: 'We had to sweep up all the mud and straw round the farm yard which was a very big one and took us most of the day ... for one penny ... I worked all the holidays driving carts and received one shilling a day ... and in haytime and harvest or other busy times. I had a day off school to drive cattle or sheep once a fortnight eight miles [to Northallerton Auction Market] to save the other workers wasting a valuable day. For this sixteen mile walk (which was often over twenty miles after chasing the cattle which strayed into people's fields through gaps in the hedges and open gates) I received 9*d*.'[44]

Finally, for the adult workers, there was the question of the relationship between themselves and their employer. On some of the larger farms there were strict conditions of service such as those in operation at Chesterton Farm on the Bathurst estate in Gloucestershire around the middle of the century. Among the regulations laid down were:

> The Carter will obtain from the Bailiff the weekly allowance of corn and serve out to the driver of each team daily the feeds appointed by the Bailiff. He is to keep the stable granary locked.'
>
> The Carter and each Ploughman on coming home at night to hang up his harness on numbers in the Harness house corresponding with those on his Boxes, and to clean their horses thoroughly morning and night.
>
> The Horses to be led to water, haltered, from April to October and to be supplied in their boxes from September to May. Every driver of a cart to stop at a gate, prop it open, lead his horse through, and stop on the other side, and close the gate excepting in the case of continuous days hauling through a gate set open for the day.
>
> Every implement not on wheels to be taken out and brought home on the sledge.
>
> All tools delivered out to labourers to be returned to the Bailiff at night, cleaned.
>
> No Servant or labourer to absent himself from his work without previous application to the Bailiff, and any labourer leaving work without notice or leave to forfeit all wages which may be due to him at the time.
>
> Any breakage or damage occasioned by negligence or carelessness to be repaired at the expense of the servant who occasioned it; the amount to be stopped out of his wages, and the Proprietors to determine whether it was the result of accidence [*sic*] or negligence.

No Servant on any pretence to get through or over any live Fence.

The Servants are required to attend to all directions given by the Bailiff, whether as to work to be done, or the mode of doing it.

During the hay and corn harvest an account to be kept by the Bailiff of all work overtime, and the servants to be paid for it after the same rates as they are paid during the regular hours of work. Those hours to be fixed by the Bailiff according to the season of the year.

Workers who ignored the regulations could have fines imposed on them. Thus infringement of the first five rules listed could be punished by a fine of sixpence, while the breaking of the regulation requiring labourers to return tools properly cleaned could lead to a fine of threepence.[45]

On other farms annually hired men might be required to sign formal contracts of employment, usually running from Michaelmas to Michaelmas. One such was entered into by a Wiltshire lad in 1889, in respect of work as a cowman for William Gauntlett, a large farmer of Collingbourne, in Wiltshire. It laid down that the 'servant' could be required to carry out 'any work ... within his power when not employed in the particular service for which he is hired'. In addition: 'The Servant further agrees to be always at his work at all times required by the Master or his Agent, and to milk not less than ten cows at a milking, and more if required. To be cleanly, quiet and quick in milking, not to ill-treat the cattle, or to use profane or indecent language.' For this he was to be paid a basic wage of seven shillings and sixpence a week, but poor workmanship could lead to fining. Thus, 'any cow found to be partially milked, the Servant shall submit to be fined a sum not exceeding Two Shillings and Sixpence'.[46]

Although such close regulation of the worker's conditions of employment was not common by the end of the Victorian era, for the annually hired men affected it imposed a considerable burden and contributed to workers' growing discontent. It was scarcely surprising that there were complaints that 'most of the smartest young men [migrated] to the towns, the railways, and into the police'.

Indeed, one aspect of the difficult last years of the nineteenth century was the growing tendency of farmers to complain about the 'quality' of their workers. In part, this was the perennial feeling that things had been better in the past, but there is evidence, too, that many of the more able and enthusiastic younger men were seeking work outside agriculture. One of the Assistant Commissioners reporting for the Royal Commission on Labour, 1892–94, commented on the 'vague restlessness which makes [men] uncertain of adhering to field work in any form, and therefore disinclined to take the trouble of acquiring any of the special arts connected with it'. He admitted that 'machinery [had] superseded much of the old skilled work' and that 'many young men show great aptitude in learning the management of it; but such things as thatching, hedge slashing or laying, drain laying, mowing, shearing, are in many parts becoming almost lost arts.' Several of his colleagues agreed and, as one of them put it: 'I think … that the more intelligent and ambitious men leave the country, and those who are left are frequently led to look down upon agricultural work altogether, and thus become unwilling to take up and learn special branches.' A similar point was made by an Oxfordshire bailiff in conversation with Rider Haggard, at the end of the century. He declared that the men 'were different from what he remembered; now when they got home in the evening they wanted to put on a nice suit of clothes and walk about with a little cane in their hands'.[47]

But other critics pointed to the fact that farmers, hit by falling prices, were economising in the use of labour anyway, and that they were less concerned with the neat appearance of their fields than they had once been. This was admitted in the early 1890s by one Norfolk agriculturist, Mr Harvey Mason of Necton Hall, and his attitude was typical of many: 'For the last ten or twelve bad years I have no doubt the farmers have cut down the labour a bit … The thistles are not cut in the corn or the docks pulled out, and the land is much more full of twitch.' In his view: 'Extra labour may have been given in past times to hedge trimming, but this work was often done just to keep men employed and to make things look nice without being profitable and was likely to be dropped somewhat when farmers had no money to spare.'[48] By the 1890s a position of financial difficulty had certainly been reached on many British farms, and economy in the use of labour was an inevitable result.

5

RURAL CRAFTS & COTTAGE INDUSTRIES

The decline in the numbers of rural craftsmen and of rural industries in general has been the result of two historical factors which often operated on a different time-scale from each other. The first was the steady decline in rural populations from some point in the first half of the nineteenth century. Inevitably the decline in numbers would mean a decline in demand for the products of the rural craftsmen ... The second factor accounting for the decrease in the numbers of craftsmen and of the rural industries was the continuing technological revolution of the nineteenth and twentieth centuries ... When cheap and rapid transport of both bulky commodities as well as consumer goods became possible, the village handicraftsmen were increasingly at a disadvantage ... Some crafts have disappeared, their products having been ousted by the mass production goods of the factory. The independent tailor is no longer found in villages and market towns ... The bootmaker is now only a repairer and even so is found to a decreasing extent in the village ... The village baker, so prominent in the nineteenth century, has been replaced by the delivery van of the bakeries in the market towns or farther afield.

John Saville, *Rural Depopulation in England and Wales 1851–1951* (1957)

For the majority of men and boys living in the Victorian countryside, agriculture provided the principal employment, while for women and girls the main outlet lay in domestic service. Nevertheless in all communities rural crafts and industries had a significant role to play. Thus in the small village of Halwell in South Devon, out of a total population of 411 in 1851 there were no less than thirteen different tradesmen – comprising a thatcher, a carpenter, two tailors, a boot and shoe maker, a baker, a blacksmith, a wheelwright, two masons, two dairymen and a marine store dealer. And at Mapledurham in South Oxfordshire, with a population of 509 at the same date, there were eight, including a shoemaker, two sawyers, a blacksmith, a baker, a carpenter, a tailor and a sheep dealer.[1] The range was typical of most country parishes, for upon the skills of the various craftsmen the smooth running of the community depended.

Only in the last years of the nineteenth century did that position begin to change, as improvements in communications and the use of mass production techniques began to erode the craftsman's central position, and with it the independence which running a small business could bestow. This applied not only to the blacksmith, whose role was threatened by the appearance of specialist agricultural implement manufacturers, but to other groups as well, like the tailor, the shoemaker and the saddler. So while the total of blacksmiths throughout England and Wales *increased* from 112,035 in 1871 to 136,752 in 1901, and of saddlers (including harness and whip makers) from 21,181 to 29,954, in many rural districts a contrary trend was apparent. In Devon there were 3,485 blacksmiths in 1871 but only 2,834 in 1901, while the saddlers declined from 503 to 482 over the same period. Similarly in Norfolk the number of blacksmiths dropped from 2,522 in 1871 to 2,386 in 1901, and of saddlers from 501 to 460. Other trades followed a similar pattern both in these counties and elsewhere.[2]

Sometimes, of course, craftsmen would take on a whole variety of jobs, according to the vagaries of seasonal employment. At Haddenham, Walter Rose's friend 'Joey', who was a mason, also knew about butchering and reverted to that just before Christmas, when the building trade was slack. He was equally prepared to clean out a well or a sewage tank or to sweep chimneys by the old method of a long rope 'with a gooseberry bush tied at its middle, the bush being pulled up and down the flues by one man at the top and another at the bottom'.[3] Similarly, Joseph Arch, the agricultural trade union leader, combined work as a prize-winning hedgecutter with employment as a carpenter's labourer for a friend. 'He used to send for me when he got very busy coffin-making, or putting on roofing, or making church work ... Then my skill at hurdle-making and gate-hanging would come in handy at odd times. Being a good all-round man I was never at a loss for a job.'[4] In Suffolk and Norfolk, young labourers would go fishing after the corn harvest and remain at sea during the autumn and early winter. When they returned after Christmas they would fill their time until haysel 'by doing seasonal jobs on the land: bark-peeling, and ditching and draining'.[5] And in Herefordshire it was reported in the early 1890s that labourers looking for winter employment would take on wood-cutting, draining, felling and sharpening hop poles and 'a little bark stripping'. Quarrying was carried out by some, while in the early autumn hop-drying provided lucrative employment for a few skilled men. However, both here and in Monmouth the total amount of labour available was affected by the state of the Welsh mining industries. 'When these are prosperous, there is a large and steady drain of labourers from Monmouth and in a less degree from Hereford. When there is a slackness in these industries, labour ceases to flow in that direction.'⁶ So, in many areas, the country craftsman or mechanic had to be 'a man with two or three strings to his bow. The thatcher might turn hay trusser for the summer season, the hurdle maker to repairing carts and wagons, the stonemason, when out of work, to jobbing carpentry'.⁷

In certain districts these various rural crafts were joined as employers of labour by cottage industries, such as lacemaking, straw plaiting (to supply the hat and bonnet trade), button making, glovemaking, knitting, chairmaking and many others. Most of them employed a high proportion of female and child labour, although in rural Northamptonshire both men and women were employed in the boot and shoe trade, which even in 1901 was carried on partly as an outwork industry. Of around 30,000 male and 12,000 female boot and shoemakers recorded in the county at the end of the nineteenth century over one-sixth worked at home or on their own account. In some counties domestic industries absorbed a still higher proportion of the total labour force, especially of young workers. Thus in mid-Victorian Bedfordshire. nearly one in three of all girls in the age range ten to fifteen was employed as a plaiter, while about one in nine of Buckinghamshire girls in the same age group worked as a lacemaker.⁸ Their position and that of others engaged in the cottage trades will be considered in detail later in the chapter.

Of all the rural craftsmen concerned with the needs of agriculture the blacksmith cum farrier was probably the most important. Often smithing ran in families, with son succeeding father at the same forge. But even in traditional businesses a youngster had to serve a formal apprenticeship of about five years, at the end of which a practical test had to be passed. Then it was common for him to go for two years as an 'improver' to another smith, before returning to his original master as a fully fledged craftsman, qualified to set up in his own right. And for those anxious to establish their own business, initial cash requirements might be quite modest. Often a shop could be rented, and the capital needed to equip it might be borrowed at interest from a local farmer or fellow tradesman who had a little cash to spare. Sun Insurance Company records indicate that the amount involved might not be large anyway; thus in 1842 Joseph and Charles Smith of Aldbourne in Wiltshire insured their blacksmith's shop for £35 and the stock and utensils therein for £25. Even if this represented an undervaluation (and the figures are confirmed by entries for other smiths in the records), it is unlikely that the total outlay would have amounted to more than a hundred or two.⁹ Certainly when a smith set up in the small village of

Bledington, Gloucestershire, early in the nineteenth century, he made very few purchases – a lock iron, a tew iron, a nail hammer, a rasp and file, a hand-vice, a square, and a 'Shop Book' in which to keep his accounts. His anvil was, no doubt, already in place in his outhouse.[10]

The work of the blacksmith was frequently heavy and tiring. Yet he had to be ready to turn his hand to a whole range of tasks, whether shoeing a horse – the most common occupation of all – making stock-bands for the hubs of heavy carts, repairing ploughs, sharpening the tines of harrows, producing chisels and hammers for the village carpenters, or merely plugging a hole in a leaking cooking pan and making pattens (clogs on iron rings to raise them out of the mud) for local housewives. One smith at Norley in Cheshire at the end of the nineteenth century even acted as a dentist, and would 'extract teeth with pincers while the victim sat on the hob'.[11] The surviving account books of blacksmiths give an idea of the range of tasks performed. Thus George Amos of Weston-sub-Edge, Gloucestershire, carried out the following jobs for one of his farmer clients during January 1904:

Date		Job	Price
January	1	Repairing Cart	2s. 0d.
		Two shoes	1s. 4d.
	3	Repairing Drill	1s. 6d.
		Two shoes	1s. 4d.
	5	Two shoes	1s. 4d.
	6	Two shoes	1s. 4d.
	7	One Pin and repairing plough	1s. 3d.
	11	Stale to plough paddle	6d.
	13	Two shoes	1s. 4d.
	14	New ironwork to bellyband	9d.
		Repairing trace chains	6d.
	18	Repairs to Drill	1s. 0d.
	19	Four shoes	2s. 8d.
	20	New end to plough spanner	1s. 0d.
	21	Two shoes	1s. 4d.
		Frostnail 4 shoes	8d.

[Frostnailing was carried out during icy weather to prevent the horse from slipping.][12]

Entries in the work records of J. Gabb, a blacksmith at Falfield in Gloucestershire during the early 1880s, similarly confirm the variety of work undertaken. In addition to shoeing, he was concerned with 'making screw-pin to carriage', 'dressing 3 Ladder Irons, 3 new washers and new nutt [*sic*]', 'grinding Two cutting knives, mending the casting for a mowing machine and providing staples for an iron fence. Ringing pigs to prevent them from digging up the floor of the sty was another task, the usual price for this being 1*d* per animal. From time to time there were also such entries as '4 removes on Gray Pony', or 'forefeet 2 removes on Old Pony'.[13] This meant that the shoe had been taken off, the hoof trimmed and the shoe replaced. And whereas shoeing might cost 8*d* or 1*s* per shoe, 'removes' were only about half that price. In his role as farrier Mr Gabb also gave veterinary treatment to animals, such as drenches for a sick cow or salves for wounds – as in February 1881, when he was concerned with 'dressing mare's foot at different Times'.

Yet, if village smiths were able to carry out almost any job involving the use of metal, most had a special line for which they were known beyond their own parish – whether repairing farm machinery or making implements like hoes, spades, shovels and mattocks. Gaius Carley, a Sussex blacksmith, was apprenticed to one man, who was an expert at making axes, scythes and similar edge tools. As he recalled it was 'hard graft aright, swinging the heavy hammer, beating the steel and iron together', but his employer's reputation was such that his 'tools were sought after in East Sussex'.[14]

Even shoeing horses could be a testing job, especially if the animal were highly strung. An apprentice had to be ready to lift up the heavy feet in order to take off the old shoe and pare the hooves. But sometimes there were accidents. Carley himself lost a finger when a spirited horse tore a nail into his forefinger and caused blood poisoning and a diseased bone. Indeed, when a colt was shod for the first time it was customary for the owner to give an extra shilling – known as the 'First Nail' – to provide the men with beer. As an old Suffolk blacksmith recalled, some of the meaner farmers would try to get out of paying this but if they did not pay up, they 'got it out of 'em in another' way – by putting an extra shilling on one of their bills'.[15]

The blacksmith's shop was always more than a mere place of work. It was a social centre, too, where men stood about gossiping and discussing market news as they waited for horses to be shod and implements to be repaired, or perhaps they merely dropped in to while away an idle moment. Rainy days were particularly busy, since the farmers sent their men off with the horses, saying: 'There's nothing for 'em to do here. Take 'em off to the blacksmith's.' Sometimes when young boys brought the animals along, the smith would allow them to play around the forge, getting themselves thoroughly dusty and dirty. At Pitstone in Buckinghamshire a favourite prank of the blacksmith was to give troublesome youngsters a slice of bread covered with treacle on both sides. This they eagerly munched, only realising afterwards that their hands and face were covered with a sticky, sooty mixture which was unlikely to endear them either to their employer or their mother. But, as one boy recalled, if they behaved well they might be allowed to pump the bellows. Nevertheless his memories of the smithy were somewhat mixed: 'The reek of the burning hoof, as the hot shoe was pressed on it, the smith's language when the horse would not "side still", the clanging anvil and the flying sparks, all conjured up a sort of Sunday School picture of hell with the smith himself as a kindly sort of devil.'[16]

Yet to many lads the blacksmith's shop possessed a character and a glamour that belonged to no other craft. At Haddenham, Walter Rose remembered the

> dim-lit smoky atmosphere, enlivened by the ruddy fire and hot glowing iron. From within a dusky recess, the large bellows emitted its deep breath as the handle was moved up and down ... The smith knew what was wanted because he was a smith; his thought pierced the molten deeps of the fire and knew the transformation that was taking place there; he judged the heat required for mere shaping, or for the more subtle process of welding or joining two pieces of iron together, and knew the precise moment when it must be withdrawn from the fire and held on the anvil, ready for the blows of his hammer.[17]

Like the blacksmith, the saddler and the wheelwright were closely involved with the daily farming round. It was the saddler who made the harness needed by the horse for the varied tasks of carting, pulling and ploughing – each process requiring slightly different items of equipment. Horsemen were usually very proud of the harness which belonged to their own team and would not use that belonging to any other. So if an article had to be repaired and could not be sent down to the shop, the horseman would often bring it himself after he had finished work, get it repaired and then take it back ready for the following day. For ploughing, the harness comprised a collar, wooden seals, a bridle and a simple 'plough-back, a light leather band fixed to the top of the collar and running down the horse's back ... and having a transverse piece of leather across the haunches'. Fixed to this on one side was a metal loop which passed through the rein; the other rein passed through a similar loop in the harness of the horse working alongside. For carting a cart-trace leather was fitted to the top of the collar and ran down the centre of the trace-horse's back, and there would also be a leading rein as well as collar and seals. It was difficult to measure a horse for a new collar and most saddlers kept a good stock of varying sizes so that they could by trial and error find one which suited the horse. The collar was stuffed with straw and padded with collar-flock, a coarse wool made from old rags which had been torn up and shredded.[18]

Both carpenters and wheelwrights required a plentiful supply of timber, and wood was purchased well in advance so as to give it time to season. Indeed, in the view of a Cotswold wheelwright, a true craftsman 'made sure he had a supply of well seasoned stocks not only for his own use but for the sons or grandsons who might come after him'.[19] Newly purchased timber was left at least a year before sawing, and then the planks and boards were allowed to season a further year for each inch of their thickness. Ash and elm were the principal woods used by the wheelwright, with elm for the boarding in the bed of the waggon and for the hubs of the wheels. When these latter had been cut and bored they were chained together and put into a stream to soak for a few months before being left to dry and season. Ash, because of its strength and flexibility, was used for the top-rails and for the shafts of the waggon, while the spokes were made of oak. But wheelwrights would often take account of the particular needs of their clients, since it was quite usual for the farmers, millers, brewers, grocers and others who utilised their services to place orders regularly with a local man. In the 1880s George Stuart recalled how in his family workshop at Farnham in Surrey the requirements of the area were catered for:

> In farm-waggon, or dung-cart, barley roller, plough, waterbarrel, or what not, the dimensions we chose, the curves we followed (and almost every piece of timber was curved) were imposed upon us by the nature of the soil on this or that farm, the gradient of this or that hill, the temper of this or that customer, or his choice perhaps in horseflesh. The carters told us their needs. To satisfy the carter, we gave another half-inch curve to the waggon-bottom, altered the hooks for harness on the shafts, hung the water-barrel an inch nearer to the horse or an inch further away, according to requirements … There was nothing for it but practice and experience of every difficulty … What we had to do was to live up to the local wisdom of our kind; to follow the customs, and work to the measurements, which had been tested and corrected long before our time in every village shop all across the country.[20]

In the workshop itself every size of chisel, awl, screwdriver and plane could be found, with graded saws hanging on hooks, each in its appointed place and kept in perfect condition. Then there was the forge, where the iron wheel-rims were heated and beaten into shape with a heavy hammer. Finally came the paint shop, which in the view of at least one Norfolk wheelwright was 'the holy of holies, with regularly sluiced down tiled floor and row upon row of paint cans, varnish, turpentine, brushes and all the paraphernalia of the finishing art'.[21]

The prices charged varied according to the skill of the craftsman and the nature of the work undertaken. Thus in 1860 the Fleming family of Gaydon, Warwickshire, charged 6s for fitting two felloes and two spokes to the fore wheel of a waggon, while the making and painting of a new nameplate for a wagon cost only 2s 6d; fitting a new wheelbarrow wheel and painting it amounted to 4s 6d; and the fixing and painting of a 'new axle casing to a cart' cost 10s 6d. There are countless similar entries in the account book; at this time the annual turnover of the business seems to have been in the region of £130 per annum.[22]

Plough-making was another wood-based craft which had for long been a specialist trade in its own right but which in the Victorian years was superseded by iron ploughs made by agricultural implement manufacturers or blacksmiths. Nevertheless, a few ploughwrights survived – like Alec Walter, who was born in Wiltshire at the end of the nineteenth century and began his career as an apprentice to a carpenter and wheelwright. Among his jobs was repairing ploughs, and on one occasion 'some ploughs came in ... to be repaired and they wanted me to take the iron turn furrows off and put wooden ones in'. Alec had never seen this job done before and so he went to a firm of timber merchants who, fortunately for him, had retained the patterns of some old wooden ploughs. Armed with these he experimented, and his work proved a success. The wooden plough worked better than iron in turning furrows on wet land, and as Alec gained in confidence he went on to make wooden ploughs for a number of other farmers.[23]

Many village craftsmen, like the builder, the carpenter and the miller, catered for the needs of the community in general as well as those of agriculture in particular. Carpenters were involved not merely in making field gates and repairing barns for farmers but also in fitting doors and windows for local cottagers. A number of them, like the men employed by the Rose family at Haddenham, stayed with the same master all their life, starting as raw youngsters around the timber yard, where they chopped and sawed and carried out the more laborious work whilst they served their apprenticeship. Then as 'helpers to experienced carpenters they had acquired a knowledge of the craft; finally becoming proficient joiners able to undertake anything that was required and with a permanent bench in the workshop. Each possessed his complete set of tools, jealously prized, cared for, and guarded.'

The work they carried out was intimately linked to the life of the village and its immediate vicinity, and as Walter Rose, the founder's grandson, recalled:

There was continual going and coming from the shop to the places for which the work was intended; a few days' work in the shop, making doors, windows, or other fitments for a house or farm, then a period at the place fixing the work, and doing what else was required ... No field for miles around but had its gate that sooner or later would need repair: no farmer who did not need his new cow-cribs, sheeptroughs, or ladders. No house from the vicarage to the labourer's cottage, but had at some time or other a defect in its woodwork for which the services of our men would be required.[24]

This is confirmed by the surviving account books of carpenters and joiners, like the Bennetts of Wortley in Gloucestershire. A random examination of their records for the year 1858 shows that a 'Sheep Trough loft with wheels &c' was made for one farmer client at a cost of 18s 6d, and a turnip box, for 3s. Window and door frames were produced for other customers, while the making of coffins provided another regular source of income. Finally, there was a miscellany of household tasks to be performed, such as those carried out for a local clergyman, the Reverend J. Fisher:[25]

1858		
Jan. 23rd	Fix^d. an Ironing board and altered a pr. of Tressels [*sic*] 8 new legs	2s. 6d.
Feb. 6th	Repair^d. a Chair & Planing Knife board	6d.
Aug. 14th	Repair^d. a Perambulator	1s. 0d.
	–do– a portable Desk and Small Box	2s. 0d.
	2 Turn^d. Privy Tops	1s. 3d.

Almost as ubiquitous as the carpenter was the miller. Virtually every parish had its mill, and although the bakers were the main customers for flour, many villagers, too, purchased a small quantity in order to make their own bread. The miller also provided fodder for the farm livestock and feeding stuff for the cottagers' pigs, ducks and fowls. He would grind their gleanings, too, often paying himself by taking a toll of the flour or, as at Five Ashes in Sussex, he might keep 'the offal, that is sharps and bran, and [give] back the flour'.[26]

Like most village tradesmen, the amount of capital needed to set up in business was comparatively modest, especially if the mill itself could be rented. In May 1841 William Moores of Piddlehinton in Dorset insured the stock and utensils of his windmill and bakehouse (including cloths for the mill sails and three pairs of mill stones) for a mere £60. Similarly, in January 1863 William Reynolds of Long Crendon, Buckinghamshire, insured the stock and utensils of his long-established watermill for £225. And at Pitstone in the same county the village windmill was sold for £400 in 1874 to Lord Brownlow, owner of the Ashridge estate. He immediately let it to the Hawkins family, who had been for many years the tenants of the surrounding Pitstone Green Farm, and they proceeded to combine their agricultural interests with their milling ones. Many other examples could be quoted.[27]

Closely associated with the trade of milling was that of baking. Though most villagers made at least some of their own bread, shortage of fuel and of suitable ovens ensured that the baker had a steady business in the majority of communities. Bread was usually sold in 2-lb or 4-lb loaves made from stone-ground flour. The baking itself was carried on in brick-built, domed ovens with tiled floors which were heated either by a furnace or by faggots of wood burnt on the floor of the oven itself until the bricks became hot. When the correct temperature was reached, the baker would carefully remove the glowing embers and wipe down the floor with a damp rag fixed to a long pole. The loaves were then slipped in and baked to a crusty, golden finish. But one of the perennial problems was that the loaf lost weight as it cooked and there was always a trickle of cases at the petty sessional courts concerning bakers who either by accident or design had sold bread at short weight or from a cart without scales. In the early 1880s, for example, at Ivinghoe petty sessions in Buckinghamshire, bakers convicted of selling bread without scales regularly faced a fine of 1s or 2s, plus costs.

Finally there were the village craftsmen who were concerned with the making of wearing apparel, such as the tailor and the boot and shoemaker. Sometimes if there were no tailor in the parish, a man would travel out from a nearby country town or larger village in order to measure up farm workers for suits or to sell them ready-made working outfits. One Stowmarket tailor and draper always travelled around the Suffolk villages at harvest time when the men had received their extra pay, collecting orders. These were then executed in the family workshop. He and his father hired a club-room in a public-house as a centre for their activities in a village:

> After we had our little bout in the tap-room they'd come in and buy what they wanted: cord trousers, hob-nail boots, shirts and so on. And they'd probably want a little bit of best wear: black jacket and waistcoat and a muffler, ... And they often bought the old *billy-cock hat* the horsemen used to wear. It was a black hat with a rather high, pointed crown; and it had a wide black band round it.[28]

Boot and shoemaking, like the other rural crafts, declined in importance in the later nineteenth century. In Devon, for example, the number of shoemakers fell from nearly 6,000 in 1871 to under 3,000 by 1901, and in other districts the trend was much the same. To some degree this was inevitable, not merely as a consequence of the migration of people from the country areas but because of the emergence of a low-cost mass-produced boot and shoe industry in the later years of the century. In the 1890s it was reckoned that a pair of machine-made boots could be purchased for about 8s a pair, as opposed to those made to order by the village shoemaker for 14s Even if the machine-made footwear did not last as long, the existence of this cheaper alternative probably meant that fewer children had to wear broken boots handed down from one member of the family to another or to walk about barefoot.[29] Most country shoemakers specialised in heavy footwear suitable for work on the land, and some also produced the long leather gaiters worn by thatchers, hedgers and carters. The boots were made of barktanned leather, stiff and clumsy, with soles handstitched and studded with rows of large hobnails. The tongues were stitched to the uppers so as to make them watertight. Uppers and soles were carefully cut out, and then the leather was pierced with an awl before the two waxed cords were threaded through, 'passed in opposite ways through the hole and vigorously pulled to right and left'. The majority of bootmakers used a split pig's bristle instead of a metal needle to thread the waxed cord through the hole, since this gave a fairly stiff point and yet, unlike a metal needle, it did not stick into the fingers of the receiving hand.

Most families purchased new boots out of their harvest earnings, and the more businesslike shoemakers planned their work programme to meet this demand. At Ludford Magna in Lincolnshire, Montagu Allwood remembered the shoemaker busily engaged in his small shop, with a trough beside him containing the liquid in which he soaked the leather to soften it, before hammering it to 'close up the pores'. His 'wall and ceiling were hung with wooden lasts on which the boots and shoes were made; his bench had little slots for nails, sprigs and wooden pegs. The shoemaker sat with his boot-jack between his knees his mouth full of brass sprigs which he spat out as required, and he knocked them into the heels and soles of the boots with the back of an old worn-down rasp.'[30]

The life of these small village bootmakers was very different from that of out-workers in the Northamptonshire shoemaking industry, where specialisation of process was the order of the day. Here each task was clearly defined, starting with the cutting out of the uppers and soles of the shoes – an operation which was often carried out on an employer's own premises. Then the various parts of the upper were put out to be sewn or 'closed'. In the early nineteenth century this was done by hand but from the 1860s sewing machines were used in an operative's home or in a small workshop. On completion the upper was returned to the employer, who would then send out uppers and soles together, usually in quantities of up to two dozen pairs, to be 'made', that is for the closed upper to be shaped on a last and the sole attached. Finally, after return to the employer's premises once more, the boots or shoes were put out for the finishing process. In the early Victorian period some of the smaller shoemakers would carry out all the manufacturing processes on their own premises, rather like the village bootmakers described above, but by the middle of the century division of labour had become increasingly common.

Shoemaking employed whole families in some of the villages of Northamptonshire. Thus at Earls Barton (with a total population in 1861 of over 1,500) between one in two and one in three of all males in the parish was a shoemaker and about one in three of the females. Agriculture employed around a sixth of the men and boys, with cottage lacemaking occupying a number of the women. Mat making was another minor industry in the parish, but it was clearly boot and shoemaking which dominated life in that community. At the nearby parish of Grendon (population in 1861: 610) about one in six of the men and a rather smaller proportion of the women and girls were similarly engaged. In these villages the women and children were largely employed as 'closers', and because of the need to work long hours, the household chores of the wife were often neglected. As in the other cottage trades, critics pointed to 'the dirty home, the slatternly habits, and the neglected children' which drove 'the husband to the public house'. And the women themselves were described by one unsympathetic observer as being 'as black as a nigger' and 'as ragged as a moulting crow'.[31] Many of the children began work at an early age. At Earls Barton a number started at six or eight years old, and there were in the village as a whole twenty-one girls and ten boys employed at the age of ten or under at the time of the 1861 Census of Population; the youngest was aged only three! Most were employed to assist with 'closing', but according to a shoe manufacturer from Hardingstone, Northamptonshire, boys also worked for 'riveters, finishers, makers (i.e. men that sew the soles to the uppers of boots) and equally with females, for closers'.[32] For this they were paid about 2s 6d a week. But in the early years of Victoria's reign, the children's first job had been to boil the pitch, resin and tallow used to make wax for the thread. The mixture was then poured into a pail of water and balls of wax were prepared by the young workers. 'Next, taking several strands of hemp, they would wax them and roll them on the knee in order to make cobblers' ... thread for sewing on the welt.' After a boy had mastered this process and had learned how to use his awl, he would be set to 'close' children's shoes.[33]

With the passage of the 1867 Factory and Workshops Regulation Act the minimum age of employment of children was established at eight, and in

1878 this was raised to ten. Between the ages of eight and thirteen a boy or girl could be employed only in accordance with the half-time system already in use in factories and workshops. In other words, each child had to attend an approved elementary school for at least ten hours per week, between 8 a.m. and 6 p.m. and had to obtain a certificate from the teacher stating that this had been done. The legislation was difficult to implement in its early days in all domestic trades, and bootmaking proved no exception. In 1886, at the village of Finedon, for example, the annual report of Her Majesty s Inspector noted that at the girls' school the 'large number of Half Timers in the 3rd Standard and upwards' was 'a hindrance to progress'; earlier reports had commented on the 'large proportion' of half-timers in attendance at the school and the problems that this presented. The 1871 Census of Population for the village recorded children as young as nine or ten working as 'knot tiers' or 'fitters' in local shoeshops. Not all were the children of shoemakers, either. Thus Mary Knowles, aged nine, was the daughter of a mason's labourer, although her mother worked as a closer. And Annie Dickens aged ten was the daughter of a labourer in an iron works. A number of other young workers were the children of agricultural labourers.[34] The great problem as regards schooling was irregularity of attendance; thus on 8 January 1877 the mistress noted that a 'great many girls' had returned to school 'who had not put in a single attendance for more than one year'. Nevertheless, as the industry became more and more factory based and as the general education legislation of 1870–80 gradually enforced compulsory attendance at school for all children, so the situation slowly improved.

In the recollection of H. E. Bates, the novelist, who was born in the early years of the twentieth century at Higham Ferrers, the adult shoemakers of Northamptonshire were a rough lot. They lived largely on 'kippers, bloaters, tea, beer, cheese, potatoes and plenty of good bread from the coal-ovened bake-houses; and the lordly inevitable roast-beef on Sundays'. For those working at home there was no clocking in at regular times. Indeed, in the mid-Victorian years there were complaints that shoemakers employed at home had 'no stated time, generally the early part of the week is wasted, and towards the close they are then obliged to work all manner of hours'.[35] This view is confirmed by Bates. At Higham Ferrers they regularly got drunk on Saturdays and Sundays and never worked on Mondays:

Either out of duty to their patron saint St Crispin or in pursuit of a cure for mountainous hangovers, they sought solace in the surrounding countryside, rabbiting, coursing, mushrooming, following hounds, walking or riding miles by devious routes to secret hide-outs where barefisted bruisers bloodily battered themselves to pulp before crowds of gentry and poor alike. With Monday behind them, shoemakers returned to their lasts, madly stitching and hammering away until midnight and even into the small hours in pursuit of cash that would, when Saturday came again, be riotously squandered on booze and the 'blues'.[36]

At haytime and harvest they would also go out to work in the fields, alongside gangs of itinerant Irish labourers who had come to England for the harvest months. But with the growth of mechanisation in the boot industry, the era of the out-worker drew to an end. Centralisation became the order of the day, largely for motives of economy. But there were other reasons as well. The National Amalgamated Union of Operative Boot and Shoe Riveters and Finishers, which was established in 1874, disliked the old system, seeing the out-workers as undermining the wages of their factory colleagues. In 1894 the Union demanded that all work, except that concerned with closing and hand-sewing, should be confined to the factories. This was conceded by the employers, who may themselves have viewed the end of outwork without too much regret. Petty embezzlement was one particular hazard which they had to face under the domestic system. 'It was easy for the finisher, with perhaps several dozen pairs of completed boots in his possession, to sell or pawn them, and then, with his small bundle of possessions, move on under an assumed name to another boot-making town to do the same.'[37] The irregularity of the work pattern was another cause for exasperation among some employers, and a further reason for them to welcome the end of outwork. Nevertheless, even in 1901 about one in six of Northamptonshire's boot and shoemakers was still working at home, and the system did not finally fade away until after the First World War.

Most of the other rural industries were affected by the same process of change as that of boots and shoes. In the case of lacemaking, the competition of machine-made lace and changes in fashion undermined the position of the cottage worker, and whereas there had been just over 20,000 female lacemakers employed in the two counties of Buckinghamshire and Bedfordshire alone in 1851, by 1871 this total had dwindled to about 14,000 and by 1901 to under 2,000. Although these figures may be an underestimate, especially in the earlier period, in that women and girls working at home did not always declare their occupation to the Census Enumerator, the trend they reveal is unmistakable. Glovemaking, buttonmaking, straw plaiting and chairmaking all followed a similar pattern. In 1919, for example, the Report on Wages and Conditions of Employment in Agriculture pointed out that thirty years before there had been about 160,000 men employed in the Chilterns of Oxfordshire and Buckinghamshire in the manufacture of chairs:

Twenty to twenty-five years ago there might have been found one hundred men employed at Beaconsbottom, to take one village out of many as an example. In 1914, I am informed that there were not ten men so employed where there used to be a hundred ... As the big factories with their machinery cheapened production, the village craftsmen were driven to expedients to save costs, and they would erect a rough temporary shed in the woods where trees had been felled, to convert into second and third class material the tops of the trees which were left behind by the fellers working for the factories. There was hardly any money to be made at the business however and all the young men went to the factories and the boys ceased to learn the trades ... One village craftsman told me that fifteen years ago he had five or six men, beside himself, working at lathe and bench; but as one man after another dropped out he did not take the trouble to find another man to take his place. To quote his words, 'So you see there was just that much in it.' For the last six years up to 1914 he employed two men as well as himself.[38]

An investigation of mid-Victorian Census Returns confirms the importance of chairmaking in some Chiltern communities. At Stokenchurch, on the Oxfordshire Buckinghamshire border, with a total male population of 795 in 1861, around one in five was employed as a chairmaker or turner. Agriculture employed only a slightly higher proportion. Among the women, five were employed as 'chair seaters', although for them lacemaking was the prime occupation.

By the end of the century, however, as we have seen, chairmaking had largely become factory based. Nevertheless, certain aspects of production continued to rely on outwork. The turners who made the chair legs, for example, frequently worked on their own account. A number of the men purchased their wood from the saw mills ready cut to chair leg length, but others cut the trunks of the felled trees into the correct sections by hand. This was done with a two-handled crosscut saw and then each section was carefully split so that from a piece of wood 12 inches in diameter two dozen legs could be obtained. The process was completed by turning the legs on an old-fashioned pole lathe. The pay was desperately poor, and around 1900 men producing a gross of legs were paid a mere 5s. Yet, according to one report, it took a man 'from seven in the mornings to seven at night and a half-day on Saturday to make three gross in the week'. In addition, the turners had to find their own tools and were also expected to provide the stretchers which formed the underframe of the chair.[39] In chairmaking communities, a few women and children were also employed in caning the seats. During fine weather they could be seen in the villages around High Wycombe – the centre of the Buckinghamshire chairmaking trade

– sitting at their doors busily caning away for the meagre return of 1s 6d a chair or less.

But it was pillow lacemaking and straw plaiting which formed the two major domestic employments for female and child labour in the early and mid-Victorian years. There were five main pillow lace centres – Northamptonshire, Devon, Oxfordshire, Bedfordshire and Buckinghamshire, with the two last counties providing three-fifths of the total labour force at the 1871 Census of Population. Straw plaiting was carried out in Hertfordshire, the northern area of Essex, parts of Cambridgeshire and Suffolk, a large part of Bedfordshire, and the eastern districts of Buckinghamshire. The great marketing centres were at Luton and Dunstable, although both St Albans and Hitchin were other significant outlets for the trade and there were many small local markets – such as Tring in Hertfordshire and Ivinghoe in Buckinghamshire. The wives and children of agricultural labourers provided the major labour force for both of the industries, although in years of good trade the families of rural craftsmen were also involved, as an investigation of the mid-Victorian Census returns confirms. At Ivinghoe even the niece of a private schoolmaster in the parish was occupied as a plaiter in 1871. And in 1860 it was noted that 'a well-ordered family' engaged in plaiting could 'obtain as much or more than the husband who [was] at work on [a] neighbouring farm'.[40]

Only with the importation of cheaper foreign plaits on a large scale from the 1870s and with changes in fashion in favour of smaller straw hats and bonnets for women, did the industry's prosperity finally decline. Even in the last decade or so of the nineteenth century, however, women could still be found who 'plaited eternally from morning till night, for a wage of about one and threepence a week'.[41]

Both lacemaking and straw plaiting had many common characteristics, with in particular a sad history of exploitation of the workers engaged upon them. Straw plaiting was, in essence, a less skilled occupation than lace, which involved the production of fabrics of complicated and delicate pattern. The lace was made on a hard round cushion, stuffed with straw, and supported either upon the knees of the worker, or partly upon her knees and partly upon a three-legged pillow-horse or a bench. On the pillow a stiff parchment pattern was fixed. The threads with which the lace was formed were wound on bobbins, made either of bone or of wood, and having something of the size and shape of a pencil. The ground of the lace was created by 'twisting and crossing the threads', while the pattern was produced by 'interweaving a thread much thicker than that forming the groundwork, according to the design picked out on the parchment'.[42] Nevertheless, for both plaiting and lace the output of the individual – and consequently her earnings depended very much upon the achievement of a high degree of dexterity through constant practice.

Children were set to work at an early age. In the case of lacemaking they were usually sent to a special lace school at about five or six. Here they would learn the rudiments of the craft from a 'mistress', whose only qualification for holding her position was her skill in her trade and perhaps her iron discipline in extracting the maximum output from her charges. A few made half-hearted attempts to teach the children to read but most were of too limited education themselves to make a success of it. The instruction was usually given in one of the living rooms of the cottage, at least during the winter months, with the fireplace stopped up to prevent draught. Ventilation was minimal and the close atmosphere of the room was made worse by the large number of 'pupils' who were packed inside – sometimes as many as twenty or thirty in a room only 12 feet square. Those aged about five or six worked between four and eight hours a day, but for the older children, between twelve and fifteen years of age, the hours could stretch from 6 a.m. to 10 p.m., or even longer if demand for lace were brisk. As it grew dark, the youngsters would struggle to produce their intricate patterns by the shared light of a candle, while earthenware pots of hot ashes, known as 'dicky pots' were placed at the feet of many of them, to provide a little warmth. Unfortunately, the acrid smoke the pots emitted added to the discomfort of the working conditions. Mrs Roberts of Spratton in Northamptonshire was one of many children who attended a lace school in the earlier years of the nineteenth century. In her village the children attended an ordinary elementary school for a few years before moving on to the lace school and this was a practice followed in certain other villages in the lacemaking areas. As she recalled:

> The girls left the day school at the age of eight years, and joined the lace school, and here the hours were from 6 a.m. to 6 p.m. in the summer, and from 8 a.m. to 8 p.m. in the winter. Half an hour was allowed for breakfast and for tea, and one hour for dinner, so that there were ten hours for actual work. The girls had to stick ten pins a minute, or six hundred an hour; and if at the end of the day they were five pins behind they had to work for another hour ... They counted to themselves every pin they stuck, and at every fiftieth pin they called out the time, and the girls used to race each other as to who should call out first.
>
> They paid twopence a week (or threepence in winter for lights), and in return they received the money realised from the sale of the lace they made, and they could earn about sixpence a day. Pay day was a great event; it came once a month.
>
> In the evenings eighteen girls worked by one tallow candle, value one penny; the 'candle-stool' stood about as high as an ordinary table with

four legs. In the middle of this was what was known as the 'pole-board', with six holes in a circle and one in the centre. In the centre hole was a long stick with a socket for the candle at one end and peg-holes through the sides, so that it could be raised or lowered at will. In the other six holes were placed pieces of wood hollowed out like a cup, and into each of these was placed a bottle made of very thin glass and filled with water. These bottles acted as strong condensers or lenses, and the eighteen girls sat round the table, three to each bottle, their stools being upon different levels, the highest nearest the bottle, which threw the light down upon the work like a burning glass. In the daytime as many as thirty girls... would work in a room about twelve feet square, with two windows, and in the winter they could have no fire for lack of room.[43]

When completed the lace was sold by the parents to one of the local dealers. Sometimes these would be village grocers and drapers who collected the lace for onward despatch to larger agents in the towns, or in London itself. In return for purchasing the lace many of these smaller dealers required their clients to take items from the shop in payment, or part payment, for their goods. And in order to tie the lacemakers closely to them, several of the shopkeepers encouraged the women to 'take goods on credit to be paid for out of their lace when they [were] able to bring it'. Clearly this was open to much exploitation and to overcharging for the items of grocery or drapery involved in the transaction. Workers were also often compelled to buy their threads, pins, patterns and other materials from the same dealers. This meant that when, as in the early 1840s, the trade was depressed, and lace was selling for only two-thirds of its former price, the makers were still forced 'to take their thread from the dealers at the same enhanced price as formerly; and if they did not buy their thread of them, they would not take their lace'. The use of the truck system persisted to the end of the cottage lace trade, even though as early as 1779 an Act had been passed specifically forbidding such abuses in the industry. Even the larger dealers, who were prepared to pay in cash, would deduct a discount 'at the rate of about $1d$ in the $1s$ in the payment' for making this 'concession'. In Devon in the mid 1870s, for example, Assistant Factory Inspector Whymper noted that the already small wages – 'a shilling a day is, I am told, above the average' – were eroded still further by the prevalence of truck. 'One of the largest merchants has informed me that somewhere about 10 per cent of his payments were in tea or some other commodity, and that payments made entirely in money were extremely exceptional ... I am told that where money alone passes the price given is considerably lowered, and that the worse the state of trade the greater the amount of truck.'[44] The fact that lace dealers were prepared to make such admissions to the Inspector gives an interesting insight into the degree of enforcement of truck legislation in that part of the country.

Like all the other domestic industries, lacemaking was brought within the terms of the Factory and Workshop Act of 1867. But observation of the regulations proved difficult to achieve, as the following extract from the report of Alexander Redgrave, Inspector of Factories, for the six months ending 30 April 1875, makes clear:

> The principal difficulties we have had to contend with have arisen in rural localities, in the pillow lace and straw plait districts, where, as in the manufacturing districts forty years ago when wages were at a minimum, and the earnings of children were absolutely a necessary part of the subsistence money of the family, it is almost impossible to insist upon the children going to school, without incurring the reproach of the parent, 'Who then is to find them bread?' There are school boards in very few of these localities, and where school boards have been established they have not taken compulsory powers, so that the whole educational force is vested in the Inspector of Factories.

Twelve months earlier Redgrave had also drawn attention to another problem, namely that many of the straw plait and pillow lace 'schoolmistresses' were only kept from pauperism by this occupation. And if the Inspectors insisted that fewer children were accommodated in the overcrowded rooms, or sought to ensure that the youngsters attended an ordinary day school for the hours laid down in the 1867 Act, they were told that the mistresses could not earn a living:

> The sum paid for a child is generally from three halfpence to twopence per week, and as many of these women have twice as many children as their rooms will hold ... the painful nature of our duties may be conceived. Having myself been through both the straw-plait and the pillow lace making districts of Bedfordshire and Hertfordshire, I speak with my own experience as well as that of the sub-inspectors, and I know how much judgment, temper, and patience are necessary in dealing with the people in these districts, looking upon the law as heartlessly interfering with their earnings and their privileges, to whom the weekly earnings of their children, small though they may be, are of vastly greater importance than prolonging, or even making regular, attendance at school.[45]

A similar point was made by Assistant Inspector Whymper in evidence before the Factory and Workshops Commission of 1876, when he noted of the Devon lace industry: 'there are still parents who think that they have brought children into the world to no purpose, if they do not become contributors to the family purse as soon as they can hold a lace pillow, or shuffle a lace stick.'[46]

Although the pressures applied by the Inspectors may have helped to bring about a decline in the employment of children during the course of the next few years, there is no doubt that the *prime* factor was the collapse of the cottage lace trade itself in the face of more intensive competition from cheaper machine made goods and of changes in women's fashions.

The child plaiter, unlike the lacemaker, normally learnt the basic skills of the craft at home from his or her mother before being sent 'usually at four years old, some at three and a half' to a plait school. This was often little more than a child-minding institution held in a local cottage, since some of the mistresses were unable to teach plaiting themselves. Their sole function was to keep the children working as hard as possible and, as with their lacemaking counterparts, slaps and canings were regarded as a normal part of the disciplinary process. In the lace schools the thread and patterns used were normally provided by the mistress, but for plaiting the bundles of split and bleached or dyed straws were supplied by the parents, who would buy them from straw dealers or sometimes from a village shop, as was the case at Harpenden in Hertfordshire. And it was the parents who normally arranged for the sale of the plait when it was made. This would take place either at one of the special weekly plait markets, the largest of which was held at Luton, or else to local dealers, who were often also shopkeepers. At Harpenden, for example, a small grocer regularly purchased quantities of plait, although with 'no money passing'. When women, wanted articles of grocery from the shop they would 'take or send along a score or half score yards of plait as the case might be'. The grocer would value it and would give as many of the required articles as he thought fit.

Plaiting was an industry dominated by women and child workers, although youths and men would also do a little at nights when they had finished their regular job, if the trade were booming. Edwin Grey who grew up at Harpenden in the 1860s and 1870s remembered the large numbers of his fellow villagers who were involved:

> Everyone when engaged in plait making, carried a bunch of splints under the left arm, pushed close up to the armpit, the elbow having to be kept fairly close to the body to retain the bunch in place. The starting was a somewhat tricky business, but once fairly started, the experienced hands moved their fingers very rapidly, turning the splints in and out, over and under, with but a moment's pause now and again to 'set in' a new splint: this insertion was always spoken of in the singular number ... whereas it should have been in the plural, for there were always a pair used when 'setting in', the rough or inner sides being face to face, the glazed or glossy

sides being outward, so that in the plait itself, only the glazed side was seen
… To ensure that the two splints were kept evenly together in the position
just indicated, they were, when placed together, passed between the lips
lengthways and lying flat, and so in this position drawn along close by
the corners of the mouth, the saliva of which moistened them, and also
caused a slight adhesion sufficient to keep the pair of splints in the even
position required for the 'setting in'. This moistening trick had to be done
with care, or a cut lip or tongue, or perhaps both, would be the result …
I have known some children, whose lips and tongues received nasty cuts,
when they were beginning to plait properly, but these cuts made them
exercise care, and they soon learned the knack of moistening their splints
with safety. Many women were accustomed to hold several splints in
the mouth whilst working, and by the feel of the tongue and movement
of the lips, would so twist, turn and manoeuvre them about, that a pair
were always ready properly placed together, glazed sides outward, when
required for 'setting in' … I might here say that this obstruction in the
mouth did not debar the women from talking, nor from the pleasure of
joining in a little gossip, when friends met friends.[47]

Older children were expected to produce about thirty yards of plait a day,
although some of the more skilled could exceed this output, especially for
the simpler patterns. But those who failed to reach their target might be
kept at work until their fingers became quite sore and bleeding with the
effort 'to get the required yards of plait finished'. Several varieties were
produced – plain, single-splint, pearl, bird's eye, and whipcord, to name but
a few – and some of the more intricate could command as much as 2s 6d
a yard, if trade were good. The most proficient plaiters might produce as
many as four hundred yards of the simpler patterns in a week. To do this a
woman had to 'sit up in bed at 4 o'clock on a summer morning and plait
for an hour or two before rising'.[48] Ruth Stombridge, a twelve-year-old from
Eaton Bray in Bedfordshire, who was interviewed in connection with the
Royal Commission on Children's Employment in 1863, and who had begun
plaiting at the age of three, gave an account of a typical working day:

At the plait school that I am at now I go only from 8 ½ till 12, and from
1 till 4 ½, but mother sets me the same to do as I did at a school where I
stayed till 9 o'clock, viz. thirty yards, ten in each of the three school times
… We sit very screwed at school. Get 10d a score, and dare say I clear
about 5s a week after paying for straw. Have two sisters younger and a
brother older than I am who plait. He goes to the writing school in the day,
and does ten yards afterwards, which takes him till 10 o'clock at night.
There are, I think, seven plait schools in the village, three of them large.
All but three of them have night schools, one till 8 ½ the others till 9, and

their hours in the day are the same as where I am. Was never at a reading
school. Can read the Testament, but not without spelling.[49]

Against this background it is no surprise to discover that infringements of
the 1867 legislation were common. All too often the 'children would slip
out through the back door when anyone in authority called at the [plaiting]
school, while the number plaiting at home was too great to be dealt with
by the Factory inspectorate or the police'. Even when prosecutions were
initiated, their effect could be nullified by the attitude of other members of
the community. Thus during the early part of 1875 in Suffolk 'an inveterate
straw plait mistress who overcrowds her cottage and openly evades the law,
and who was prosecuted a year ago' was again brought before the courts
by the Factory Inspector. But, as he complained, on the previous occasion
'the fines and costs were ... paid for her by a farmer, by whose support and
advice she has been again overcrowding and illegally working. I have been
again obliged to direct her prosecution, and she again leans upon the farmer,
who evidently wishes to secure to her that immunity from the Workshops
Act which he enjoys from the Agricultural Children's Act.' (This latter, it
will be recalled, was an attempt made in 1873 to prohibit the employment
of children in agriculture below the age of eight but which proved utterly
ineffective in operation.)

Complaints from elementary school teachers confirm the irregularity of
attendance of young plaiters at the day schools, and the constant flouting of
the Workshops Regulation Act. At Ivinghoe, a Buckinghamshire plait centre,
for example, the master noted on 24 November 1876: 'The attendance poor
for this week, especially that of the half-timers. The Factory Inspector visited
Ivinghoe on Thursday and called at the school. I trust his visit may do good.'
But these hopes were soon dashed, and on 8 June of the next year, following
a further visit by the Inspector, the master once more expressed the wish
that this would 'be the means of getting more of them to school and to
attend better.' Not until the end of the decade did the situation improve.[50]
Similarly at Shillington in Bedfordshire, the poor attendance of the girls was
attributed to plaiting. In October 1875 the master noted that there were five
plaiting schools in the parish, and that children were being withdrawn from
the ordinary day school to attend them. Only with the decline of the English
plait trade itself, following cheap imports from China in the 1870s and from
Japan in the 1890s, were these problems at last solved and the exploitation
of the young workers brought to an end.

In other parts of the country smaller-scale cottage industries also
existed. Thus in the dales of the north-west of Yorkshire women and
children occupied themselves in the mid-Victorian years with knitting
stockings, jackets and sailor caps, while in the villages around Abingdon
(then in Berkshire) a good deal of 'slop' work was carried out. Even in the

1890s women were paid only 2¼d to 3½d per pair for finishing trousers, 'for which they have to find their own cotton and thread. They have also to deliver the goods themselves, or to pay their carriage to Abingdon.' In Worcestershire, Somerset, and around the small town of Woodstock in Oxfordshire, it was glovemaking that provided the principal employment for women and girls, while on the coast in the fishing villages the making and repairing of nets was an important form of work. In Cornwall late in 1849 a correspondent of the *Morning Chronicle* noted that while many of the nets were 'home-made', being produced by the fisherman's wife and daughters, at other times 'girls and children are hired for the purpose. A girl, if she works early and late, can work off about two skeins a day ... Her remuneration is one shilling a week and her food.'[51] Elsewhere, as in the villages round Leicester, Hinckley and Lutterworth in Leicestershire, stocking-making and seaming employed 'almost all the women and children in the parishes where they exist', while in South Derbyshire, Oxfordshire and Nottinghamshire, osier stripping engaged large numbers each spring. When the rods had been cut and peeled they were dried and then sold for basket weaving – another task which employed women. Large quantities of the willow were also worked up unpeeled 'into hampers of all kinds'.[52]

There can be no doubt that many of the cottage industries imposed great physical strain upon the women and children they engaged. Youngsters were often forced to work long hours for pitifully low wages – as the *Morning Chronicle* correspondent noted in respect of the plait trade: 'As soon as they are able to earn a few pence during the week by their exertions, they are almost certain to be kept constantly to it, and no opportunity is afforded for giving any education.' Nevertheless, given the low wages normally paid to male agricultural labourers in much of southern and central England, the contributions of a wife and children to the family budget were of vital importance. The *Morning Chronicle* correspondent himself admitted that such 'employment has the effect of relieving to a great extent the pressure which would otherwise rest upon the [Bedfordshire] agricultural labourer ... Were it not for the assistance which he obtains from the earnings of his family at the straw plait, his condition would not be one jot better than the great majority of his brother labourers in other counties.' Similar arguments were used to justify the other domestic industries.

Only in the last years of the century did that position change, as mass production techniques and changes in fashion undermined most of the cottage trades, and as many farm workers, enjoying improved real wages as compared to the mid-Victorian years, were now able to support their families by their own efforts. It is to these wage changes that attention must now be turned.

6

Agricultural wages, Trade Unionism & Politics

Wages rose sharply in 1853 and 1854, the years of the Crimean War, and from this period until 1871 the upward movement continued, with slight interruptions coincident with falls in the price of corn. In 1872 and 1873, just after the Franco-German War, rates of wages again rose considerably, and the agitation amongst the labourers, led by Joseph Arch, helped to maintain the high level until the period of agricultural depression which followed the disastrous season of 1879. The upward movement was resumed in 1889 and, with the exception of slight decreases in 1893 and 1894 (a period of general agricultural and commercial depression), it continued up to 1902 ... Speaking generally, ordinary agricultural labourers in England get comparatively few allowances in kind excepting potato ground and beer at harvest. But in the northern and some of the western counties cottages and fuel are also frequently given free, and in some counties in the latter group cider is often given as a daily allowance ... As regards the rates for piecework, they have, as would be expected, gradually increased along with the increase of weekly wages, and they are now about 50 per cent higher than they were in 1850.

A. Wilson Fox, 'Agricultural Wages in England
and Wales during the Last Fifty Years',
*Journal of the Royal Statistical
Society*, LXVI (1903)

Throughout the nineteenth century the wages of agricultural labourers remained low compared to those of most workers in manufacturing industry. Even in the 1880s and 1890s they only reached about 55 or 56 per cent of the average industrial rate and in the middle of the century they had been a mere 49 per cent of that average level. Admittedly within this general picture there were considerable regional variations as well as wide differences between individual workers according to age, experience and post held. A skilled stockman, for example, would expect to earn 1s or 2s per week more than an ordinary day labourer, partly because he had to work on Sundays and partly in recognition of his extra responsibility. Likewise a man who was getting on in years would earn at a lower rate, in recognition of the fact that his physical strength could not match that of younger colleagues. Thus, to quote one example, on the Blount estate at Mapledurham in South Oxfordshire during 1890–91, at a time when the head carter was earning a basic wage of 15s a week and the general labourers 12s or 13s, a seventy-year-old man who had been employed on the estate for about fifty years was earning 7s 6d per week on miscellaneous 'jobbing', while a slightly younger colleague was paid 8s 6d for similar duties. This situation is reflected in the records of other estates and farms.[1]

But it was on a regional basis that the greatest variations occurred. In 1837 it was estimated that average weekly wage rates in Hereford, Wiltshire and Devon were a mere 8s a week and in Dorset and parts of Wales only 7s 6d at a time when they had reached 13s in Cheshire and 12s in many other northern counties – thanks to the proximity of higher paid alternative employment in urban factories and the mining industry.[2] By 1851, when James Caird completed his survey of English agriculture, the position had changed little, with average wages in the north standing at 11s 6d a week, while in the southern and eastern counties they amounted to 8s 5d and 9s 1d, respectively. The lowest rate of all encountered by Caird was 6s a week paid in South Wiltshire; the highest, 15s a week, in parts of Lancashire. And he noted that while the 'redundance of labour oppresses property and depreciates wages in the South', the 'influence of manufacturing enterprise' had added '37 per cent to the wages of the agricultural labourers of the Northern counties, as compared with those of the South'.[3] (See also Appendix G)

The building of the railways helped to reduce some of the problems of the southern counties by absorbing men who would otherwise have remained unemployed or underemployed, while in other cases emigration to Australasia and North America or migration to the towns of England also reduced numbers. But although some of the regional differences had in this manner been ironed out by the end of the century, even then the range of weekly earnings remained 'astonishingly great', with the 14s 6d obtained by Oxfordshire men contrasted with the 22s 6d which could be secured in Durham. Similarly, in the south-western counties, workers who had been earning in 1870 about 13 per cent below the national average were still earning about 9 per cent below the then average in 1898.[4] East Anglia, too, continued to fare badly, and by 1900 'wages in Suffolk, [averaging 11s 5d a week] were probably the lowest in England

and only Caithness and Orkney and Shetland denied the county the distinction of being the worst-paid in Britain.'[5]

Piecework earnings could supplement low basic wages, while for the annually hired stockman there were additional lump sums of perhaps £2 10s to £6 payable at Michaelmas or Lady Day, whenever the year's hiring came to an end. In the late 1860s on one small estate in South Oxfordshire, where the carter-cowman earned 14s a week, he also received £2 10s at Michaelmas, plus a rent-free cottage and occasional piecework earnings, including payments for killing rats. The young under carter-cowman was paid 8s a week, with £4 for Michaelmas money.[6] Likewise in Northamptonshire at around the same time it was calculated that although the average basic wage rates for able-bodied adult labourers varied between 11s and 14s per week, piecework earnings could push this up by several shillings. A man who received 12s a week as his basic rate could have an average weekly *income* of perhaps 15s when the extras were taken into account. In Norfolk, too, where 'the weekly wage ... was 12s it was estimated that the total annual earnings of an able-bodied labourer, including his piecework, would range from £37 to £40 ... the annual earnings of a farm labourer, who loses no time and gets his fair allowance of piecework would give an average throughout the year of about 2s per week in excess of the current weekly wages'.[7]

The harvest season was, of course, a particularly fruitful period for piecework earnings. Thus Caleb Prior, a general labourer employed on the Dillon estate at Ditchley in Oxfordshire at a daily rate of 2s or 2s 2d, abandoned his day work for employment on contract during the harvest season of 1872. He earned £13 1s 9½d as his share of piecework at this time – after a deduction of 3s 4½d had been made, as was the custom on this farm, to cover half the cost of measuring the work carried out. Prior was obviously a versatile man who seized every opportunity for contract work, including, for example, thatching ricks. Consequently during the twelve months from mid-June 1872 to mid-June 1873 his annual income amounted to £42 18s 9½d, whereas at basic rates only it would have been £33 14s. On the other hand, another labourer, Thomas Scuse, also paid at the basic rate of 2s or 2s 2d per day, achieved an annual income of only £39 6s 10½d over the same period (including 10s for working on ten Sundays 'assisting shepherd') because of his more limited piecework earnings.[8]

Yet if task work in its varied forms provided a valuable addition to the weekly wage, not all men were able to take full advantage of it, especially in the later years of the century. For with the wider use of machinery to replace hand labour in such operations as hay mowing, corn harvest and threshing, and with a reduction in the area of land under arable cultivation, especially from the 1880s, there were fewer opportunities available. The financial difficulties of farmers from the 1870s onwards also encouraged them to leave undone routine jobs like hoeing, weeding, hedging and ditching. Then, too, except for the annually hired labourer there was always a danger that during the winter or in very wet weather, when work was in short supply, men would be laid off without pay, and in this way would lose much of the benefit derived from earlier piecework earnings. In North Essex as late as 1914 basic wages were quoted at 13s a week, but 'in the winter, time lost through bad weather sometimes brought them down as low as 6s or 7s.' A Lincolnshire farmer at around the same time estimated that the average amount of time lost by workers through 'standing off' was between ten and fourteen days a year. On some farms, winter wages were in any case always lower than those paid in summer, because the men worked shorter hours. At farms at Wootton Bassett in Wiltshire, labourers who were paid 8s 6d a week during the summer months in the early 1850s received only 7s 6d a week in winter. By the end of the decade these levels had increased to 10s 6d and 9s 6d, respectively, and by the late 1860s had jumped a further shilling to 11s 6d and 10s 6d. But despite the overall upward movement in the levels, the *differential* between summer and winter payments was maintained. Similarly, at Wereham in Norfolk, mid-century winter rates were 9s or 9s 6d a week; in the summer they were a shilling more.[9]

Another source of financial uncertainty was illness. A minority of employers made their men an allowance when they were sick as on the Hackwood estate in Hampshire, where the usual amount in the early 1870s was 1s 4d a week, while on the Dillon estate at Ditchley at about the same time the payment was 1s per day. Where the illness was prolonged, however, this allowance was discontinued after a few weeks.[10] But most men received no pay at all, and were forced instead to rely upon poor relief or upon the benefit of a friendly society to which they had contributed during good health.

The effect of all these factors on the money earnings of workers is demonstrated by the following breakdown of the annual income of two labourers: one employed at Tolleshunt D'Arcy in Essex and the other at Aspley Guise in Bedfordshire. Both were quoted by the Royal Commission on Labour:

(*1*). *Earnings of a general labourer at a farm at Tolleshunt D'Arcy in the Maldon Union, Essex—Michaelmas 1891 to Michaelmas 1892*

	£	s.	d.
48 weeks at 12s., less five days' wet, 10s.	28	6	0
Hoeing wheat, peas, barley, and beans, over 2s. a day	1	6	8
Hoeing and chopping out swedes and mangold, over 2s. a day		10	8
Mowing red clover, over 2s. a day	1	1	0
Extra pay and overtime, in haying, over 2s. a day	1	2	1
28 days with threshing machine, at 4d. a day extra		9	4
4 weeks harvest piecework	9	5	0
Total	42	0	9
Average per week		16	2

(*2*). *Earnings of a general labourer at a farm at Aspley Guise in the Woburn Union, Bedfordshire—1891–92*

	£	s.	d.
Ordinary wages, four weeks, two days, at 12s. a week	2	12	0
Ordinary wages, 48 weeks, at 13s. a week	31	4	0
Total ordinary wages if no time had been lost	33	16	0
Less loss of time, one week through illness, and 11¾ days on visit and on his allotment	1	17	3½
Actual ordinary wages	31	18	8½
Extra earnings during harvest, including 15s. for other work during that period of 4½ weeks	4	5	1
Other extra earnings	2	19	6
Total earnings during 12 months	39	3	3½
Average per week		15	0

[This man was a total abstainer and received money when other workers had beer.]

As can be seen, although the Tolleshunt D'Arcy labourer had a lower weekly wage *rate* than his colleague at Aspley Guise, thanks to piecework earnings and better health his average weekly *earnings* for the period were higher.

The amount of money income received might be complicated in some cases, too, by the practice of workers of buying meat, butter, eggs, coal and pigs from their employers on an instalment system. Although this doubtless had the advantage that the items involved were purchased at a lower price than was available in the shops, it did mean that in certain months workers received very little cash. Elsewhere the custom of paying part of the wages in alcoholic liquor also had the effect of reducing take-home pay. John Dent, a landowner and Member of Parliament, pinpointed this in 1871 when he wrote: 'Perhaps one of the greatest evils which affect the condition of the labourer in the Southern, Western and South Midland Counties, is the practice of giving beer or cider to the men in lieu of wages. This custom not only prevents a fair share of the wages going for the support of the family, but it generates that love of drink, which ... [is] the curse of the labourer.'[11] It is significant that when the agricultural trade unions became established in the 1870s, one of their early demands was for the payment of wages in cash instead of partly in cash and partly in kind. But the practice of paying in alcohol was only finally made illegal with the passage of the Truck Act in 1887. Even then its restrictions were sometimes ignored – not only during harvest, as we shall see in Chapter 7, but at other times as well. A farmer from North Petherton in the Bridgwater district of Somerset, informed Rider Haggard in 1900 that in his district, the average weekly wage of 12s was supplemented by 'two quarts of cider per diem, the Truck Amendment Act being ... a dead letter which was equally ignored by master and men'.[12]

It is not surprising that given the low wages of most labourers, particularly between the 1830s and the 1870s, and with work for a good many men also irregular, the earnings of wives and children were required to make ends meet. In some areas, as we saw in the last chapter, this family contribution took the form of employment in cottage industries like lacemaking, straw plaiting and glovemaking. Elsewhere the tasks taken up might include washing, sewing and charing for better-off members of village society – at a wage of perhaps 2s or 3s per week. As one Hampshire lad remembered, with a family of eight children his father's weekly 11s was not sufficient to feed and clothe them all and so his mother took in washing. 'When the weather was bad and the washing had to dry, she used to chase us all off to bed and then used to hang the washing up all round the house.' The discomfort of wet sheets and clothing ranged around a small crowded house is not difficult to imagine. Many town families also sent their laundry into the villages to be washed and this, too, provided employment for country women. Wives and daughters at Headington Quarry, for example, laundered clothes sent out from Oxford, while in certain villages in Buckinghamshire and Bedfordshire, washing was even received from London households.[13] Other women did washing and ironing in their employer's home. Mrs Dowrick of Coombe in Cornwall recalls that when her mother worked in this way during the 1890s 'for farmers she would have some butter and milk as reward and her meal'.[14]

But for many the securing of extra earnings meant work on the land. Rates of pay for women in agriculture by the middle of the nineteenth century varied between 6d and 1s per day, according to the nature of the work and the availability (or otherwise) of alternative non-agricultural employment. In some places slightly higher wages were earned at the busy haymaking and harvest seasons. Young children, on the other hand, could obtain as little as 1s a week – like the 'two bits of wenches, ten or eleven years old', whom Arthur Munby met near Jervaux Abbey in September 1863. They were 'minding' cows grazing in the lane and worked from 9 a.m. till 5 p.m. for six days a week.[15] However, as such youngsters grew in strength and experience, the amount paid to them rose until it approximated, in the case of boys, to the rate paid to the men. An idea of the scale of these additional contributions can be gained from the example of families at Long Sutton in Lincolnshire during 1868. According to a large farmer in the village, women and children were employed each year during the late summer and autumn at daily rates of pay of 1s 3d for the women, 1s for the older girls, and 9d for the younger boys and girls. In all, for a family of a mother and two children this could amount to 3s a day – or around £8 for the full period: 'Reckoning the husband's wage at 15s a week ... throughout the year, supposing him to make £4 additional in harvest, a boy to earn 4s a week for a portion of the year, and the wife also to earn £3 or £4 in spring to summer the total income of the family is, say, £56 a year ... and thus the £8 autumnal earnings of the wife and two children is one-seventh of the whole livelihood of the family. In fact, a loss of this source of income would be equivalent to a deprivation of one day's living per week.'[16]

But as mechanisation progressed and as male workers secured higher cash wages, so the role of women and children diminished. In the early 1890s, in fact, the Senior Assistant Agricultural Commissioner in connection with the Royal Commission on Labour, commented on the 'lessened employment of women in farm work' and added: 'The universal withdrawal of women from field work is evidence of an improvement in the circumstances of the labourers.' Even in Norfolk, where women and girls were still engaged in singling, pulling and cleaning roots, weeding com, and raking after the waggons in hay and corn harvest, numbers had fallen sharply as compared to earlier years. And interviews carried out with male workers showed that almost all of them approved of the change.

It was not until the last thirty or so years of the nineteenth century that general wage rates began to edge noticeably upwards. The average money wage for the lowest-paid male labourers, which had been about 7s in 1850 jumped to around 10s by 1869–70 and to between 11s and 13s by 1872. Indeed, according to Hasbach, the average rate for the whole of England and Wales – a calculation which eliminates the important regional variations – stood at 12s 3d in 1869–70 and around 14s 8d by 1872. In part this change can be attributed to the general buoyancy of trade and the opportunity for men to leave the land for better-paid urban employment. Then too, agriculture itself had enjoyed a period of prosperity during the previous decade or so, and the labourers had shared in this improvement to a limited extent. But the situation was also influenced by another factor – namely the growth of rural trade unionism. This development owed something to the publicity surrounding the passage of the 1871 Trade Union Act, which confirmed the legal status of trade unions and gave protection to their funds, as well as to the success of a movement for a nine-hour working day among men in the building and engineering industries.

The union movement of the late 1860s and early 1870s was not the first attempt at organisation among farm labourers. As early as 1833–34 an attempt had been made to form a combination at the small village of Tolpuddle in Dorset, but the six most active members had been arrested. They were found guilty as 'evil disposed persons' under a statute of 1797 which had been intended for the suppression of seditious societies after the naval mutinies of that year. The six were eventually sentenced to seven years' transportation for administering an illegal oath in connection with the formation of their union. But public anger at the sentences proved so intense that the government was induced in March 1836 to grant the men a pardon. Even then their return from Australia was delayed and it was not until 1839 that the last of them reached England.[17]

The treatment accorded to these six men became a symbol of the early struggles of the trade union movement but in the years that followed they had few imitators. Admittedly, during the agitation for the repeal of the Corn Laws in the 1840s there are accounts of meetings of labourers demanding repeal – and cheaper bread. One such was organised at the hamlet of Bremhill in Wiltshire during early February 1846. According to the local press about 1,500 labourers and their wives attended from the surrounding area, to demand changes. For as one of the speakers, a middle-aged woman named Lucy Simpkins, declared: 'I have been obliged to tell my children that I would beat them if they cried for hunger … if Free-Trade will make bread cheap, then I want Free-Trade.'[18] Similarly, in May 1840 a Justice of the Peace from Saxmundham in Suffolk wrote to the Home Secretary expressing concern at the actions of a Mr James Acland, an Anti-Corn Law lecturer, in his area: 'it is causing considerable excitement amongst the labouring population so much that I am told some Farmers yesterday declined attending their market at Saxmundham being apprehensive of a riot.'[19] Yet, despite these fears, support for the reform campaign proved limited among villagers and the most vociferous hostility to the Corn Laws remained in the towns.

So it was not until the mid-1860s, at a time of rising prices and of demands among urban workers for an extension of the parliamentary franchise, that agricultural trade unionism again emerged on a firm basis. Then, in 1866, a short-lived union called the Agricultural Labourers' Protection Association was established in Kent, while in June of that same year a similar attempt at independent organisation was made around the village of Great Glen, near Leicester. Here workers came out on strike to support their demand for an increase of 2s in their basic weekly wage of 10s. The employers responded by evicting all of the strikers living in tied cottages and in face of their opposition the combination soon died away. In 1867 a fresh attempt was made to establish a union, this time centred on the town of Buckingham and seeking to organise workers in nearby parishes in Buckinghamshire, Northamptonshire and Oxfordshire. The strike of labourers in the Buckinghamshire village of Gawcott, which was called in connection with this union, aroused the attention of the national press and of the *Annual Register*. Yet, once again, the opposition was too great and the movement, lacking effective leadership, faded away.[20] Other attempts followed but it was only in 1871 that a more permanent organisation was at last established, when a number of labourers in Shropshire and Herefordshire joined together to form the North Herefordshire and South Shropshire Agricultural Labourers' Improvement Society. It was an essentially peaceful body, whose watchword was 'Emigration, Migration but not Strikes'. As a result of this approach one of its main achievements was the sending of 'surplus' labour from Herefordshire to employment in Yorkshire, Lancashire and Staffordshire at substantially higher wages than those obtainable in Herefordshire. Some men also emigrated to America and even to Queensland under the auspices of the Union. In all, it was to recruit members in six different counties and to claim a membership of about 30,000 at its peak.

In the months that followed, similar organisations appeared in Leicestershire and Lincolnshire – each with the principal objective of improving wage rates at a time of sharply rising prices and general trade boom. But it was from agitation among the men of South Warwickshire that the prime inspiration of the rural union movement was to derive. The Warwickshire labourers began to combine in February 1872, under the leadership of Joseph Arch, a stocky, forty-five-year-old hedgecutter from the village of Barford and a Primitive Methodist local preacher. Arch was a man of great determination and he was able to transmit something of this quality to his followers. Night after night during the wet spring of 1872 he tramped from village to village addressing meetings. It was an exhausting programme but his belief in the importance of the cause enabled him to carry on. For he was convinced that a beacon had been lit 'which would prove a rallying point for the agricultural labourers throughout the country'. And so it proved.

Once the Warwickshire men had started to form their union they were anxious to achieve some positive benefits as quickly as possible. Consequently, early in March they put forward demands for an increase in wages to 2s 8d a day and a reduction in the hours of work, so that they started at 6 a.m. and ended at 5 p.m. on weekdays 'and to close at three on Saturday'. Over and above this, overtime was to be paid at the rate of 4d per hour. These proposals were incorporated in a circular letter which was sent out to local farmers, with Arch's approval, by men in the Wellesbourne area. The employers, for their part, ignored the letter, believing that the new organisation would prove too weak to support effective industrial action. But on 11 March that confidence was rudely shattered. The men came out on strike.

Press publicity followed rapidly in the wake of this action and the strikers were helped by favourable reports of their case published not only in the local *Royal Leamington Chronicle* but also in national newspapers, like the Liberal *Daily News* and the *Daily Telegraph*. From early on money began to flow into the union's reserves, sent by a sympathetic general public anxious to help provide strike pay. For very few of the men had any cash of their own to fall back upon. A number of the strikers migrated to alternative employment in the north of England, while a few emigrated to New Zealand and even Brazil. But most stuck it out and were eventually rewarded by the granting of an increase in pay. The dispute was finally wound up in the middle of April.

Meanwhile on 29 March 1872 at a large demonstration held at Leamington, rules were drawn up for merging all existing union organisations in the county into one body, to be known as the Warwickshire Agricultural Labourers' Union, under the leadership of Joseph Arch.

By now Arch's fame had spread far beyond his own county. And there was a sudden mushrooming of local combinations as labourers in most of the low-wage counties of southern and central England joined together to demand a better deal. To such men the union seemed to offer both the promise of a more prosperous future and a means of achieving self-reliance and self-respect. In Kent organisation began in the middle of April, as a direct result of news of Arch's movement reaching the Kentish villages, while in Dorset meetings were held from May. In Oxfordshire action was taken still more quickly. As early as 9 March, *Jackson's Oxford Journal* mentions 'a good deal of agitation' among labourers in the Banbury district, and reports that in two parishes at least this had led to a 1s per week rise in wages being secured. Norfolk, soon to be at the heart of the union movement, was another area involved. Meetings were held all over the county, in chapels, in public houses and often in the open air. At many the lead was taken by men who were also Primitive Methodist local preachers – like Arch himself. At Thetford, for example, an assembly was held in the Temperance Hall. It began with a prayer and 'at the close of the meeting some men signed the pledge'. This kind of response was typical, and in the months ahead there were claims by clergymen that the Nonconformist leadership of the movement was alienating villagers from the Church. Characteristic of these was the complaint of the incumbent of Easington and Cuxham, Oxfordshire, who informed the Bishop of Oxford that his congregation had decreased 'in consequence of a spirit of insubordination and disaffection towards employers and clergy being raised by inflammatory speeches and publications' of the agricultural union.[21] This particular aspect of the union's activities is examined further in Chapter 8.

Within weeks of its formation the Warwickshire union was swamped with appeals for help, and especially with requests for Arch's attendance at meetings. And in south-west Oxfordshire, where the union movement centred around the parish of Milton-under-Wychwood, the local leaders were pressing for his attendance at a meeting within three weeks of their union's formation.[22] It was against this background, therefore, that the Warwickshire men decided to organise a further conference at Leamington to establish a *national* union. With the help of outsiders, including Liberal politicians from Birmingham and non-agricultural trade unionists from Leamington, this second meeting opened amidst considerable press publicity, on 29 May 1872. About sixty delegates attended, from most counties south of the Trent, and discussions were soon under way. Many of the speeches were punctuated with 'devout utterances of "Amen" and "Praise Him" ... Numbers of the speakers used phrase's redolent of the village pulpit. "My Christian friends," "Beloved brethren," "Dear fellow Christians," slipped out incessantly.'

According to the Revd F. S. Attenborough, a Leamington Congregational minister who attended the gathering, about half of the delegates were local preachers. And he added: 'In the hands of such men the movement is safe.'

Once the preliminaries had been completed Arch was unanimously elected president of the new National Agricultural Labourers' Union (NALU), while the general secretary was Henry Taylor, a unionist from Leamington who was already treasurer of his local branch of the Amalgamated Society of Carpenters and Joiners. On being appointed to the NALU post, however, Taylor gave up his other employment. The treasurer was a sympathetic newspaper owner and journalist, also from Leamington, J. E. Matthew Vincent, whose paper, the *Royal Leamington Chronicle,* had already given extensive coverage to the labourers' activities. With his backing the National Union decided to establish its own newspaper, and in June 1872 the first edition of the *Labourers' Union Chronicle* appeared. It was to act as a valuable link in the movement, for in its pages were reports of village and district assemblies from all parts of the country. Labourers could read of the doings of their fellows elsewhere and perhaps derive inspiration from them. The newspaper continued publication, although with a change of name in 1877 to the *English Labourers' Chronicle,* until 1894 – shortly before the demise of the National Union itself.

In the months that followed the formation of the NALU the workers' pressure for higher wages continued. Sometimes their efforts encountered severe opposition from employers as at the village of Wootton in Oxfordshire, where in late June 1872 farmers not only turned down the men's demands for a wage increase from 11s to 16s a week but also formed their own defence association to oppose the agricultural union movement. Then, on the first Friday of July about 120 labourers in Wootton and its immediate vicinity ceased work – some because they had been locked out by their employers and others because they had struck in support of their wage claim. The dispute was to drag on for several weeks and in the middle of July a number of unionists and their families migrated to Sheffield in order to seek alternative employment. But most stayed to continue the struggle.

With the approach of harvest, the farmers grew anxious about the gathering of their crops. Yet they were still unwilling to negotiate with their workers. So they decided to apply instead to the military authorities at Aldershot for soldiers to work in the harvest fields. In the end perhaps fifty servicemen were so engaged, but their intervention in the dispute aroused immediate controversy. Both the secretary of the NALU and the secretary of the London Trades Council wrote to the Secretary of State for War to protest, and their efforts led to an amendment of the

Queen's Regulations designed to prevent a similar situation arising in future. The dispute finally petered out in August, when most of the remaining labourers returned to work – many having secured at least some increase in pay to compensate them for their bitter fight.

Other, rather shorter, disputes occurred in various parts of the country, and in April 1873 an anti-union farmers' association on the Essex-Suffolk border discharged about a thousand union members. Dispute pay could only be continued for a little over a month, and in the end the men either gave in or left the area.[23] In 1873, also, Arch was sent by the union to Canada to investigate the possibilities of labourers emigrating to that Dominion. He returned with assurances from the Canadian Government that any men sent would be well looked after and settled on the land. In the mid-1870s a number of labourers were despatched to Canada and Australasia under NALU auspices.[24]

Yet, if the union encountered difficulties and opposition from some quarters during its first months of existence, at the same time membership was rising steadily – from around 71,000 in 1873 to over 86,000 by 1874 – and in many areas the men were winning advances in pay without resort to strike action. An examination of farm accounts bears this out; thus on the Butler farm near Blandford in Dorset adult labourers had been paid – on a monthly basis – at the rate of 9s a week since the mid-1860s. But after the harvest of 1872, rates increased to 10s and 11s per week, paid fortnightly. And in the spring of 1873 the rate moved up again, so that by that date most of the general labourers were taking home 12s per week. Similarly on Viscount Dillon's model farm at Ditchley in Oxfordshire, weekly wage rates increased from 11s or 12s in 1871 to 12s and 13s in May 1872 and then went up by a further shilling in July of that year. Among the women workers the daily rate increased from 10d at the beginning of 1872 to 1s in July. And at Audley End Park Farm in Essex, Lord Braybrooke's property, the rates advanced from 11s or 12s per week in the early months of 1872 to 13s and 14s about a year later. In all cases the advances were secured without industrial action and were retained at the new level to the end of the decade. Only in the depressed 1880s did a change occur, with *some* of the men once more losing 1s or 2s per week.[25]

Unionists were also learning to co-operate in other ways. Many branches, for example, set up an 'incidental fund' from which they made payments to sick or unemployed members. In other parishes efforts were made to obtain allotments or to investigate the distribution of local charities. All of these functions were to continue throughout the union's existence as were the various social gatherings organised by branches from time to time. At these, NALU leaders would combine business with pleasure – as the following account of events at Witchampton in Dorset during September 1873 demonstrates:

> An open-air meeting of members and friends of the Witchampton branch of the NALU took place on Wednesday ... in a field kindly lent by Mr H. Tripp, the local secretary. Early in the afternoon a procession was formed, which started from the old malthouse, headed by the Witchampton brass band, over whom waved a gaily-painted banner with the expressive motto, 'Each for all, and all for each,' composed of members of the Union, wearing blue favours and dressed in holiday style. After parading the village, a bountiful spread of tea and cake awaited them in the large yard adjoining Mr Tripp's house. Again and again the tables were filled, and for some two hours the order of the day was eating and drinking. Meanwhile all sorts of amusements were going on in the field, where the youths and maidens were making fun for each other, and soon after five o'clock some hundreds of persons gathered round a waggon, which served as a rostrum for those who were to address the assemblage. Mr H. Mayor, district secretary, presided at the meeting ... The meeting was closed with three hearty cheers for Mr Arch, the speakers, and the Union.[26]

Even the small branches had their festivals – as at Garford near Newbury, where there were only twenty-six members. In the summer of 1873 they and their families had a tea provided by the labourers' wives. 'After tea, speeches, songs, and about to do accounts, when a friend came in and put five shillings on our books, wishing us every success.'[27]

Yet despite this brighter side, the NALU was soon to face a major test. One of its perennial problems was that even in the best unionised counties it was unable to recruit more than about one in three or one in four of the men. On a national basis it could not even reach a level of membership of one labourer in ten. Nevertheless, East Anglia was one of the best organised areas in the country and it was here in the spring of 1874 that the union had to face a counter-attack by employers, who resented what they saw as the 'dictatorial' attitude of the NALU leaders. The demands of labourers for what were, in essence, modest increases in pay were attributed by farmers to the influence of these outside 'agitators' who had to be defeated at all costs.

The immediate cause of the trouble in 1874 was a dispute involving workers in the small Suffolk village of Exning. As early as September 1872 the Exning labourers had asked for a 2s per week increase in their basic wages to bring them up to 14s, but had been met with a firm rebuff from their employers. The latter had joined with other farmers in the surrounding area of Suffolk and Cambridgeshire to form the Newmarket Farmers' Defence Association, with the avowed aim of taking co-operative action in the face of any future dispute between their workers and themselves. At about the same time other East Anglian farmers followed along the same lines by forming defence associations of their own. Then in the spring of 1873 a further wage demand was put forward by the men of Exning. This time the farmers decided to give a rise of 1s per week, although they denied that their action was influenced by trade union pressure. Not surprisingly the men thought otherwise. And in February 1874 they came forward with a demand for a further shilling a week increase in their pay. When this request was turned down they came out on strike.

The members of the Newmarket Farmers' Defence Association, for their part, showed equal solidarity and they responded to the strike by locking out all union men in their employ. So it was in this virtually unplanned, almost casual, fashion that the great Eastern Counties dispute began. It soon spread beyond the confines of Exning and the Newmarket area. By 23 March at least 2,500 members had been locked out in Suffolk, Cambridgeshire, Norfolk, Essex, Bedfordshire, Lincolnshire and Hampshire, and a Union Lock-out Fund had been established.

The pressures on both farmers and labourers were tremendous. But for the latter there was the additional burden of obtaining money to feed their families, for the union dispute pay of 9s per week scarcely sufficed for this. Many were forced to sell their already scanty possessions in order to continue the struggle. Yet for them, as for Arch and his fellow leaders, the issue was 'not a rise of a shilling a week but, Shall these labourers have a Union?' It was for the basic right to combine that they were fighting.

In all the lock-out lasted about five months and involved an expenditure of £24,432 10s 7d by the National Union Executive Committee in support of the 6,000 or so men who were eventually sucked into the conflict. Local funds were also disbursed, bringing the total expenditure to perhaps £29,000. In these circumstances fund raising became a major problem for the NALU leaders. Furthermore, as some of the men were sent to alternative work in other parts of England or migrated overseas, particularly to Canada, their transport had to be arranged as well. Arch himself set off on an intensive fundraising campaign in the towns and cities of the Midlands and the North addressing numerous mass meetings in an effort to obtain funds to continue the struggle. Urban and rural unionists elsewhere also contributed. For example, the minute book of the Oxford district of the union has several entries to this effect – as on 14 April 1874: 'remit to Leamington £87-3-1 which we have collected as lock out fund'.[28] Individual branches held meetings and demonstrations on their own account for the same cause. Among the urban unionists, the Amalgamated Society of Engineers sent about £2,000 and many others responded on a smaller scale.

Yet despite this wholehearted support, the large scale on which relief had to be disbursed and the ability of farmers to economise on their work force or to use non-union labourers and machinery to replace the strikers meant that in the end the NALU was forced to accept defeat. At a meeting of the executive committee on 27 July it was decided to recommend all those still out to return to work. In the event, many found difficulty in doing so, while others were only re-employed on the understanding they left the union. Although the executive's decision was probably inevitable in view of the NALU's financial plight, there is no doubt that it gave rise to feelings of betrayal among many members. Out of this disillusionment there developed conflicts between the union leaders themselves. And in the summer of 1875 J. E. Matthew Vincent, the NALU treasurer and proprietor of the union newspaper, decided to break away to form a new (albeit short-lived) union of his own called the National Farm Labourers' Union. This had as its main aims the provision of allotments and smallholdings and the avoidance of strikes.

In the months that followed the leaders of this new organisation and of the old proceeded to cast doubts upon one another's personal probity, while to add to the confusion there were also a few smaller independent organisations which had never affiliated to the NALU. These included the Kent and Sussex Union and the Lincolnshire Amalgamated Labour League, and their leaders, too, joined in the general mood of recrimination. All were tasting the bitter. fruits of defeat and finding them little to their liking. In addition, agriculture itself was moving into difficult times, particularly at the end of the 1870s, as bad harvests at home and growing imports of foreign grain cut farmers' profits.

In 1877, in a desperate effort to tie members more firmly to it, the NALU established its own sick-benefit society. Unfortunately, however worthwhile the aim, this move served only to weaken the Union still further, since withdrawals from the fund soon began to exceed payments in. As Arch later wrote: 'So it came about that for almost every ten shillings paid in, twenty shillings had to be paid out. Then the neglect of enforcing a proper entrance fee, the amount of which should have been regulated by the age of the applicant, deprived the fund of considerable sums.'

Nor was this all. Wage rates, too, were cut back by employers and although they did not, in general, return to pre-1872 levels, the fact that the Union could offer so little protection on the sensitive issue of pay weakened its appeal further. Paradoxically, of course, thanks to the fall in food prices in the last quarter of the century, *real* wages were moving upwards – and were by 1898 perhaps 30 per cent above the level of 1873.[29]

The subscription for membership of the NALU was 2½d per week. Soon some of the men – and their wives, on whom family budgeting problems principally fell – were asking where the money was going. Arch was accused, wrongly, of spending funds on himself, and wives discouraged their husbands from contributing precious pennies by asking 'why [they] wanted to keep ol' Joey Arch a gennelman'. In these circumstances union membership dropped, until by the end of 1879 it had reached 20,000 – or less than one-quarter of the 1874 peak.

Nevertheless, despite the failures on the wages front, in the early 1880s a number of unionists did concern themselves with action in the political field. In particular, there were demands for a widening of the franchise to include the rural householder, matching his voting rights with those given to the townsman in 1867. This had been a feature of NALU policy from early days, and by June 1873 the *Labourers' Union Chronicle* was putting the acquisition of the vote second only to higher wages as a union aim. In both 1876 and 1877 the Oxford and Banbury districts of the NALU were active in sponsoring petitions to Parliament for franchise extension, while in Norfolk a group of local leaders met in Norwich to form the County Franchise Association. Like their Oxfordshire counterparts they immediately began to organise petitions to Parliament.[30] And in May 1876 a large-scale demonstration was held with NALU support at the Memorial Hall, Farringdon Street, London, and was attended by labourers from all over the country. Several Liberal MPs were also present. For from the start rural enfranchisement had had the support of the Radical wing of that party, who no doubt saw it as a way of 'dishing' Conservatives in their traditional agricultural strongholds.

Although in the final push for the county franchise in 1884 the influence of the union was weakened by its loss of membership – support had fallen to a mere 15,000 by the end of 1883 – neither Arch nor his immediate supporters allowed themselves to be cast down by this. In a speech made on the Reform Bill at Radford in Warwickshire, for example, during March 1884 Arch declared that in that community a few 'good men and true' had kept 'the fire of unionism burning'. He then added: 'In view of the new duties they would soon have to discharge, he wished to urge upon them the importance of combining together so that they might learn to act in concert so that they might be able to secure for themselves and their families the greatest measure of benefit.' But many of the village meetings he attended at this time were sponsored by the Liberal Party rather than by his own organisation. Nevertheless, during these months there was a modest revival in the union and membership temporarily rose to about 18,000 in 1884 – only to slide back to 10,700 in the following year.

Early in December 1884 rural workers were at last admitted to full political rights. In these circumstances it now became the aim of Arch and most active unionists to persuade them to give their support to the Liberal Party. Time and again Arch warned them against expecting 'Tory parsons and Tory squires or any of their agents' to provide political guidance, declaring, 'You must read and think for yourselves.' Indeed, if anything, he was inclined to overstress the value and significance of the vote, as when he told a meeting at Swaffham in Norfolk, 'Now the welfare of the country depends upon you, and I should like you to use your power for the good of the country.' With such statements he must have aroused the hopes and expectations of the labourers to a pitch far in excess of what was justified by the facts. When their aspirations were not fulfilled, disillusionment inevitably set in.

Yet, despite these weaknesses, there is no doubt that Arch and the NALU did carry out much useful work in the country districts. They were able to instruct the labourers on the simple mechanics of voting and to advise them how they could get their names on the electoral register. Reassurance was given on the secrecy of the ballot and it was emphasised that there was no way in which their employers could find out for whom they had voted. Arch suggested that on polling day 'all the working men of the village meet together, and march to the polling booth, with one of your best men at the head'. This advice was designed to overcome the timidity a worker might feel if he saw his employer in the vicinity of the polling booth and knew that he was going to vote for a different candidate from that favoured by his master.

In some parishes, 'mock polls' were held in the last weeks before the election to encourage the men to turn up on election day itself – and to vote Liberal. At Alderton in Suffolk, for example, a large meeting was held on 18 November 1885: 'After the meeting eighty ballot papers were issued, seventy-eight of which filled up were in favour of the Liberal candidate and two in favour of the Conservatives.' And in the Sawston area of Cambridgeshire the district secretary reported in late November that over the preceding week 'good meetings have been held with the Test Ballot at six places ... Thank the great Liberal party for your power to vote, and for the power to use it as you like, and of course, as it was given you by the Liberals, I shall be surprised if you do not give your vote to them.'[31]

When the general election was held in the closing weeks of 1885 Arch himself stood as a Liberal candidate for the North-West Norfolk division. Needless to say, in an 'Address to the New Voters' published in the *English Labourers' Chronicle* early in November, he, too, called upon the labourers to return 'good sound Liberals to Parliament ... You have very largely the future destiny of the country in your hand; let me beg you to do your duty like sensible Englishmen by placing Mr Gladstone in power once more, as Prime Minister of England.' This address was later published as a separate pamphlet by the London and Counties Liberal Association.

Meanwhile the NALU leaders were calling on the labourers of north-west Norfolk to make sure that they elected Arch. And at national level the Radical wing of the Liberal Party was also making a play for the farm workers' vote. Joseph Chamberlain in his so-called 'unauthorised programme' proposed free elementary education; land reform, particularly designed to give the labourer 'a stake in the soil'; manhood suffrage, with payment of MPs; and disestablishment of the Church of England – the latter being of particular interest to the Nonconformist voter.

In the event the various efforts met with success. Arch himself was elected by a margin of 640 votes over his Conservative opponent, Lord Henry Bentinck, polling 4,461 to Lord Henry's 3,821. The *English Labourers' Chronicle*, no doubt expressing the elation felt by Arch himself, declared: 'It will be a memorable return in Parliamentary history for he is the first agricultural labourer ever elected a member of Parliament in this country ... The agricultural labourers have done their duty at the polls nobly.'

Joseph's success in North-West Norfolk was indicative of the result in other rural areas, where Liberal gains were also registered. Consequently, despite the defection of many Irish and urban voters at this election, the Liberal Party managed to secure a majority of eighty-six seats over its Conservative opponents. But the issue was complicated by the fact that alongside the two major parties, a third – the Irish Nationalists – was also represented, and with exactly eighty-six seats. It was they who were to hold the balance of power.

With the problem of Ireland overshadowing it from the beginning, the new Parliament had but a short life and in the early summer of 1886 the Liberal Party split over the issue of Home Rule for Ireland. Arch was among the supporters of William Gladstone who lost their seats at the general election held shortly afterwards. The *English Labourers' Chronicle*, realising that the fight was to be a close one, sought to extract the last ounce of loyalty for the NALU President, declaring: 'To Mr Arch the farm labourers owe the vote more than to any other man ... Before he commenced his great life work they were like "dumb driven cattle," today they are "heroes in the strife" ... To reject Mr Arch would be an act of ingratitude, of which we can never believe the labourers will be guilty.'

On the day preceding the poll Arch received a telegram of support from Mr Gladstone, stating that he hoped 'the electors of North-West Norfolk [would] show undiminished confidence in the representative who [had] well justified it'. Joseph proudly carried this round with him on the final stages of his campaign. But despite all exertions he was unsuccessful. Fellow unionists blamed the defeat on the unfair electoral tactics of the Conservatives, while the *Pall Mall Gazette* of 15 July claimed that 'some suffrages [had] been bought by the bribe of a two-shilling meat tea' provided by Tory party workers for 'sixpence per head'. Arch himself attributed his defeat mainly to a shortage of carriages to convey his supporters to the polling stations and to 'great territorial influence'. Nevertheless, even the *English Labourers' Chronicle* admitted that *some* defections had taken place over the Home Rule issue, and that Arch's support for Gladstonian Home Rule policies had done him electoral damage. Elsewhere in the country similar Liberal losses were recorded, and the Conservatives again returned to power.

Although in the years that followed, Arch loyally spoke on behalf of the Liberal Party and also continued to prop up his ailing union, on neither counts could he have viewed the future with optimism. By 1889 NALU membership had dwindled to a mere 4,254. The demise of the whole organisation seemed imminent. Then, thanks to a general revival of trade within the country and to the successful outcome of a strike by London dockers in August 1889, a brief reprieve was gained. For the victory of the unskilled dockers gave a new confidence to poorly paid workers everywhere. In the early 1890s, indeed, new unions were formed among farm labourers in a number of countries – including Suffolk, Norfolk, Wiltshire, Berkshire, Hertfordshire and Warwickshire. Most were associated with a Radical organisation called the English Land Restoration League, which had been set up in 1884 to promote policies of land tax reform designed to 'restore the land to the people'. Later It decided to extend its activities by sending out 'missionaries' to the rural areas in order to convert farm workers to its views on land reform and to secure the 'abolition of landlordism'. It also called for higher farm wages, better cottage accommodation, payment of overtime and similar matters. The establishment of trade unions was a further objective. The first tour organised by the League was in 1891 in Suffolk, where the missioners worked in conjunction with the newly established Eastern Counties Labour Federation. But others quickly followed.[32]

The National Union shared in the revival of interest, especially in Norfolk where by the end of 1891 over 12,000 men had been recruited thanks to the enthusiasm of a local organiser and Methodist lay preacher named Zacharias Walker. The NALU's total membership was now around 15,000. But then came general economic recession plus, in rural areas, the serious effects of drought upon crop yields. Arable farmers were hit by the continuing importation of cheap foreign grain, and even the meat and dairy producers were facing competition from abroad. In these circumstances the bargaining position of the unions weakened. One by one they collapsed. The NALU itself was finally wound up in 1896, but many of its younger competitors had predeceased it. The English Land Restoration League gave up its rural propaganda campaigns in the following year.

Nevertheless, the agitation of the early 1890s, plus the influence of the general revival in trade, had led to an increase in wage rates among many farm workers, and these gains were largely retained in the years that followed. By contrast, on the political and union front there was little progress once this final burst of activity had spent itself. Admittedly in East Anglia a number of the workers retained their enthusiasm for the Liberal Party – as Charles Slater recalled when he moved from Hertfordshire to Norfolk in the 1890s. He found that 'nearly all the working class were Liberals. and they all seemed to know what a man was if he was a Liberal or a Conservative, they soon wanted to know what I was ... Some of them used to think a tory was a bitter enemy. I have heard them say when a tory has passed by he votes against the working man ... I saw a poor crippled man, they said ... poor fellow but he will go against the working man, and if a man failed in business they would say serve him right he would go against the working man, that was if he was a tory.'[33] Furthermore, at the general election of 1892 Arch was again returned to Parliament as Liberal MP for north-west Norfolk, a position he was to hold until 1900, when he finally retired. (He eventually died in his native Barford in 1919, aged ninety-two.)

To some observers the establishment of parish councils in 1894 was also seen as an opportunity to encourage the political consciousness of rural workers. In July 1894, for example, the English Land Restoration League called a conference of delegates from the labourers' unions to discuss 'the action to be taken with the forthcoming elections of Parish and District Councils'. In subsequent months League supporters toured the villages encouraging farm workers to put up for election. And in some areas the careful preparations did lead to victory at the polls. Thus, according to one contemporary: 'The success of the Norfolk labourers [placed] them in the van of the army of labour; they have without doubt achieved a signal victory.' In Suffolk, too, progress was recorded, while in the south-western counties the villagers were said to have 'carried out the new law with an energy and enthusiasm never witnessed in rural England for many generations. The parish meetings seem to have been well attended; the labourers, and in fact all classes, were properly represented ... we find the rural mind waking up everywhere, and with more or less resoluteness, determined to leap on the horse Opportunity. Thus we are not surprised to hear that even the sweetest and gentlest of our rural labourers, the people of Dorsetshire, have displayed great activity in the elections, defeating in several places their employers at the polls.'[34] In Warwickshire, ninety-one 'Labourers' Candidates' were elected with the support of the county agricultural labourers' union – fifty-four of them being farm workers and the rest 'artisans and tradesmen adopted and run by the local branches of the union'.

Nevertheless, there were many parishes where labourers were still too diffident to put themselves forward for election against more influential members of village society. And even the limited progress recorded in 1894 was not maintained at subsequent contests. By the end of the 1890s most labourers took little part in parish council elections – perhaps through indifference or through fear of reprisals, if they appeared over-zealous in the wrong cause. The days of Arch had passed and most men who were dissatisfied with village life were now voting with their feet and leaving the land for good. The situation was summarised in 1903 by Redlich and Hurst in their book, *Local Government in England*:

> So deeply rooted in social prejudice, so intertwined in the baffling complexities of land laws, is the dependence of the man who tills the soil ... that he has hardly been able to employ a single weapon out of the whole armoury of formal democracy which has been hung up by Parliament in his cottage.

It was, then, the village tradesmen, farmers and smallholders who, like Joseph Ashby of Tysoe, felt able to take advantage of the new opportunities to exercise democratic rights, rather than the agricultural workers. At Tysoe, according to Joseph's daughter, the first parish council election 'was as lively an affair as a parliamentary one. The day of village radicals had come at last!' But there were many routine matters to consider as well – the maintenance of footpaths and greens, the care of bridges, and pressure for sanitary and highway improvements. Yet however trivial the work might appear, 'the men of Tysoe felt it was policy and their duty to use to the utmost such powers as had been allotted to their new Parish Council. The sound discharge of its functions would provide an argument another day for larger responsibilities.'[35]

7

HOLIDAYS & RECREATION

Home has no attractions for the young labourer. When he goes there tired and chilly he is in the way amidst domestic discomforts; the cottage is small, the children are troublesome and the fire is diminished, the solitary candle is lighted late and extinguished early; he treads on the children amidst an uproar of screams, is perpetually taking his father's chair by the chimney corner, and frequently leaving dirty thumbmarks on the linen his mother is getting up for the squire's lady. If he goes to bed early, his elder brother who sleeps with him, wakes him after an hour with a kick; if late, he is scolded by his mother for disturbing the four children who sleep in the next bed to his own. He naturally, then, goes to the public house where a cheerful fire and jovial society are found.

Quoted in L. Marion Springall, *Labouring Life in Norfolk Villages 1834–1914* (1936)

When their working day came to an end most farm labourers returned home for the evening meal, which was usually the main one of the day. Then, if the weather were fine, many of them would go out to their allotment or garden to see how the crops were faring and, at the appropriate seasons, to dig, set, weed and harvest their produce. In the busiest months the women and children would also lend a hand – and it was quite common for youngsters to be kept away from school in the autumn to help pick the family's potatoes. For, as an old Buckinghamshire labourer declared: 'Nobody can realise what a blessing it is to have a good crap a taiaturs stoared in yur barn for the winter, only them as a bin through hard times.'[1] Celery, peas, beans, cabbages, carrots, cauliflowers and marrows were all grown, and seed was obtained either by saving some from the previous year, or by exchanging a few precious samples with a friend or neighbour. In the autumn the large cabbages were often dug up 'by the roots and tied head downurds under the roof a the barn with the dirt on. Then in winter ye used to goo and cut a bit out, jest as much as ivver ye wantid'.[2]

But apart from economic necessity a man's pride in his garden might be stimulated by the holding of flower or vegetable shows, where there would be considerable competition to see who could grow the best peas or the largest onions. In other cases, as at Ablington in Gloucestershire, a prize was given for the 'prettiest garden among all the cottagers'.[3]

For the younger, unmarried men, however, gardening had little appeal. For them the parish reading room or club and the inn were the village social centres. And here the older men, too, would join them when they had finished their outdoor work, or during the winter months, when gardening in the evening was impossible. In some parishes – like Combe in Oxfordshire – these clubs were established by well-wishers as a counterattraction to the public house. They stocked a variety of periodicals such as the *Illustrated Times* or the *Churchmen's Magazine,* and a few also offered 'innocent amusements' like bagatelle, billiards and non-alcoholic beverages.[4] Several of the reading rooms were used as debating centres as well, like that at Ivinghoe in Buckinghamshire, where the minute book records that during the 1890s members discussed such topics as 'Capital Punishment' and Lord Winchilsea's plans to establish a National Agricultural Union to represent the views of landlords, farmers and labourers. The minute book notes that the 'labouring class' was well represented at these gatherings. Elsewhere musical talent was developed by the formation of brass bands, often – as at Bledington in Gloucestershire – in association with a local temperance society. Needless to say, not all of the bandsmen took that connection seriously.

> Practices were held in the small Sunday School wing of the chapel. Boys were taught in special sessions to read staff notation and to play their instruments and their parts: the band-master led them up and down Heath Lane, puffing and blowing with the difficulty of marching and playing at the same time ... The band played for all Bledington fetes and for festivities in other villages also. They charged modest fees or collected money to pay for the costly instruments and keep them in repair. (A euphonium cost ten guineas and a cornet as much.) A special activity was playing at Methodist Camp Meetings in a number of nearby villages – Chadlington, Milton, Lyneham, Chilson and Churchill.[5]

Fifes and drums or, as in Thomas Hardy's *Under the Greenwood Tree,* a small string band of violins and violoncello, satisfied the musical needs of other communities.

Another entertainment provided from time to time during the long winter evenings was 'penny readings'. For a modest outlay the audience could hear volunteers reading from Dickens or some other popular author, or perhaps reciting such well established favourites as *Excelsior* and the *Wreck of the Hesperus*. Francis Kilvert, curate of Clyro in Radnorshire, noted the local enthusiasm for these meetings – as on 3 February 1871, when the parish's '4th Penny Reading' of the winter was held and the room 'was fuller than ever, crammed, people almost standing on each other's heads, some sitting up on the high window-seats ... Numbers could not get into the room and hung and clustered round the windows outside trying to get in at the windows. The heat was fearful.' Kilvert himself recited one of his own compositions, entitled 'Fairy Ride', but the interest of the audience was perhaps due not so. much to the literary merit of the pieces selected as to the lack of alternative amusements.

In the clubroom of the public house, members of the local friendly society would hold their meetings, while in the skittles yard adjoining there was more energetic fun available for those who desired it. According to the agricultural trade union leader Joseph Arch, the village lad had only two kinds of recreation open to him. 'He could take his choice between lounging and boozing in the public house, or playing bowls in the bowling alley.'[6]

Some parishes had their cricket and football teams but in general these were a product of the later Victorian years. rather than the earlier, and they appealed to the village tradesmen, craftsmen and young farmers rather than to agricultural workers, who were often unable to afford either the necessary time or the equipment to play. This was especially true of cricket when matches were organised in the busy summer months. But even if they were not able to play, most villagers would eagerly watch local contests, and some of the older men would keep score 'by cutting notches on a stick'. Because of shortage of transport many teams had to restrict their away matches to villages within walking distance. Occasionally a local landowner might take the initiative to promote a club – as did William Chute of the Vyne estate near Basingstoke. A young farmer's son from nearby Bramley recalled that when the pitch had been laid out and marked: 'We were all asked to join the cricket club ... Sometimes the old Squire would play in a match... The Cricket season was finished about the end of September with a wind up match and a supper at the Swan Inn, when the chair was taken by the old Squire and a very pleasant evening used to be spent.'[7]

A number of other young men played quoits 'and if those of orthodox make could not be procured, the lads would play the game with horseshoes'. Some arranged extemporised football, using a pig's bladder as a ball. At Langley Burrell in Wiltshire certain of the bolder ones even ignored the solemnities of the Sabbath in order to play a game. But this the rector would not tolerate and so he 'used to come round quietly under the trees and bide his time till the football came near him when he would catch up the ball and pierce the bladder with a pin, But some of the young fellows would be even with the parson for they would bring a spare bladder, blow it, and soon have the football flying again.'[8]

Among more lawless elements, especially up to the middle of the century, cock-fighting and badger-baiting provided a surreptitious Sunday recreation. At Nafferton in Yorkshire, the young William Blades remembered that cock-fights would often be organised on Sunday at about 11 a.m. 'when the people were in church. These contests took place in the malt-kiln of a certain mill situated in the village. A barrel of beer would be provided for the occasion, when about fifteen spectators would be present. A good deal of betting went on, and many who did not attend would put bets on the cocks.'[9]

Where several lads worked together on the same farm as hired servants, however, they had to make their fun among themselves, for they were often prevented from leaving the farm, even after their day's work had ended. Those who ignored this restriction ran the risk of being hauled before petty sessional courts for the offence – like two young workers from Great Ashby in Leicestershire. In August 1869 they were charged by their employer at Lutterworth Petty Sessions with 'going out at night for a short time, after they had done work for the day'. The employer admitted that they had committed no actual wrong but said he was bringing the case because he 'wished to show them that they could not go out where they liked'. The court ordered that they be fined 7s each.[10] In such circumstances youngsters had little choice but to amuse themselves as best they could, perhaps by playing a tune on a mouth-organ, or singing familiar ballads and songs, or some similar diversion. Fred Kitchen remembered many such evenings on the Yorkshire farm where he began his working life at the turn of the century. Here the lads would gather together in the stable to sing ballads about 'soldiers sighing for their native land' or 'heart-broken lovers'.

> Another diversion, when not singing was playing dominoes, draughts, or fox-and-goose on the lid of the corn-bin, or seated on the floor with a stable-lantern beside us ... I enjoyed these musical evenings singing old English songs; but alas for the fly in the ointment, if I offered to oblige with Hearts of Oak, or some well-known school song, the missus's voice would come from the kitchen door, 'George! George! en yer owt for 'im to do a minute?' and I should be sent to another odd job.

1. The village fair. (From *Illustrated London News*, 27 May 1843)

2. The Easter Bread dole at Tring, Hertfordshire, in the 1870s, showng the smock frocks worn by some of the men, as well as their military campaign medals. The army recruited widely in country districts at this time.

3. May Day was a celebration enjoyed by schoolchildren in many villages. Children from Iffley, Oxford, parading with their May garland, *c.* 1905.

4. Chadlington National School pupils in Oxfordshire during the 1890s.

Right: 5. Joseph Arch's grave at Barford, Warwickshire, *c.* 1970.

Below: 6. Hop pickers in Kent, *c.* 1900.

Left: 7. Sarah Jane Cook of Ivinghoe, one of the last Buckinhamshire straw plaiters, with split straws under her left arm and moistened straws in her mouth ready for use.

Below: 8. A country market. (From Jeffreys Taylor, *The Farm*, 1832)

9. Girl peeling potatoes in an East Anglian cottage garden. (From P. H. Emerson's *Pictures from Life in Field and Fen*)

10. Joseph Arch, the pioneering Warwickshire-born agricultural trade union leader, with his wife and family in the early 1870s. Standing: younger daughter Annie; eldest son John, who was in the Army; Joseph Jnr; elder daughter Hannah. Seated: Joseph Snr, Mrs Arch and younger sons Edward and Thomas.

11. The Mangold Harvest. (From P. H. Emerson's *Pictures of Life in Field and Fen*, 1887)

Above: 12. One-man
band at Kelmscott,
Oxfordshire, in the late
nineteenth century.

Right: 13. A
saddler's workshop.
(From Tomlinson's
*Illustrations of Useful
Arts, Manufactures
and Trades*, 1858)

Left: 14. Baking oven and kneading trough with one man fetching loaves from the oven and the other kneading dough. (From Tomlinson's *Illustrations of Useful Arts, Manufactures and Trades*)

Below: 15. Bedfordshire lacemakers at the end of the nineteenth century.

16. Agricultural trade union meeting at Whitnash, Warwickshire, 1872, at the start of Joseph Arch's campaign.

17. The carrier's cart. It was the village carrier, in this case William Thomas of Leckhampstead, who took people and produce to market and brought back groceries, medicaments and even clothing for their neighbours.

18. Reaping in Oxfordshire, *c.* 1900 with a horse-drawn reaper foreshadowing future mechanisation.

When we tired of singing, we told tales; at least, the men did folklore tales – whilst I sat with my ears open, and probably my mouth, taking it all in... Some nights we went sparrow-catching with a riddle fastened to a long hayfork. We held the riddle on the sides of the stacks or on the ivy where the sparrows roosted on the house-side.

Occasionally Fred was sent down to the village to get a plough-coulter 'laid' or to carry out some other errand for his mistress. Then he would stand, together with a few other lads, in the blacksmith's shop, waiting for the job to be completed. The local blacksmith was 'a bit of a politician', and the youngsters used to listen with open-mouthed admiration to his political opinions. Finally, when the snow came they went sleighing down the mill field, which had a steep slope of several hundred yards: 'All the village turned out to sleigh, or to watch others go speeding down the slope, for the older folk, whose sleighing days were over, couldn't resist the pleasure of watching lads and lassies all in a mix-up, floundering in the deep snow at the bottom of the track.'[11]

However, for the older or more staid it was the inn which provided the main entertainment. Here there was contact with the world beyond the village, through travellers' gossip over a tankard of beer and a pipe of tobacco or, in later years, through the newspapers that appeared on the table. Even those who could not read were able to learn the facts from friends who could.

Many labourers, feeling they could talk more freely in the absence of their masters, preferred the taproom or the kitchen to the main bar, where farmers and tradesmen gathered, or else they went to the humbler beer shops. These latter had come into existence as a result of the Beer Act of 1830 and were held in a room attached to a cottage. They were kept by labourers, carpenters, blacksmiths and other petty tradesmen, whose own humble origins brought them close to their labourer clients. Beershops would appear on the edges of commons, in remote hamlets and on the outskirts of the village, wherever profitable trade seemed likely. They were widely condemned by the better off members of rural society as encouraging drunkenness, and as the resort of 'poachers, thieves and incendiaries' who would corrupt the labourer's morals. Yet, despite such fears, most of the men who frequented them spent their time not in discussion or contemplation of crime, but in conversation about the humdrum events of their daily lives. As Charles Slater, a Hertfordshire labourer, commented, thanks to the dulling effect of a life spent working alone in the open air and seeing 'nothing but hedges and ditches and fields', the chief topics of conversation were 'how many cart loads they filled in a day and who could spread a row of [dung] heaps up the field ... And on different farms ... which

Master had got the best horses or cows or had the best cattle or who could drink so many pints before he was drunk.'[12] There were anecdotes about fellow villagers, too. And humour as natural as a spring, would bubble up and find expression in discussions of the sayings and doings of neighbours. Many were identified only by their nicknames – like 'Yicker' and 'Jinx' Healey of Ivinghoe, Buckinghamshire, who earned their living as hay tiers, travelling around the villages measuring ricks and cutting the hay into trusses ready for sale. Then there was 'Doughy' Dollimore, who worked for a local baker, 'Blondin' Horn, a drover and horse dealer, who was named after the well-known acrobat, and 'Sotchel' Puddifoot, who dragged his feet as he walked – 'sotchel' being an Ivinghoe dialect word for this kind of gait. Similarly, at Haddenham Walter Rose remembered 'Squirrel' Smith, who lived a carefree hand-to-mouth existence, depending for his food and clothing upon the charity of fellow villagers. But his almost childish light-heartedness was welcome to men who were often bowed down with the cares of the world.[13]

Beer (or in the west of England, cider) was cheap – at $2d$ a pint – and drinking it in modest half-pints at the local inn provided a comfortable means of spending precious free time for those who had few other pleasures. It is significant that when well-meaning philanthropists tried to discourage village friendly societies from meeting in the public houses they had little success.

As one writer has said, 'a club was not acceptable to the village labourer if it had no beer, no feast and no fire'. The traditional feast day had to be adopted by the patrons as an inducement to the poor to enter a club. The Rector of Charlton Mackrell in Somerset, for example, described the formation of his society: 'Our Society was started in January 1855, with only eight Members; the many waited and looked on. But ... as soon as it was announced that there would be a "walking day", several others joined, and by the end of the year, forty-three members were enrolled.'[14] Nevertheless, the rule books of most village friendly societies sought to discourage drunkenness and bad behaviour, as at Marnhull in Dorset, where the singing of immoral songs at meetings was forbidden. And at Meare in Somerset the heavy fine of $2s 6d$ was imposed on anyone found guilty of 'drunkenness, cursing, swearing, or using uncivil language' or speaking words reflecting on the government. Arguments on religion or state affairs, quarrelling, gambling or challenging 'another member about trade or business' were likewise penalised.

But it was the feast day of the friendly society that was the real 'fete of the labourer' – a day when, for once, he would have plenty to eat and drink and there would be singing, dancing and much laughter. The club celebrations were often held around Whitsuntide, and on the chosen date all work in the village would cease. There would be 'a sabbath stillness, a repose, a display of holiday costume'. Groups of men would gather early in the streets, talking quietly, while the shrill, excited voices of children could be heard at play.

Preparations would already be well in hand for the erection of stalls selling sweetmeats and toys – spotted black-and-white wooden horses, monkeys on sticks, tin trumpets, whips and tops, dolls, and tin money boxes. Ribbons, beads, gloves and combs would fill another stall, while on yet another stone bottles of ginger beer and bottles of lemonade would be offered. In the larger villages there would also be swingboats and a rifle gallery where a young man could show his prowess – or lack of it – to a group of admiring, giggling girls. But all this lay in the future when suddenly the church bells began to ring and from the club room there streamed the procession of members, arrayed in their Sunday best, and wearing ribbons and rosettes in the colours of their society. Before them marched the band – 'drums, bassoons, hautboys, flutes, and clarionets' gaily playing – as together they proudly paraded to the church, with a 'broad banner of peace and union' flapping over their heads and their staffs held aloft like the 'spears of an ancient army'. After the special service had been held, there would be another procession before the serious business of feasting began. And serious it was. At one such celebration held at Swanbourne, Buckinghamshire, in 1844, the club feast cost the substantial sum of £13 19s 4d to cater for forty-eight members. The biggest items of expenditure were £4 4s 1d for meat, £3 17s 4d for beer and £2 for the band.[15] Similarly Alfred Williams recalled that in his home village of South Marston in Wiltshire, the members sat down at one o'clock to 'a substantial hot dinner of roast beef, and other cooked meats and vegetables... the band played selections; the foaming ale was brought in large two-gallon cans; the greatest good nature prevailed. Farmers and all belonged to the gathering; it was no one-sided affair, and a great number of folk attended from the neighbouring villages.'[16] But for young Alfred and the other boys the real excitement lay in the sideshows and stalls. There was a Punch and Judy, coconut shies and roundabouts as well as other more unusual displays – like the man who 'brought a small menagerie with a "Rooshan" bear and a gorilla' to amaze the small rustics of South Marston. For the older folk the day would be rounded off with a dance, when they could romp to such old country tunes as 'Hunt the Squirrel' or 'Four-hand Reels'. The Dorset dialect poet, William Barnes, describes the conclusion of a typical feast day in his own county:

An' then went down to Narley Hall
An' had some beer, an' danc'd between
The elem trees upon the green.
An' down along the road they done
All sorts o' mad-cap things vor fun;
An' danc'd, a-poken out their poles,
An' pushen bwoys down into holes.[17]

Yet, although much beer was drunk on the annual feast day, this was regarded with less general disapproval than was the custom of supplying alcohol as part of the labourer's wages. In 1887 a new Truck Act made it illegal for employers to pay their workers in any form of alcoholic liquor, but despite this, the practice of giving drink as a perquisite, particularly at haymaking and harvest continued – usually with the approval of the labourers concerned. All too often, however, excessive drinking at harvest time led to quarrels among the men – as in a case reported by the *Reading Mercury* in October 1882. Here a labourer was sent to prison for a month for assaulting a fellow harvester who would not 'stand' their gang a quart of beer. And in 1878 a North Leicestershire farmer explained why he was now giving money to the men instead of beer at harvest: 'Formerly I had great difficulty in keeping them from getting "muddled" towards the end of the day, and quarrels were not infrequent; but these evils have now altogether ceased, and neither I nor my men would return to the old system upon any account. I am paying men 1s per diem, and lads and boys 9d and 6d according to age.'[18] Nevertheless, most men felt that they needed beer to give them strength to carry out their heavy tasks, and so the old ways continued.

In East Anglia, the custom of 'largesse' was also blamed for adding to the problem of drunkenness: 'After harvest supper, the labourers started begging from house to house throughout the district, wherever a friend or tradesman of their employer was to be found. At some places they got beer, at others money which they spent at the public-houses on the way. Habitually sober men and young boys were compelled by custom to drink more than was good for them.' By the middle of the century, however, efforts were being made by parsons and squires to discourage the 'largesse' system and the holding of harvest suppers in barns and public houses where these led to uncontrolled drinking. 'Many parishes tried public parochial dinners, including beer, with tea and sports, or dancing for the wives and children afterwards, in the rectory grounds or the squire's park. They were arranged with the best intentions, but never really captured the imagination of village people. The men disliked the restraint, and perhaps the unfamiliar cutlery and crockery in unaccustomed surroundings. They missed the spirit of the old harvest supper, the traditional songs, hardly fit for the vicar's ears, the cheering and spontaneous dancing to the fiddler's tunes.'[19]

But in most places harvest homes continued. At one such gathering attended by Joseph Ashby at Tysoe in Warwickshire at the end of the century, proceedings began with the saying of grace. Next came 'the distribution of Yorkshire pudding, after which came smoking joints of beef and mutton, followed by plum-puddings, all attended with a plentiful supply of the English workman's "nut-brown" beverage. There were no distractions at the table. The employer drank his beer from a pint cup, as did his guests, in the same manner in which it was served to his workpeople. By the time the plum-puddings were being brought upon the table, we had become a gleeful company. All the jokes of the harvest field were passing around, and ere long no adventure which smacked of what was comical or amusing remained to be told.' Then the farmer stood up and thanked the men for their help in the harvest. They all drank to the success of agriculture – a toast which was drunk with enthusiasm – before the jollifications ended with songs and a toast to 'the health and prosperity of our employer'.[20]

The women and children were denied many of these pleasures, however, since only a few of the more daring or dissolute of the former would venture to drink with the men in an inn. They were even excluded from many harvest homes and village friendly society gatherings, although in a few communities there would be a club especially for the women. One was at the village of Drayton, near Langport, in Somerset, and the annual feast was held on the second Wednesday of June: 'What a washing of white finery went on the week before. What a goffering of the many frills under and on top. For it used to be the custom to wear a white frock adorned with a rose-pink sash worn crosswise. Knotted at the waist, and ... the smart bonnets that made their appearance ... The tea was held in a large tent.'[21] Like the feast day for the men in that village, proceedings were 'carried on ... with a fun Fair'. Before the celebrations began the members marched in procession to church behind a band, bearing appropriate banners.

But few women shared in these activities, and for most a gossip with a friend, over the garden fence or in the village street, provided the major entertainment. Sometimes they would invite neighbours into the cottage for a cup of tea during the afternoon, while the more energetic clergymen's wives would organise sewing parties or mothers' meetings at the parsonage for those who cared to attend. But the majority of wives with large families and small incomes had little time for such social events, or indeed for any other leisure activity.

During the winter months dances were held from time to time in the schoolroom or perhaps a large barn, while if there were a wedding in the family, householders might have a dance in their own home. Then all the furniture of the small living room would be pushed to one side to make the maximum space. The same was true at Christmas, and Thomas Hardy, in *Under the Greenwood Tree,* describes one such assembly in the house of Reuben Dewy, the tranter (or carrier). On the afternoon of the party the greatest activity could be seen around the cottage: 'The flagstone floor was swept of dust, and a sprinkling of the finest yellow sand from the innermost stratum of the adjoining sand-pit lightly scattered thereupon. Then were produced large knives and forks, which had been shrouded in darkness and grease since the last occasion of the kind, and bearing upon their sides "Shear-steel, warranted," in such emphatic letters of assurance, that the warranter's name was not required as further proof, and not given. The key was left in the tap of the ciderbarrel instead of being carried in a pocket.' Just after midnight the dancing commenced with a country tune called 'The Triumph' or 'Follow my Lover'. Then men and women jigged madly round to the squeak of the fiddles, as dance followed dance in an unending stream.

> The ear-rings of the ladies now flung themselves wildly about, turning violent somersaults, banging this way and that, and then swinging quietly against the ears sustaining them ...
>
>   It was the time of night when a guest may write his name in the dust upon the tables and chairs, and a bluish mist pervades the atmosphere, becoming a distinct halo round the candles; when people's nostrils, wrinkles, and crevices in general seem to be getting gradually plastered up; when the very fiddlers as well as the dancers get red in the face, the dancers having advanced further still towards incandescence, and entered the cadaverous phase; the fiddlers no longer sit down, but kick back their chairs and saw madly at the strings with legs firmly spread and eyes closed, regardless of the visible world.[22]

The children were, of course, left out of such affairs. They enjoyed themselves in their own way, running over fields and along hedgerows, fishing in the streams, bowling hoops, skipping, spinning tops and playing with marbles or fivestones. An impromptu see-saw could easily be rigged up from a plank and a log of wood, while in the autumn home-made pop guns were greatly prized. As one girl recalled: 'There was always the hunt for a thick piece of elder wood about nine inches long. We scooped all the pith from the centre to make the barrel after which we put half an acorn in each end. Then a firm piece of stick to push (from one's chest) from one end to the other to make a loud pop.'[23] Some enjoyed formal rhyming games, like 'Oranges and Lemons' or 'Here we go round the Mulberry Bush', which could be played on the roads undisturbed save for the occasional horse and cart or herd of cattle. During the winter evenings knitting, sewing or crocheting occupied the attention of the girls before an early bedtime, although most children had household chores to perform as well – water to fetch, younger brothers and sisters to look after, wood to collect, and so on. There were very few toys available, and youngsters had to make a plaything of whatever they could get hold of. A mother might make her little girl a doll by dressing up a clothes peg, or turning a bunch of rags into a doll shape and dressing it, 'whilst a little stool made a capital make-believe engine for the small boy'. A wooden doll or Noah's ark or penny monkey on a stick might be purchased from the local fair or market, while in some parishes pedlars would bring simple toys to amuse the little ones.

Most children looked forward with particular excitement to the special celebrations, the 'highdays and holidays' of the year.

On 14 February, St Valentine's Day, they would get up early, dress and then rush out to sing 'Good morrow to your Valentine' at the doors of all those they thought likely to give pennies. Any money collected would then be spent in the local shop on marbles, sweets or perhaps a toy.

May Day was another cause for celebration, and as Walter Rose declared: 'Of all the yearly celebrations Mayday lasted the latest in continuous observance. None was more truly beautiful in its expression, or more historic.' At Haddenham the children went round either singly, with a small garland on a stick, or in pairs with an interwoven festoon held between them, singing songs, wishing each household a happy day and collecting their pennies. But in some villages a Mayday procession would be organised. At Spelsbury in Oxfordshire the schoolmistress recorded in her log book on 1 May 1885: 'The children assembled at nine o'clock, when the Queen who had been previously elected, was robed and crowned. Preceded by the banner, the children marched in procession to the church, at the door they were met by the choristers whom they followed up the aisle, singing "Brightly gleams our banner", portions of the Morning Prayer followed, with a short address from the Vicar; after singing the hymn for "St Philip and St James" from Sullivan's book, they left the church and proceeded through the villages singing May carols from house to house, returning in the afternoon to tea in the schoolroom. The evening finished up with games and dancing.' Entries in subsequent years make clear that this was the normal pattern of Mayday celebrations in that community.

During the summer months both Church and Chapel organised Sunday school outings for the children, while chapels also provided the Anniversary when the Sunday school children, carefully dressed in their best, would sing or recite suitably improving texts to an admiring audience of parents and friends (see also Chapter 8). One girl, who attended church at Swanton Novers in Norfolk, compared her own summer treat – a trip to Sheringham by wagonette – with the celebrations held by the village chapel:

> I always felt a bit envious of the Chapel children at Anniversary time. A Barn was decorated with bracken and flowers, and the children were on a waggon with the Harmonium, which our Rector's wife played on that day, and no Church services were held. All the girls had new dresses, and each child had its own moment of glory, when even the smallest had a verse or a few lines of 'piece' to say. The elder ones of course had long poems to recite. The following day they paraded the village in the waggon singing hymns, till the Chapel was reached, where they had tea. Later all went to the recreation ground, to scramble for nuts and sweets. I was not allowed to go until my Mother was sure that was over, in case I, a Church child, got one! But I enjoyed the singing games which followed, traditionally the last was 'kiss in the ring'. This is the last verse of one:

> > Now you are married, you must be good,
> > And help your wife to chop the wood,
> > Chop it fine and carry it in,
> > And kiss each other in the ring.[24]

In certain parishes Oakapple Day, 29 May, was observed even into the twentieth century, in honour of the escape of Charles II from the Battle of Worcester. In Northamptonshire villages, for example, the children wore sprigs of oak and carried bunches of nettles with which to attack anyone bold enough to appear without the requisite signs of loyalty, while in Wiltshire and Berkshire youngsters without their sprigs were pinched by fellow pupils.[25] The fifth of November was another date widely commemorated, with bonfires, the burning of effigies of Guy Fawkes and the roasting of chestnuts and potatoes. And in Oxfordshire it was still possible to see the morris dancers at Whitsuntide going the round of the villages. They performed in groups of six, dressed in white shirt and white trousers with tall black hats, decorated with plenty of gay ribbons and many little bells which jangled with the movements of the dance. The dancers were usually accompanied by a fiddler and by a 'Squire' or 'Fool', who was the jester: 'He carried a stick with a calf's tail at one end and an inflated bladder at the other, with which he kept a clear space for the dancers, bestowed hearty thwacks upon the backs and sides of any among the crowd who encroached too much. He also collected the bystanders' contributions in a tin box. Among the dances performed was one with sticks, each man striking the stick of the opposite dancer, keeping time to the music, something after the manner of a melodramatic backsword combat, whilst there were other dances in which handkerchiefs were prominent features.'[26]

But Christmas was perhaps the most welcome feast of all. Even the men had a holiday on this day, and they were often presented with meat, coal or clothing by their employer or the local gentry. Country newspapers abounded at this time of the year with notices inserted by villagers acknowledging with suitable gratitude a whole range of gifts. Typical of the many thousands which could be quoted was one which appeared in the *Leicester Chronicle* of 23 January 1864: 'Croft. The poor of this village have received a liberal supply of coal from Captain Brookes, to whom they desire to return their sincere thanks ... They desire also thankfully to acknowledge Mr Swain's kind donation of bread.' The same issue contained another acknowledgment from 'the poor' of Kibworth for the coal they had received 'through the kindness of the gentry and farmers'.

With a large joint of meat, a good fire and perhaps a bottle of homemade wine, families prepared to spend Christmas day in unaccustomed ease. Children would receive few presents, but the fortunate ones who hung up a stocking might get oranges and nuts and perhaps a penny or two and a toy to celebrate the occasion. The walls of the living room would be gaily decorated with holly and ivy, while colourful sugar mice or tinsel stars made a bright contrast with the dark fir branches of the Christmas tree. In some country districts the older kissing-bough was retained in place of the Christmas tree. This consisted of 'iron hoops bent into the form of a crown ... covered with greenery and decorated with apples and lighted candles. Usually a bunch of mistletoe [was] fixed to the underside, and in the North of England small presents ... hung from it on long streamers of coloured ribbon.'[27]

In certain parishes, too, there would be visits from the Mummers, who performed the traditional fight between St George and the Turkish Knight to an appreciative audience of parents and children. A little later, on the first Monday after Epiphany, came Plough Monday. On this day the young ploughmen would drag a decorated plough from house to house, asking for money or other gifts. If they did not meet with a favourable response, they might plough up the lawn or the ground in front of the house or, in the case of farmers, lift field gates off their hinges. In some villages the children took part, too, blackening their faces, and joining in the appeals for money. And on the evening of Plough Monday in the Lotting Fen area of Huntingdonshire, there was yet another ceremony-that of the 'Straw Bear'. According to Kate Edwards:

A party of men would choose one of their gang to be 'straw bear' and they'd start a-dressing him in the morning ready for their travels round the fen. They saved some of the straightest, cleanest and shiniest oat straw and bound it all over the man until he seemed to be made of straw from head to foot, with just his face showing. When night came they'd set out from pub to pub and house to house, leading the straw bear on a chain. When they were asked in, the bear would go down on his hands and knees and caper about and sing and so on. Some parties used to do a play about 'Here I come I, old Beelzebub', and there was another place where one man knocked another down, and then stood over him and said:

> Pains within and pains without
> If the devil's in, I'll fetch him out
> Rise up and fight again.[28]

Except for Christmas day and the annual village feast, holidays were few and far between for country people. Even the children usually enjoyed 'working' holidays from school. Nevertheless the occasion of the local hiring fair was celebrated with days off in many parts of the country. Annually hired men who lived in – like Fred Kitchen – usually had a week or a fortnight off, so that they could visit their family and friends, but the rest of the work force had to be content with a day only. These fairs, which were also known as Statutes or Mops, had the dual-purpose of acting as a rudimentary labour exchange and as a place of entertainment. However, the former role was much diminished in the second half of the nineteenth century as registry offices and newspaper advertisements took over the task of matching workers and vacancies. Nevertheless up to the First World War in many towns up and down the country, men could be seen at the hiring fair, dressed in their Sunday best, and 'each usually wearing his insignia of wool, whipcord, etc., while in some towns it was customary for a servant girl to carry a broom ... at Ulveston a match stick stuck in a man's hat meant he was for hire.'[29]

Fred Kitchen, who attended the Doncaster Martlemas Fair at the turn of the century, remembered it as the annual hiring fair 'for farm servants from South Yorkshire, North Notts, North Lincolnshire, and a small portion of Derby, and represented the biggest babel of dialects since the time of Noah'. But the men were distinguished not only by their differing modes of speech but also by their appearance: 'the Lincolnshire "fenners" by their fancy for bright blue cords, set off with as many pearl buttons as could be conveniently carried on a pair of breeches and leggings. They were usually of heavier build than the "woadies" (men from the Yorkshire and Lincolnshire wolds), being of the broad, chubby kind, while the "woadies" were tall, raw-boned, and straight on the leg. The "Yorkeys", too, often wore carters' smocks, with a whip hanging over their necks.'[30] At the fair there were 'fights and uproars', as well as the meeting of old friends and the making of new ones. Men would compare notes on the past year and, indeed, the choice at hiring fairs was not all on one side, for workers would discuss among themselves the merits of farmers and their wives. Those who lived in were anxious to get a 'good meat house', and in this regard a lot depended on the farmer's wife. When an agreement had been reached between farmer and worker, the hiring shilling was exchanged and the labourer was then free to enjoy the rest of the day as he liked. Music and singing belched forth from every pub, with the popular tunes of the day played on concertina, melodeon, mouth-organ and tin whistle, and the beer flowed freely. Bustle and noise were on every side.

Needless to say, there were always a few 'scrimshankers who strolled round the fair hiring themselves to several farmers', in order to obtain the 'fastening penny'. According to a Warwickshire farmer, one such 'hired himself to three or four, accepting their shillings, then he joined the army, taking the King's shilling from a recruiting sergeant who was also at the Fair'. But the breaking of even a verbal hiring could be, and sometimes was, brought to court.[31] And, on the other side of the coin, there were those who condemned the fairs for the degrading slave market atmosphere which they engendered or the moral hazards they offered. Thus, at the beginning of the 1860s, the Superintendent of Police for King's Heath declared that in his view 'Statute Fairs were one of the greatest evils in existence. I have seen married and single conducting themselves with the greatest impropriety, and young girls, or rather children, stopping all night, dancing and drinking, and allowing most indecent liberties to be taken with them ... I have upon several occasions heard of cases of affiliation before the magistrates, when young girls have dated their ruin from the Statute Fairs.' His colleague at Worcester agreed: 'After the Mop ... is over, drinking, cursing and swearing, and fighting are carried on to a fearful extent, and I have been many times called out to quell the disturbances. I have known young women entrapped by procuresses, and have often been employed by their distracted friends to find and restore them. But when they have once been tainted, they often break out again. "Mops" are calculated to bring trouble and misery, without producing the least benefit to Society.'[32]

Yet, despite such fears most of those attending the fairs escaped the dire fate predicted for them. Relations between servant girls and farm lads rarely got beyond the flirting stage, while the 'fastening penny' was spent not just in drink but at boxing booths, coconut shies and roundabouts, or in seeing the sights – 'the tall man, and the short woman, and the calf with two heads ... the dancing dogs ... the wonders of the menagerie'.[33] At many of the fairs, produce was also bought and sold, and on the roads leading to them there would be not only carts crammed with passengers but 'droves of pigs, flocks of sheep; herds of cattle; strings of horses'.

At a time when most poorer people were restricted to visiting places within walking distance, the fair brought a welcome opportunity to join the activities and excitements of a wider world. The same was true of the peep shows and circuses which occasionally stopped in country districts on their journeys to the large towns which provided their main business. 'Lord' George Sanger describes several such impromptu shows in his autobiography – including one at the village of Long Sutton, which was held when his circus was on its way to Norwich fair.

On a wide space in the turnpike road we put down a few seats and something in the shape of a ring, made up a few of the old-fashioned grease-spot lights with tallow and rags for wicks, and announced a grand performance. There was no charge to view the latter, as the ring was perfectly open, but we charged a penny to all who wanted a seat. We presented a lively little programme of juggling, rope-walking, trick-riding, etc. ... The last item was my fortune-telling pony, who did very well until I came to the finish. This always was to tell the pony to go round and find out the biggest rogue in the company. The proper response was to walk up to the ringmaster, so pointing him out as the biggest rogue in question.

I never knew him to do a wrong thing before, but on this occasion, after I had given him his order, and stood with my back to him waiting for him to come and push his head against me, I heard the people laughing.

Turning round, I saw the pony with his head resting on the shoulder of the village constable, who looked very red and unhappy. I at once threw the whip forward, driving the pony round the ring, at the same time saying: 'You have made a mistake, sir!' and with this I gave him the usual cue. But it was no use. The pony, instead of coming up to me, merely walked some ten paces on, then turned and came back to the unfortunate constable, while the crowds shrieked with laughter. I was now really vexed, so I cracked the whip... but the crowd wouldn't have it. 'No, no,' they shouted; 'pony knows better than you! Pony's all right! ... Us know p'leeceman, and so do pony, it appears!' Here the laughter and jeering broke out afresh, and we had to leave the matter where it stood.[34]

But opportunities for fun like this were few and far between. Equally limited for most were the cheap day excursions which country people took by train or boat, particularly in the second half of the nineteenth century. The London barrister, Arthur Munby, met one such party of men, women and children when he was visiting Ullswater in August 1863. They had just landed from one of the steamers and 'were walking up in procession behind a good brass band ... They were picnickers, from... up the lake; farm-servants, male and female, and labourers, who had paid for their journey: and nowadays nearly every village about has its annual picnic of this kind.'

Despite such events it was not until the very last years of the century that rural isolation began to break down altogether, notably following the appearance of bicycles. These opened up opportunities for regular visits to nearby towns in search of amusement. They had other uses as well. John Purser of Ilmington remembered how in the 1890s he used to ride off on errands for his fellow villagers. 'There were perhaps only six bikes in the village, and all of an inferior sort. Mine was only a boneshaker, too, but it did good service.'[35]

Of course, even in 1900 most country folk still found the greater part of their recreation within the village. As Donovan Thomas, a Berkshire carrier's son, recalls: 'You had to make your own entertainment in those years. There was no Saturday afternoon off. The only day was Sunday, and being Methodists we attended [Chapel] as boys three times on a Sunday. That was the only change we experienced. If there was nothing on at the Chapel that was it.'[36] For the rest of the week men gossiped about their employers, their work and their wages; they argued about county cricket or exchanged notes 'about blight, or new buildings, or the latest public sensation; and all this in endless detail, endlessly interesting to them ... And it may well be conceived that in an existence so empty of other pleasures, the pleasures to be derived from company [were] held precious.'[37]

8

THE INFLUENCE OF RELIGION

Indifferentism, if not Infidelity, I fear is the prevailing characteristic of the day in most country parishes.

Comment by the incumbent of Farnborough, Berkshire, in the
1875 Clergy Visitation Returns for the Oxford Diocese,
at the Bodleian Library, Oxford.

The village radical placed disestablishment and disendowment of the Church first in his programme. Religious differences had nothing to do with this opposition to the Church except in isolated parishes where 'high church' practices had offended. It came because the parson stood in the way of any great alterations in the administration of public business. He controlled the vestry and the management of the public charities, as a guardian he administered the hated Poor Law, and his influence in the village school ensured that education should take place in an atmosphere favourable to the existing social order. He personified the impediment to reform, and upon him was concentrated the full force of the radical attack.

L. Marion Springall, *Labouring Life in
Norfolk Villages 1834–1914* (1936)

The influence of the Church of England clergy on the day-to-day lives of country people was well-established in Victorian England, even if by more committed Nonconformists it was accepted with considerable reservation. It extended not only to their priestly duties but also to the spheres of education, charity and the administration of justice, since many clergymen were also Justices of the Peace. Indeed, despite the gloomy comments of some clerics, the power of the Established Church remained strong in the rural areas at a time when its authority in towns was already under attack from the supporters of religious dissent and of secularism. It tended to be greatest in the smaller parishes where squire and parson were linked by birth or marriage, or by upbringing and common interests. In the larger 'open' parishes, where a more democratic spirit prevailed,

Nonconformity claimed its adherents, too, and small brick-built chapels could be seen in the main streets of most such communities.

In the earlier Victorian years, when plurality of livings and non-residence were still characteristic of the Church in certain areas, Nonconformity was able to strengthen its hold. Much the same was true of neglected parishes like Danby in Yorkshire, where up to the mid-1840s the parson sometimes did not bother to hold a service on Sunday. His successor, the Revd J. C. Atkinson, was shocked to find that even the altar itself consisted of a rickety table covered by a piece of ragged green baize cloth and sprinkled with the crumbs of the Sunday school teachers' lunch! Here the Wesleyans and Primitive Methodists had stepped in to fill the gap left by the failures of the incumbent, and as Atkinson admitted, 'if it had not been for them and their influence, religion would practically have died altogether in the Danby area'. But by the middle of the century such slack methods as these were being eliminated by a new generation of churchmen.

Although some families (labelled 'devil dodgers') attended both Church and Chapel, and thereby had a foot in each of the competing religious camps, in many cases rivalry between the two groups was bitter. Nonconformists resented the privileged position of the Church and called for its disestablishment, while Anglican clerics regarded their Nonconformist counterparts as members of an inferior breed. In May 1848, for example, Samuel Wilberforce, as Bishop of Oxford, wrote in strong terms to Thomas Curme, the vicar of Sandford St Martin, reproving him for attending 'a public meeting in a place of Dissenting worship'. As he declared: 'If there is no difference between us & dissenters what can our Ordinal and all our reformed liturgy mean? How can we justify in God's sight continuing in a body which by refusing to acknowledge their ministry is guilty of the highest breach of charity if there is no sufficient reason for maintaining separation? Either we Churchmen have ground from God's word for being thus distinctively Churchmen, or we are the most miserable schismatics.'[1] And in 1872 his successor as Bishop of Oxford, John Fielder Mackarness, devoted his first address to the clergy to an attack on Nonconformists. He denied to their ministers and preachers 'the validity of their call' and went on to accuse them of filching 'promising sons of the church'. He taunted the ministers, too, with 'desiring a social equality with the parish clergy which nothing, not even a revolution, would give them.'[2]

At parish level there are many similar examples – as at Clipston in Northamptonshire, where the incumbent claimed that his pastoral duties were hindered by the 'excessive bigotry of the Baptists – who never cease assuring church people that they must "come out of her".'

And at Fenny Stratford in Buckinghamshire there were complaints that congregations were adversely affected because 'some 3 or 4 Dissenting Tradesmen make *a point of having the poor people in their debt* and so *compel* them to attend the [Nonconformist] Meeting Houses'.[3]

In Wales these feelings ran still stronger for here the landowners, who were usually English and churchmen, were opposed by the mass of the population – the small peasant farmers and labourers – who were Welsh and normally attended chapel. Nonconformity and political radicalism both grew rapidly in Wales during the period 1815–70 and already in the 1840s there were comments on the 'wide-spread alienation from the doctrines and disciplines of the Established Church, which [was] so prominent a feature in many districts of the country'.[4]

Disagreements between Anglicans and Roman Catholics were, by contrast, much rarer in the country areas, since the main strength of the Catholic Church in the nineteenth century lay in the towns. Nevertheless, in some villages, especially where the squire was a Roman Catholic, a number of his fellow parishioners might share his faith. This was true, for example, of East Hendred (then in Berkshire), of Lulworth in Dorset, and of Mapledurham in Oxfordshire. In the latter parish relations between squire and vicar varied over time according to the character of the individuals concerned. Thus in 1860 the incumbent sourly wrote to his Bishop: 'The most serious Evil in the parish is this; that the only resident gentleman is a Roman Catholic. I do not think that he or his Family now take much pains to draw the Poor from the Church. But he, of course, gives no aid to Church Objects.' At that date between a fifth and a quarter of the inhabitants were Roman Catholics. Similarly at mid-century Enstone in the same county Lord Shrewsbury, the Roman Catholic owner of Heythrop Park, was blamed for 'importing' Catholic families into the parish. And in certain parts of the country, like the Lancashire Fylde or the North Riding of Yorkshire, where the old faith had endured more strongly, the number and influence of Catholic families and their priests were still greater.

Nevertheless, despite these rivalries, in England at least the Anglican clergyman saw himself, and was largely accepted by others, as the arbiter of conventional morality within the parish. Nowhere was this seen more clearly than in the provision of the village school. In the eyes of both himself and his contemporaries 'the duty of educating the people had always been a religious one'. So those clergymen who lacked the financial resources to carry out their duty in this direction often felt a deep sense of guilt and failure. But most were able to make the effort and in rural parishes even at the end of the nineteenth century Church of England schools outnumbered those of the Nonconformists and also the rate-aided board schools. In 1895 it was estimated that

61.6 per cent of all elementary schools in England and Wales were Church of England ones – as opposed to 24.2 per cent connected with school boards and 6.2 per cent with the most important Nonconformist educational organisation, the British and Foreign School Society.[5] And in a rural county like Lincolnshire Church schools comprised no less than 71.7 per cent of the total. Although under the 1870 Education Act the children of non-churchmen could be withdrawn from class during the periods of religious instruction comparatively few took advantage of the concession. And prior to that date the schools associated with the Church of England National Society laid down clear rules and regulations on the religious issue. The Society's printed 'Terms of Union' included such provisions as:

> The Children are to be regularly assembled for the purpose of attending Divine Service in the Parish Church, or other place of worship under the Establishment, unless such reason be assigned for their non-attendance as is satisfactory to the Managers of the School.
> The Education in such Schools is to be conducted on the principles of the Established Church and by Masters and Mistresses who are Members of the same ...[6]

Scripture lessons were under the superintendence of the incumbent and were sometimes conducted by him or his curate in person – as at Cottisford in Oxfordshire. Here Flora Thompson recalled the rector's religious instruction as consisting of 'Bible reading ... of reciting from memory the names of the kings of Israel and repeating the Church Catechism. After that, he would deliver a little lecture on morals and behaviour ... From his lips the children heard nothing of that God who is Truth and Beauty and Love; but they learned from him and repeated to him long passages from the Authorised Version, thus laying up treasure for themselves; so the lessons, in spite of much aridity, were valuable.'[7]

However, if the school provided the clergy with one important means of influencing village life, another – for those who attended the services – was through the sermon. Each week he would exhort his congregation to put away their sinful ways – their drunkenness and quarrelling; their jealousies and petty weaknesses – and to embark instead upon a purer and holier life. Many clergymen certainly felt their pastoral work to be seriously impeded by the large number of public houses in country districts. Typical of complaints on this score was that of the incumbent of Cassington, Oxfordshire, who attributed the decline in his mid-nineteenth century congregation to the 'demoralising' influence of the railroad labourers who were engaged in building the Oxford to Worcester railway, and to 'five Public and Beer Houses in so small a Parish' having 'their usual bad effects upon the morals of our young men'. His colleague at Northmoor likewise bewailed the existence of 'four Public Houses' in the parish, 'i.e. about one Public House to about seventeen Heads of Families (Farmers not included). I can suggest no remedy save an alteration of the law of the land respecting the licensing etc. of Public Houses and Beer Shops'[8] At Ecton in Northamptonshire the clergyman was equally firm: 'Drinking, more than any thing here, I think, interferes with the welfare of the Church – as a remedy, I believe that the sale of drink over the counter & the prevention of drinking on the premises of the "Public" would be beneficial to the parish.'[9]

Another favoured subject for sermons was to impress upon the congregation the need to support the 'supreme rightness of the social order as it then existed. God, in his infinite wisdom, had appointed a place for every man, woman and child on this earth and it was their bounden duty to remain contentedly in their niches.' Anyone who denied this precept was offending against the divine order – an order which was, incidentally, reflected in the seating arrangements within the church itself, with the families of the squire and clergyman sitting in special pews, carefully segregated from the rank and file of the congregation. Even these humbler beings were graded so that farmers and tradesmen were kept apart from the cottagers, who were pushed into the lowliest places of all, in the side aisles or at the back of the nave. It is to the credit of some incumbents that this pew system was strongly criticised as an affront to the symbolism of the Church and to its spiritual professions. Among the opponents of the system was the incumbent of Oundle, who informed the Bishop of Peterborough that the chief hindrance to his work in the parish was 'the legalised system of selfishness in the ... Church commonly known by the name of "Faculty Pews", which virtually shuts out the poor from the House of God – and hands them over to the Dissenting Chapels'.[10]

Many clerics also emphasised the necessity for regular churchgoing. At Cottisford Flora Thompson remembered that the rector would 'hammer away at that for forty-five minutes, never seeming to realise that he was preaching to the absent, that all those present were regular attendants, and that the stray sheep of his flock were snoring upon their beds a mile and a half away'.[11] Rarely did he touch on the ordinary human griefs and joys of his parishioners or upon the bonds which joined man to man. 'It was not religion he preached, but a narrow code of ethics, imposed from above upon the lower orders.' In these circumstances it was small wonder that many working people saw the Church of England as something for the well-to-do rather than for the ordinary man.

Not all clergymen, however, adopted an autocratic stance. A number were concerned instead to help and guide their flock to the best of their ability. They gave charitable assistance – coal and clothing to the poor in winter, food and wine to the sick. Some even established small dispensaries from which they supplied medicine, and in Oxfordshire during the 1870s there were at least three instances of clergymen qualifying and practicing as doctors of medicine. Again, at Yarnton in that county the vicar distributed lime in an effort to combat dirt and infection during the cholera epidemic of 1853–54 and issued warnings to his parishioners against eating raw fruit and keeping late hours; he also, rather pathetically, advocated the wearing of flannel belly-bands and waterproof boots as a means of combating the disease.[12]

The diary of the Revd Francis Kilvert, curate of Clyro in Radnorshire, shows still more clearly the warmth of feeling which could develop between clergy and villagers. Thus in February 1870, at a time of bitterly cold weather, Kilvert called on one of his parishioners who was ill, and seeing that the man had no blankets on his bed, he immediately gave an order for a pair to be supplied, to be paid for out of the surplus Communion Alms. He also provided some wine. Other members of the congregation benefited in a similar way from his generosity. And when Kilvert left the parish in 1872, his departure was deeply mourned. As he wrote: 'these people will break my heart with their affectionate lamentations... What am I that these people should so care for me?' The school children even saved up precious pennies to present him with a small gold pencil to hang on his watch chain. Their gesture moved him greatly: 'I tried to speak to tell them what I felt, but my heart was full. "Please not to forget us," said the children. Dear children, there is no danger. I did not want this to help to keep you in mind.'[13]

At Byfield, another Victorian country parish, Richard Hillyer has similarly described how the elderly rector, Mr Driffield, regularly visited all the houses in the village in strict rotation, 'making no difference between church and chapel'.

> Every woman in the village knew the Rector's day as well as she knew the butcher's or the baker's ... Where there was any particular need he would leave a gift behind, half-a-crown or so, laid unobtrusively on the corner of the table where he had been sitting or put on the window ledge as he went out. Nothing to hurt anybody's feelings. If people who were ill needed medicines, or special food, they got it from the rectory; only then it would be given out by one of his daughters. He had a lot of them, all unmarried, and they visited as regularly as he did, though they were not so stately about it.[14]

And, of course, there were countless men and women who found consolation for the hardships of their daily existence by attendance at the Sunday services. When visiting the small parish church at Pyrford in Surrey during May 1864, Arthur Munby was deeply impressed by the general atmosphere of 'rustic simplicity and antique reverence' which he found. The school children 'and the poorer folk filled the free seats, which are stout ancient benches near the door, but they are to be found in the pews also'. He noticed with approval that there 'was no squire's pew, no squire's family or servants, nothing that is to shame the dress and manners of the rustics, nor weaken their self-respect nor make one suspect their devotion'. Many country congregations elsewhere displayed equal sincerity, while others found an outlet for their devotions in serving the Church. Perhaps they would clean and polish its silver and brass, ring its bells, act as sexton or parish clerk and sing in its choir. Lucy Edwards of Eydon in Northamptonshire was one such. She 'sang in the choir all the days of her life and cleaned and dusted it for donkeys' years. How she loved the church with all her heart, mind and soul.'[15]

For many, the great events of life were also associated with the Church – the baptism of a child, the celebration of a marriage and the burial of a loved one. Even those who in the normal course of events were not regular attenders resorted to it on such occasions. For there were, needless to say, always a number of backsliders who showed their independence by attending neither church nor chapel on Sunday – like the parishioners of the shoemaking village of Earls Barton in Northamptonshire. Here the incumbent complained of: 'Dissent, lukewarmness and indifference, drinking especially on Sunday. Half the population dissenters. But many profess no religion.' Out of a total population of around 1,900 in the early 1870s only 300 attended church regularly.[16] Although many modern clergymen would no doubt welcome a congregation as large as this, to the mid-Victorian cleric such a response smacked of failure. Those who did not attend preferred instead to get up late, eat the best dinner of the week in a leisurely manner, and then spend the rest of the day in drinking, visiting relatives, and walking round to examine with an expert eye the state of the crops in the neighbouring fields or allotments. Perhaps, like the west country parishioners described by Richard Jefferies, they 'cleaned their boots on a Sunday morning while the bells were ringing, and walked down to their allotments, and came home and ate their cabbage, and were as oblivious of the vicar as the wind that blew. They had no present quarrel with the Church ... nor apparently any old memory or grudge; yet there was something, a blank space as it were, between them and the Church.' And when the clergyman questioned them as to why they did not attend, they had a hundred excuses ready: the rain, a bad foot, illness of the infant, a cow taken ill and requiring attention, and so on.[17]

Others moved between Church and Chapel according to current whim; as the incumbent of Mollington, Oxfordshire, bitterly observed: 'I find that when a married couple have a child shortly after the marriage & I speak to them on the sin of it they are almost sure to go off to the Dissenting Chapel for the Ranters make so light of sin ... Again when I find fault with young people for misbehaviour in Church they will sometimes go to Chapel for a time as there they may do as they like.'[18]

The men were always the worst offenders on these occasions and, as we saw in Chapter 6, when the agricultural labourers' trade union movement was established in southern and central England during 1872–73 many clergymen noted the adverse effects this had on attendance by male parishioners. Not only was the situation aggravated by the fact that the union was mainly led by Nonconformist local preachers who had little love for the Church at the best of times but in 1874 the union newspaper, the *Labourers' Union Chronicle,* assumed the sub-title of 'an independent Advocate of the British Toilers' Rights to Free Land, Freedom from Priestcraft, and from the Tyranny of Capital'.

Most clergymen, for their part, were hostile to the movement and thereby earned the dislike and distrust of the younger men for the Church of England as a whole. Typical of the comments was that of the incumbent of Great Coxwell, Berkshire, in 1875 : 'Since the agitation carried on by the Agricultural Labourers' Union, there has been a very evident coolness & sullenness evinced on the part of the Labourers, who have not attended the Church services as heretofore, tho' I have studiously refrained from taking any part in the dispute, *pro* or *con.*' His colleague at Byfield in Northamptonshire also lamented that 'the Labour Movement has made the Labourers suspicious of the Clergy as taking the side of Landowners & Farmers. It is very difficult to have influence with them without taking their side in a particular spirit.'[19] A number of other incumbents registered similar complaints and the bitter feelings reached a peak in the years 1876–78, when there was the so-called 'battle of the vestries' as unionists sought in many villages to get their candidate elected as the people's warden, so as to have a say in the running of parish affairs and the distribution of the charities. For under the 1869 Parochial Rate Assessment Act every householder had the right to vote at the annual vestry meeting. Thereafter, as the union weakened, anti-Church sentiments also diminished, but as late as 1881 the incumbent of Kirtlington, Oxfordshire (to quote one example) could declare: 'The Parish has never recovered the effects of the Labourers' Union.'[20] And three years later a pro-union pamphlet, *The Farm Labourer's Catechism,* still expressed much of the old hostility towards the clergy, who had 'condescended' to distribute among us

soup, coals, and blankets... they have preached unto us contentment
with the station into which we have been called, it being our duty to
bear and suffer, and complain not.'

But if the *adult* members of a family could choose how to pass
the Sabbath, for the children there was rarely any freedom of choice.
Attendance at church or chapel two or three times a day, including
Sunday school, was the usual order of things. A girl from Saxlingham
in Norfolk remembered the dreary monotony to which this led: 'I used
to be taken to Church three times on Sunday: Matins in the morning,
Sunday school in the afternoon, and Evensong at night ... We were never
allowed to knit or sew on Sundays nor even read a newspaper. Saturday
night, the work basket, knitting and sewing, with the weekly newspaper
folded on top were all put away in the cupboard till Monday.'[21] Her
feelings were echoed by Flora Thompson: 'The afternoon service, with
not a prayer left out or a creed spared, seemed to the children everlasting.
The schoolchildren, under the stern eye of the Manor House, dared not
so much as wriggle; they sat in their stiff, stuffy, best clothes, their
stomachs lined with heavy Sunday dinner, in a kind of waking doze,
through which ... the Rector's voice buzzed beelike.'[22]

Sunday school was little better and until the passage of the 1870
Education Act it was quite common for the rules of denominational
schools to demand the attendance of day pupils at Sunday services. Thus
at Kirton-in-Lindsey Endowed School in the mid-1850s the regulations
clearly laid down: 'All the Scholars are to attend both services in the
Parish Church on Sunday, parents who prefer taking charge of their own
Children to Church, are to state the same in writing on their admission.
All others are to assemble at the School on Sundays at half-past 9
o'clock, a.m., and 2 o'clock, p.m.'[23]

Yet, perhaps surprisingly, despite all this emphasis on religious
instruction, it was still possible for gross ignorance on the simplest
of Christian doctrine to persist. In the late 1860s the incumbent of
Cottingham in Northamptonshire was pained to discover that: 'Out
of a confirmation class of sixteen boys, one did not know the Lord's
prayer, and five could not say two consecutive articles of the Apostles
Creed.' His equally shocked colleague at Cranford in the same county
encountered a boy of sixteen who declared: '*he had never heard of Jesus
Christ*'; and he added, 'the boy was not particularly dull'.[24]

The one compensation for the children for this monotonous Sabbath
routine was the annual Sunday school treat, when the pupils might be
taken on an expedition to the seaside, or at the very least would be
provided with a special tea and games. At Ilmington in Warwickshire the
young John Purser recalled the children being marched to the Rectory
park by the schoolmaster. 'There they would enjoy themselves, till called

to sit in a circle for tea, a thing most of them had been looking forward to for days. Some boys would have no dinner, so that they could have a good "tuck in".' It was good food, such as they were not used to: 'fresh bread and butter, tea brought round in big jugs to fill their tin mugs, and two sorts of cake. The Rector, with his wife and four daughters, enjoyed the fun of serving, and seeing them eat. It was all done in perfect order: they said grace as they stood; and at the close, sang a retiring hymn, cheered their thanks, and left with a few nuts each in their mugs.' To youngsters who had few pleasures even this modest celebration was an occasion to remember.

John Purser was the son of Methodist parents, and in his home Church and Chapel seemed to mix fairly easily. But not all families saw matters in this light. Some of the more independent Nonconformists resented the attempts of the clergy to 'dictate' to them, as they saw it, or to impose their views upon them. Typical of the hostile stories which circulated on this point was that of Charles Slater, who was born at Barley, Hertfordshire, in 1868. He claimed that when a friend of his was short of money, the clergyman offered to give him a gold sovereign, if he would 'come to church and leave the Chapple ... and he did but afterwards he went and was found drowned in a pond'.[25] Whether such tales were true or not they were an expression of the ill-feeling which could develop. Even the quiet and order-loving Joseph Ashby of Tysoe, whose mother was a regular churchgoer, felt he could no longer attend the church when its leading members in and around the village opposed the labourers' trade union movement. From his middle teens Joseph began to attend one or other of the local chapels – visiting the Primitive Methodist and Wesleyan chapels in his own village and sometimes going off across the fields to chapels and churches in nearby communities.

But to him and to others who felt like him the chapel did not merely represent an opportunity to express their independence, or even to learn to run an organisation of their own democratically – it meant far more. It gave consolation and comfort with its warm and beautiful phrases like 'Beulah Land' or 'Jerusalem the Golden'. Its preachers were often fellow villagers – labourers, craftsmen and small farmers – whose theology might be crude and whose language was hesitant and yet who shared the same hardships and difficulties as themselves. Chapel life could also provide fellowship to people who had migrated from their home village and were cut off from friends and family. In the informal atmosphere of the Sunday and weekday evening cottage meetings held by so many local Nonconformist groups, new friendships were forged. These meetings provided an answer to feelings of individual isolation and loneliness. They presented the chapel as a home where all could find peace and brotherly love. And at the same time they had their own community links, for 'woven into the fabric of the Dissenting "connection" there was usually a nexus of local dynasties, whose history and relationships were inextricably bound up with its own story and gradually came to form a focus of interest and loyalty in themselves.'[26]

There was proof, too, of the power of religion in the example of men who had given up drinking or gambling or neglect of their families because of their newfound faith. At Tysoe, Joseph Ashby recalled that the grace of God and the love of Christ were the central themes of the homespun sermons. 'These were praised and adored till the chapels were full of happiness. Faces glowed as the people left the little brick chapels, and some of them developed a permanent saintly warmth of expression.'[27] Nor was the influence lost away from the chapel, for Bibles and hymn books were easy to purchase and hawkers brought round copies of books like *Pilgrim's Progress,* or short religious tracts which could be perused at leisure; there were also demands for suitable biblical pictures and texts to hang on cottage walls.

Some of the more ambitious young men sought to become local preachers themselves. Before they could be accredited an examination had to be passed in front of the local preachers' meeting. Every statement made by the candidate had to be supported by the 'quotation of a passage from the Bible; this needed both a good memory and thorough knowledge of the Bible'. Once they had passed their test these local preachers would, like the young Northamptonshire village tailor, Joseph Tyrrell, willingly walk miles to conduct services each Sunday.[28]

Apart from the well-established Nonconformist sects – the Baptists, Wesleyans, Primitive Methodists, Independents and Congregationalists – there were many minor groupings, such as the Bible Christians or Bryanites, who were founded in the obscure Devon parish of Shebbear in 1815. Like most of their fellow dissenters they sought to end the 'unscriptural alliance' between Church and state and the payment of tithes by those unconnected with the Anglican Church, but they called forth a sharp emotional response as well. One of their favourite activities was said to be hunting 'the devil out', with the aid of sticks. All the lights would be extinguished in the chapel and the devil would then be hunted and beaten in the darkness: 'Peculiar scenes certainly took place in rural chapels. Women would lie down on the floor during the course of a service, passing into hysterical fits, crying and screaming. Congregations also indulged in "love feasts" which sometimes lasted for hours with men and women clasping one another, crying out and throwing themselves on the floor in a kind of ecstasy.'[29] Yet despite these excesses, the Bible Christian eschewed pleasures like playing cards or dancing, and they made their life as far as possible a pilgrim's progress. Nor was 'devil hunting' confined to this particular sect. Indeed, as late as 1915 a small boy attending the chapel at Wood Norton, Norfolk, could remember the passion with which visiting preachers condemned the powers of darkness: 'Their prayers would mount into a frenzy, spell-binding to themselves and their congregation. "There's the Devil, Brother," cried one, roaring into the aisle. "Howlld him, Brother Daniel," shouted another, grabbing the first. The spell would break and each would return somewhat sheepishly to his seat; but it had been wonderful while it lasted, and quite unforgettable.'[30]

In a rather different vein, during the last fifteen years of the nineteenth century, Methodist leaders, anxious to maintain the 'evangelistic glow' in rural chapels, also embarked upon a revivalist campaign with the aid of 'missionaries' who travelled through the countryside in horse-drawn caravans. The first of these Methodist vans took to the road in the mid-1880s – with the Wesleyans and later the Primitive Methodists both taking part in the scheme. The Primitive Methodist vans were 'staffed with men who [could] sing, preach a sermon, give a temperance address, conduct a prayer meeting, and engage in house-to-house visitation'. Vans were parked on village greens and in the evening supporters would march in procession, singing as they went, to the local chapel for a meeting. Mostly the evangelists were welcomed in the villages and gifts of potatoes, eggs and cream were received. But occasionally there was resistance and then stones were thrown at the preachers, and outdoor services disrupted. Nevertheless, in the communities they visited they do seem to have strengthened support for Methodism.[31]

Local persecution of dissenters of all persuasions occurred wherever bigotry reared its head – as at Iddlesleigh in Devon, where it was reported that the clergyman, who was also a magistrate, had combined with almost all the farmers in the parish to sign 'a paper to withhold parish relief and refuse employment to any follower of the Methodists'. In this instance the prohibition was contested by a widow named Mary Lock, who took her complaint concerning the non-payment of parish poor relief to the Quarter Sessions, and had her claim upheld by the bench.[32] Unfortunately, not all disputes were settled as easily as this. In many villages sectarian bias continued to poison relations between Church and Chapel. There were clergy, like the rector of Well with Dexthorpe and Claxby, Lincolnshire, who stressed the need for Church infant schools not on educational grounds but because they would 'get possession of the Children of the villages before their minds were affected with dissent'.[33] Nonconformists could be equally rigid as to the rectitude of their cause and the error of all others. As has been said, 'in the heat of the controversies that raged during the seventies and eighties "the Primitives" may have fomented distrust and hatred in the villages'. Certainly at Bozeat in Northamptonshire, to quote but one example, the incumbent believed that the large number of dissenting farmers in his parish was adversely affecting his congregation, because of the pressures they were exerting on their workers.[34] And at Wheatley, Oxfordshire, in the early months of 1881 a dispute was carried on through the columns of a local newspaper as to whether or not the Nonconformist poor of the parish were excluded from gifts of food and fuel provided by the incumbent. The Baptist minister claimed that they were, and the incumbent stoutly denied it.

Yet it was, inappropriately enough, on the matter of burials that some of the sharpest Church/Chapel conflicts arose. Until the passage of the 1880 Burial Laws Amendment Act Nonconformist clergy were not allowed to conduct funeral services in a churchyard even for members of their own flock. This right remained the sole prerogative of the Church of England. Furthermore, an Anglican clergyman could refuse a Christian burial to those who had not been baptised – a matter of some concern to the Baptists, who believed in adult baptism only.

The burial controversy came to public notice on more than one occasion. Thus in 1862 Benjamin Armstrong, vicar of East Dereham, noted in his diary on 13 June that he had been 'impelled to get up a petition' against a proposed 'Burial Bill, which enacts that any dissenter may officiate at funerals in our churchyards. This, of course, is only a prelude to their officiating in our churches. Impudence can go no further.'[35] On that occasion, the opposition was sufficient to prevent any change in the law.

But in the summer of 1878 the whole question again came to the fore – thanks to events in the quiet Suffolk churchyard of Akenham. Here an eccentric rector, the Revd George Drury, who was already in dispute with his Bishop over his 'high church' tendencies, refused to officiate at the burial of a two-year-old labourer's son. The parents of the boy, Joseph Ramsay, were Baptists and Drury's action was based on the fact that the child had not been baptised and was, therefore, in his view, not a Christian. He declared that the child could only be buried in unconsecrated ground, reserved for stillborn infants, at the rear of the church, and without benefit of any funeral service. Furthermore, when the parents arrived for the interment a few days later accompanied by an Independent minister from Ipswich and fellow mourners, the rector intervened to prevent a service being conducted over the child's body in a meadow just outside the boundaries of the churchyard. An unseemly squabble developed between the Independent minister and the rector before Drury walked off, locking the churchyard behind him. According to the *East Anglian Daily Times* of 26 August 1878, the burial then continued in solemn silence, a way being made to the freshly dug grave through a private gateway. The party afterwards returned to the main entrance of the churchyard, where 'the usual burial service was read, and the ceremony concluded'.

Drury's unsympathetic attitude was widely criticised in the press, even though some protagonists suggested that the Nonconformists were also to blame for attempting to flout the law on the burials issue. But the local newspapers proved so hostile to Drury that he decided to sue for libel one of the worst offenders, Frederick Wilson, editor and proprietor of the *East Anglian Daily Times,* in the Court of Common Pleas. The case was heard in March 1879, and although Drury proved successful, his damages amounted to the derisory sum of only 40s.[36]

Nevertheless, public opinion on a wider front was now aroused, and the passage of the 1880 Burial Act was the eventual outcome of the controversy. Needless to say, its appearance on the statute book was by no means universally welcomed by all Anglican clergymen. At East Dereham, Benjamin Armstrong expressed his dismay in a diary entry on 6 September 1880: 'The Burials Bill is passed whereby any dissenter may be buried in the churchyard by whatever minister and with whatever service the relatives may desire. The worst of it is that the two archbishops and several bishops have advocated the bill.'[37]

Yet, happily, as the Victorian era drew to its close this sectarian bitterness began to wane, so that the passage of the 1880 Act might be seen as the precursor of a more broad-minded approach. Although feelings on particular issues could still run high – as witness the opposition of Nonconformists to the Education Act, with its authorisation of rate aid to denominational schools (many of which were Anglican) – the deepest divisions were slowly healed. In, the early 1880s the Bishop of Gloucester bade his clergy to 'recognise that Nonconformists "served the same Lord" though they must uphold to the full "the theology and claims of the Church of England". There could now be mutual respect between the two most influential groups "Church and Chapel".' Other clerics, like the Devon parson; Arnold Taylor, strongly called on churchmen to get rid of their 'haunting fears of disestablishment' and to try to reduce the barriers between 'Church' and 'Dissent'.[38]

In this process of reconciliation the career of Joseph Arch, the agricultural trade union leader, provides an exemplar. Arch was born in the Warwickshire village of Barford in 1826 and in the later 1840s he became a Primitive Methodist local preacher, being, as he stated in his autobiography, 'a Nonconformist by nature and by conviction'. And he defiantly added: 'I did not believe in Church doctrine, as preached by the parson. I did not believe either in ordering myself "lowly and reverently to all my betters", because they were never able to tell me who my betters were.' Nevertheless, by the 1890s his attitude had begun to change, and when he married for the second time in 1899 it was the local parish church that he chose for the ceremony, rather than a Methodist chapel. Although he still spoke out against his 'parson-ridden' neighbours at Barford this did not prevent him from becoming friendly with at least one of the curates, the Reverend Douglas Long, who was at Barford between 1899 and 1901 And when Long left to go to a living at Pershore in Worcestershire, Arch expressed his regret in an amicable letter: 'Have spoken to several of your leaving Barford, and there's only one remark – we liked him very much, sorry he is gone away.'[39]

It was fitting that when Arch died in 1919, the *Church Times* should comment: 'It is regrettable, when we look back to the early days of the agitation he led, to recall the loss of a great opportunity by the country clergy. They might have won the labourers to the Church, but, largely ranging themselves on the side of the squirearchy, they alienated, in too many instances, their struggling parishioners. Since then a more enlightened spirit has prevailed but there remains much leeway to be made up.' It was to be the task of the twentieth century to seek to repair that damage and to promote the growth of ecumenism.

9

Sickness, Medical Care & Death

*It might be thought that the farm labourers shared the poverty of the
unskilled men in the towns. Their weekly wages were actually lower ...
Yet families were brought up, and healthy ones too. Evidence ... shows
that farm labourers as a body had a lower death-rate than any other
manual occupation except the gardeners and the railway engine drivers
– a rate lower even than the schoolmasters' and the civil servants',
only a half that of the coal heavers and glassworkers, little more than a
quarter that of the general labourers ... The explanation is partly that
the country was a healthier place to live in, partly that the farm labourer
had much less to pay out on rent than the urban workman and usually
nothing on fares, but probably most of all that the weekly money wage
made up a smaller part of his effective income than of the townsman's.
The children would earn some thing ... A garden and allotment and a
pig in the sty would provide substantial supplies of food.*

E. H. Phelps Brown, *The Growth of
British Industrial Relations* (1959)

As early as 1842 Edwin Chadwick had pointed out in his Report on
the Sanitary Condition of the Labouring Population of Great Britain,
that agricultural labourers were among the healthiest of working men.
He had shown, for example, that the average age at death among the
working classes of Manchester in 1837 was less than half that of the
agricultural labourers of Rutland, and investigations into conditions in
the county of Wiltshire and the Kendal area of Westmorland confirmed
this trend.[1] Fifty years later the views he expressed were still valid. Even
in the period 1880–92 the Registrar of Births, Deaths and Marriages in
England and Wales pointed out that mortality rates among farm workers
were only 66 per cent of 'standard mortality among all occupied males'.[2]
Despite the fact that the land worker received only two-thirds of the
average industrial wage (even taking into account payments in kind) and
that his living conditions were often uncomfortable and insanitary, he
was nearly the healthiest manual worker in the country. Low earnings

could not entirely cancel out the benefits to health of fresh air and a country environment. In the matter of accidents, too, the agricultural labourer fared better than the national average despite the hazards of farm machinery, with hands and fingers lost in mowing machines, and the risk of serious falls from overloaded hay and corn carts.

But for those who became ill, respiratory diseases, including bronchitis pneumonia and tuberculosis, were particularly common. As one Wiltshire doctor recalled, pneumonia 'had a dreadful crisis, during which the patient often died. During this crisis they would have a very high temperature, would be blue in colour with a hacking cough, if they picked at their bedclothes it was a bad sign. If they lived their temperature would suddenly drop, and an hour or two later they would be sitting up in bed demanding a beef steak.' Even then they had to be carefully watched, and stimulants 'kept handy, to see they did not slip away'.[3]

Among children and the younger men and women the great fear was tuberculosis. Although agricultural labourers had a less than average chance of dying from this disease – mortality rates among them in the 1890s ran at only 62 per cent of standard mortality for it – it was sufficiently prevalent to strike dread into the hearts of many. As Walter Rose recalled of his early life at the end of the nineteenth century in Haddenham, Buckinghamshire, the community was never free from it: 'The symptoms were always the same: a delicate flush on an otherwise pale face, accompanied by a short, hacking cough; this continued for about three years, the sick one becoming weaker, until the end ... It was only too easy to note that their disposition resembled one's own, and that they had weaknesses to be found also in oneself. This thought, brooded on, became a perpetual secret fear.' Rose himself, on hearing that the eating of garden snails had saved the life of one victim, began a regular diet of them.[4]

For older people, rheumatism was a perennial problem, arising out of dietary deficiencies and the long hours spent in the open in all weathers, without proper shelter. In many country areas, villagers would take opium in one of its varied forms to relieve their pain, since this was virtually the only analgesic available.

The British Medical Association reported in 1867, indeed, that more than half of the opium imported into the country was consumed in Norfolk and Lincolnshire alone. In the marshlands of the west of Norfolk rheumatism and neuralgia were particularly bad and it was said that there was not a labourer's house 'without its penny stick or pill of opium, and not a child that did not have it in some form. Godfrey's Cordial, a mixture of opium, treacle, and infusion of sassafras, was the usual comfort administered to a squalling baby when its mother was too busy working in the fields to feed it.'[5]

But despite the ravages of Godfrey's Cordial, mortality rates were lower in the villages than in the towns for the youngest members of society as for their elders. Infants under the age of one year were, indeed, more seriously affected by the unhealthy conditions of urban life than any other age group. In 1893, when the average proportion of deaths of infants under one year of age to registered births stood at 161 per 1,000 for the whole of England and Wales, in a rural county like Rutland it was only 100 per 1,000 births, in Wiltshire, Dorset and Westmorland 102, and in Herefordshire 105, whereas in Lancashire it stood at a dreadful 193. Although the loss of around one in ten of all babies born in country districts each year could not be regarded with complacency, at least it was far better than the situation elsewhere.

Among children in both town and country, stomach disorders – diarrhoea, dysentery, enteritis – were major killers, emphasising the need to improve water supplies and to raise the general standard of hygiene. But 'atrophy', or death from lack of sufficient suitable food, was another common hazard and, disturbingly, in country districts caused more deaths than any other single cause, accounting for around one-fifth of all infant deaths in rural areas at the end of the century.[6] Partly this was a result of family poverty, but in the rural areas there were also bitter complaints of the shortage of milk to feed to youngsters. As one East Anglian clergyman put it: 'In many a country parish the labourer's wife and children can almost as easily buy fresh salmon [as milk]. It would be difficult to estimate the very serious, the momentous effect which this one want must inevitably produce upon the physique of the rural population in a few generations.'[17] However, the situation was not *all* loss in so far as most milk at that time was heavily infected with tuberculosis; a large consumption of milk coupled with a generally inadequate diet might have caused more deaths from TB (see also Chapter 2 on the milk question).

For those who did become ill, medical care was often rudimentary. Few could afford to pay a doctor's fees or even join a friendly society or medical club which would promise – like the Friendly and Benefit Society of Butleigh, Somerset – to provide for 'the comfortable relief of its respective members in cases of Sickness, &c.' for the modest outlay of 4s a quarter.[8] Most of the societies paid benefits to members of around 3s 6d to 6s per week whilst they were ill, while a club doctor was usually appointed to provide necessary medical care, at a fee of 2s 6d or so per member per annum.[9]

For those without such medical advice, self-help, charity and the poor laws were the main alternatives – despite the fact that medical relief from the poor law authorities carried with it the penalty of investigation into family means and, until 1885, the social stigma of pauperism as well. In that year the clumsily styled Medical Relief (Disqualification

Removal) Act ended the disfranchisement of men merely because they, or members of their families had taken advantage of poor law medical treatment or hospital facilities. Henceforth medical relief alone did not disqualify a voter or cause him to be classed as a pauper.

Nevertheless, self-help was the first line of defence in most families and even for confinements women would try to manage without professional help. Usually they would depend upon the help of an older neighbour, whose only justification for acting as midwife was practical experience and perhaps the large number of children she had herself borne. For as little as 2s 6d such women would attend at the birth and then return each night and morning for a few days, until the mother was able to struggle to her feet again. Only if complications were feared would the doctor be called in. In a number of cases this would mean reliance on the poor law medical officer – as at Piddington, Oxfordshire, during May 1846, where one of the Bicester Poor Law Union medical men noted that he had attended the confinement of a forty-one-year-old labourer's wife who was 'weakly and badly'. He had recommended the provision of 1 lb of mutton as extra food to aid her recovery. A twenty-four-year-old woman in the same village who had suffered a miscarriage was prescribed 'broth' because of weakness, but in other cases oatmeal or milk might be ordered for a new mother who had called in poor law assistance.[10] The doctors, for their part, received extra fees for attending at confinements; in the Pershore area of Worcestershire, these amounted to 10s 6d per case on average during the 1860s, although for more seriously ill patients the fee might rise to as much as £2.

Yet most women were either unable or unwilling to avail themselves of this kind of aid, and for them the help of neighbours was vital. Clothing and even groceries were provided for many of the 'respectable' poor by village lying-in charities. At Harpenden in. Hertfordshire, to quote one example, parcels of linen and other items were regularly loaned to any who cared to apply for them. They contained, besides linen articles for mother and child, a pair of sheets and a counterpane, which were kept in repair by 'lady members' of the Church. 'These "baby bundles" were loaned for a month, the borrowers undertaking to return same at the end of the period, with the contents properly washed, clean, ironed, and if possible intact … However, at the time of the handing over the sum of three shillings was in many cases, if not all, sent or given to the expectant mother wherewith to buy groceries, imperative among which articles must be a certain quantity of soap.[11] In other parishes 'linen tickets' were also provided for those who were ill from other causes than childbirth. The diaries of the Revd W. C. Risley, a former incumbent of Deddington, Oxfordshire, show that on 8 August 1868 'Widow Cowley came for a Linen Ticket for her son, Jacob – he being very ill indeed.' And about six weeks later, on 15 September, Risley noted: 'Widow Gibbs came for a Lying in Box for Martha Clarke at the Windmill.'[12]

For more general use, there was a whole range of homely medicines, such as 'salts and senna, brimstone and treacle', as well as the dubious products of quack doctors and herbalists who plied their trade in country towns and even from door to door in the villages. Most cottagers attached great importance to herbs for treating sickness. Stewed groundsel was used for poultices, marshmallow leaves and flowers were made into ointment for boils, lily leaves were used for cuts, 'dock leaves for galled feet, green broom for kidneys, and dandelion roots for liver troubles, coltsfoot leaves for bronchitis and asthma, rue pills for tonic, and so on, whilst the leaves of camomile, yarrow and agrimony were used for making what was termed "Yarb tea", this tea being drunk for general health.'[13] For earache, the core of a small shallot would be heated and placed in the affected ear, while goose grease was rubbed on chest and throat to relieve coughs and sore throats. Some, however, preferred to cure their sore throats by making 'a very strong decoction of carrots' and gargling with this frequently or applying hartshorn and oil to a piece of flannel worn round the neck.[14] Mistletoe was regarded as a 'sure cure' for whooping cough, though in East Anglia the most effective remedy was thought to be the eating of a fried mouse. More than one child could testify to the nausea felt when taking this cure.

Some of the treatment seemed to be based more on superstition than on effective medication and, as any reader of such Thomas Hardy tales as *The Return of the Native* or *The Withered Arm* will recall, a belief in witchcraft survived in many of the more remote rural areas into the second half of the nineteenth century. One old Norfolk labourer recalled that even in the 1860s his grandmother considered that a cure for a 'bleeding tumour' was to place the hand of a 'dead person upon the part affected'. And if a child were born with a rupture, 'The Father would go out and search about till he found a strait young ash plant, which he could put his knife through and split down. Then they would bring the Child and holding the ash sapling apart, draw the child through the split. The split parts were pulled together again and bound with string.'[15] If the sapling grew together it was believed that the child's rupture would be healed.

In such circumstances it is scarcely surprising that the Revd Benjamin Armstrong, vicar of East Dereham, should record in his diary on 1 April 1864: 'I have been with two parishioners this week who are really and truly persuaded that they are bewitched, a notion that is very far from being extirpated yet in these country parts.' And sixteen years later he remonstrated with an elderly woman who had 'said the Lord's Prayer backwards to get rid of an infliction which had been "put" on her. She promised me to say it forwards three times a day, but added "unless the trouble comes back, and then I shall say it backwards again."'

Among less sinister remedies of this kind was the custom of Hertfordshire labourers of carrying a small potato in their trouser pocket, about the size of a walnut, to ward off rheumatism. In Norfolk men would carry the bone of a pig's foot, or pieces of brass, zinc and copper in a bag, for the same purpose. But in the view of at least one old labourer such efforts were in vain – 'the rhumatics' were 'uncurable'. A common remedy for warts was to 'rub a bit of bacon fat on the wart and bury it in an ant hill, or rub a snail on it and bury the snail', while rabbit-skin socks in shoes were believed to prevent pleurisy, and moles' feet carried inside dress or jacket would 'prevent almost any disease'.[16]

If these remedies failed, then more professional medical help had to be sought. Here charity could once again play a part. Not only did some doctors treat their neediest patients free of charge, but subscribers to voluntary hospitals in rural areas would recommend suitable cases for charitable treatment – a policy which was often criticised, since those most in need of treatment were not necessarily the ones selected. At Deddington, Mr Risley was a subscriber to the Radcliffe Infirmary in Oxford and in his diary there are such entries as that for 23 July 1868: 'Mrs Hicks the school mistress came for an out patient Infirmary Ticket for a Daughter which I gave her.'

However, in many country districts there was no hospital available except for the infirmary wards of the local workhouse with their cheerless, whitewashed walls and uncurtained windows. As a woman workhouse visitor from Bristol pointed out in 1861, the furniture in such infirmaries was often

> unsuited to its destination. The same rough beds (generally made with one thin mattress laid on iron bars) which are allotted to the rude able-bodied paupers, are equally given to the poor, emaciated, bed-ridden patient, whose frame is probably sore all over, and whose aching head must remain, for want of pillows, in nearly a horizontal position for months together. Hardly in any workhouse is there a chair on which the sufferers in asthma or dropsy, or those fading away slowly in decline, could relieve themselves by sitting for a few hours, instead of on the edge of their beds, gasping and fainting from weariness ... In new country workhouses the walls of these sick-rooms are commonly of stone – not plastered, but constantly whitewashed – and the floor not seldom of stone also. Conceive a winter spent in such a prison: no shutters or curtains, of course, to the windows, or shelter to the beds, where some dozen sufferers lie writhing in rheumatism, and ten or fifteen more coughing away the last chances of life and recovery.[17]

It was to combat this kind of situation that the cottage hospital movement was established in the 1860s. It was designed to provide residential care for village people who had no other hospital available. As the name suggests, the hospitals were set up in converted cottages and catered for about six to ten patients at any one time. Medical treatment was provided by a resident nurse and by regular visits from the general practitioner. Patients were usually expected to pay something towards the cost of the scheme, even if that were as little as 2s 6d a week. The remainder of the funds came from charity. Equipment and medicaments were minimal – chloroform inhalers, fracture splints, an ear syringe and a stomach pump being among the modest list of instruments recommended for cottage hospitals in the 1870s – but food was both plentiful and wholesome. In 1870, indeed, it was suggested that the cost of food for patients would probably work out at 11¼d per day; the cost of drugs at just over 1d a day![18] Sometimes, as at Fowey in Cornwall, a large proportion of the funds were given in kind, 'dinner fruit, wine &c., being sent from the rich man's table to his sick neighbour'. Another example is the Basingstoke Village Hospital, formed in the mid-1870s at a cost of about £600, to provide for eight patients. Each inmate was expected to pay between 2s and 8s a week, 'the amount ... to be fixed by the patient's employer or person recommending with the concurrence of the medical officers'. In return, 'every requisite except personal clothing' was provided by the hospital.[19] By 1870, around seventy cottage hospitals had been established all over the country, and the improved diet and rest they offered to their patients were often sufficient to effect a recovery.

Elsewhere attempts were made to help the sick by the appointment of a district nurse, as in Stansted Mountfitchet in Essex, where it was 'unanimously resolved' at a parish meeting held in December 1890 that a nurse should be engaged. Her salary was to be £1 per week, and although the bulk of the funds were to be met by public subscription, cottagers were to be asked to contribute 6d a year towards the cost, plus 2s 6d for the nurse's attendance at confinements and a 'small sum when they can afford it, in other cases'. By the end of the first year, the scheme's success was assured, particularly as it had had to cope with epidemics of whooping cough and influenza which had affected the locality.[20] Similarly, at Burnham in Buckinghamshire a Nursing Association was set up in 1892, and committee members were encouraged to 'make some flannelette jackets for women and night gowns and jackets for children to send to the labouring class of patients'. But there was also an interesting moral touch here in that 'unmarried women were to pay double fees when they required the services of the midwife'.[21]

Yet, however welcome such charitable aid might be, it was by its very nature patchy, and for those who were seriously ill, application to the local poor law authorities for medical assistance had often to be made.

In accordance with the 1834 Poor Law Amendment Act, every union was required to appoint district medical officers. In the early days the standard of care provided was minimal, thanks to the prevailing anxiety of the poor law guardians to keep down expenditure. In some cases so keen were they to cut costs that they required medical men to tender for the position, and the doctor submitting the lowest tender would be accepted, irrespective of his abilities or of the convenience of his surgery for the majority of the inhabitants of the district. There were cases both then and later of villagers having to walk 4–6 miles to visit the doctor or to call in his services for a member of the family. In 1842 medical officers were put on a salaried basis, but even then the payments offered were small – salaries of £60 to £70 being common with, in many cases, the doctors expecting to provide medicines for their patients out of this sum. Perhaps not surprisingly these remedies were usually restricted to cheap items like Epsom salts, although some doctors dispensed their own special 'cough mixtures', which were much valued by patients. But an example of the generally cheeseparing attitude of the authorities can be found as late as 1895 when the Local Government Board in London queried the decision of the Ledbury poor law guardians to reappoint one of their medical officers at a salary of £70 per annum, 'his salary hitherto having been £60 a year'.

The problems to which this approach gave rise were pinpointed by witnesses to the 1854 Select Committee on Medical Relief. As the Revd C. Oxenden, Rector of Barham in Kent, noted, in his parish the medical officer would not provide 'such an expensive class of medicine' as quinine for cases of fever but would prescribe wine instead, since the poor law guardians were compelled to supply meat, wine, spirits and porter for patients on the doctor's recommendation. Another witness, the Reverend Charles Kingsley (poet and novelist as well as incumbent of Eversley in Hampshire), agreed that all too often medical officers substituted 'necessaries for medicines'. He cited a case 'in the Newton Abbot Union, where ... the officers' salary was calculated ... at about half-a-crown a case: now, one of them assures me that even that barely covers the expense of medicines, and would prevent him giving, except in charity, the more expensive medicines, cod-liver oil and quinine; I think if you calculate the expense of such medicines as cod-liver oil, quinine, or sarsaparilla, you will find that those cannot be given at the average salary of the greater number of men... and they are very often out of pocket for a very long time by permanent cases'. Kingsley estimated that the cost of cod-liver oil would be about 2½*d* or 3*d* a day, so that if the doctor supplied it for a fortnight or three weeks to a patient for whom he was paid at the rate of 2*s* 6*d* a case, he would soon be out of pocket.[22] Only for midwifery cases and the setting of fractures were extra fees payable and in Kingsley's view, the former at least was 'the most lucrative part of a medical officer's profession'.

Not until 1865 was this position changed. It was in that year that the Poor Law Board issued a circular letter recommending that in future 'Cod Liver Oil, Quinine, and other expensive medicines, shall be provided at the. expense of the Guardians'. Within two years nearly two-thirds of the unions had acted on this, with stocks of cod-liver oil being held at the workhouse 'in the same way as Wine, or other extras recommended by the Medical Officers'. But not all followed suit. Even in 1876, a Return of Poor Relief (Expensive Medicines) revealed that out of six poor law unions in Bedfordshire, only one – Biggleswade – provided cod-liver oil and quinine; the rest made no provision at all. Likewise in Wiltshire, eight out of seventeen unions made no arrangements for 'expensive medicines'. On the other hand, in Buckinghamshire, all seven of the unions made the requisite provisions, and all eight of those in Herefordshire. Some areas supplied leeches and linseed meal as well as cod-liver oil and quinine, while a few provided sarsaparilla.[23]

Nevertheless, an inspection of medical officers' relief books reveals that prescriptions of meat and alcohol were still, all too often, the only treatment suggested, although by the 1870s and 1880s milk and eggs were being added to the list, especially for children. The contemporary faith in stimulants is shown by such provision as that in the Hungerford Poor Law Union in Berkshire where, during May 1875, the medical officer prescribed half-a-pint of brandy each to a woman recovering from childbirth, an elderly man suffering from tuberculosis, two influenza victims, and a pregnant woman; seven more patients were prescribed daily doses of porter and one patient received a pint of gin a week. Gin was a common remedy for dropsy and was prescribed for this complaint by most poor law medical men. Nor was it only the older patients who were so treated. In March of that same year a boy of eight suffering from an abscess was prescribed 2 lb of meat a week and half-a-pint of porter daily, while in the Kingsclere Union of Hampshire at about the same time a lad of fourteen suffering from fever was given beef and wine; and another fourteen-year-old suffering from typhoid received eggs, beef, milk and porter – as well as quinine.[24]

The overall significance of prescriptions in kind as opposed to those of medicines can be seen by analysing in detail the treatment recommended. For example, during the week ending 4 January 1873, one of the medical officers in the Kingsclere Union, Hampshire, saw thirty-two patients. Of these, he recommended that twenty-two be provided with mutton, two with cod-liver oil and one with gin; in addition, six of the twenty-two were supplied with porter as well as mutton, one received brandy and mutton and one (suffering from meningitis) wine and mutton. Two more patients obtained gin and mutton. Eleven of the total group of patients were prescribed medicines (unspecified) and five secured neither medicines nor dietary extras. Mutton was given for debility, gangrene, rheumatism and a whole range of other ills, while the cod-liver oil was prescribed for two tubercular children.[25]

Similarly, a random examination of the Hungerford district medical records shows that during the first week of July 1875, of sixteen patients treated, five obtained 2 lb of meat a week, six obtained porter (including four of those also receiving meat), and two received half-a-pint of brandy. Three obtained medicines only. But by the end of the century – here as elsewhere – the reliance on dietary extras was weakening. In the four weeks ending 29 September 1888 the Hungerford district medical officer treated twenty-six patients. Three were prescribed eggs (in two cases with milk as well), two received meat and gin, one obtained ale, and one, suffering from a rupture, obtained a truss. Four were given medicine and the rest made do with advice only.[26]

Yet although such reliance on treatment 'in kind' appears totally inadequate to deal with the illnesses concerned, it should not be entirely condemned, for in many families, food was in short supply and these extras could at least help to compensate for general dietary deficiencies.

Of the epidemic diseases, smallpox, typhoid and diphtheria were perhaps the most feared. Although from 1854 every infant was supposed to be compulsorily vaccinated against smallpox, it was not until 1871 that the legislation began to be effectively implemented, following a severe outbreak of the disease. Nevertheless, many parents objected to the vaccination campaign. Even in remote Radnorshire, the Revd Francis Kilvert, curate of Clyro, records in his diary for 27 February 1871 that 'Fifteen people [were] summoned for neglecting to have their children vaccinated.' They 'got off by paying costs', but protesters elsewhere were not always so fortunate, and prison sentences were from time to time doled out to parents who refused to obey the law. Protesters claimed that the lymph provided for free vaccination by the arm-to-arm method was likely to make their children ill. In 1866, an Anti-compulsory Vaccination League was set up and after years of lobbying its efforts were rewarded when in 1898 parents who objected on grounds of conscience to having their children vaccinated were allowed to apply to the local magistrate for exemption. But by then the vaccination campaign had done its work (aided perhaps by a decline in the virulence of the disease), and smallpox as a major killer had been eliminated. Even at the small village of Haddenham, in the middle of the nineteenth century the disease had been a scourge, and Walter Rose recalled that his father often told him that it was impossible to imagine 'the perpetual dread of smallpox at the time of his youth, when it was usual to see one out of every three faces pitted with scars'. In the 1830s and 1840s, the mortality of children from this disease had been especially severe; during the 1839 epidemic just over one-quarter of the 8,714 deaths recorded were accounted for by children under the age of one. And the annual rate of mortality from small-pox in that year for children up to and including the age of four, was 2.73 per 1,000 living – a rate far in excess of that for any of the other age-groups quoted. By 1873–77, however, the disease was responsible for only 0.1 infant deaths per 1,000 births in the country districts, and in 1892–1902 the number was so tiny that it could not be registered at all.[27]

When a smallpox death did occur, it was often difficult to find anyone to assist at the burial. At Debenham, Suffolk, during the 1870s when the elder son of a farm bailiff died the vicar had great problems in arranging for the interment. Eventually 'several men volunteered and the funeral was arranged to take place at midnight'. But even then the men were reluctant to lift the corpse into the coffin and the vicar had to take the lead. 'When the churchyard was reached and the coffin carried to the grave, all the bearers lit their pipes, for smoking was supposed to guard against infection.'[28] Night burials were common for small-pox in many villages.

Typhoid fever, though less dreaded than smallpox, was an even greater hazard – at Debenham and elsewhere. Wells were not sufficiently deep, and in many places in that part of East Anglia, there was a layer of sand underneath the clay soil, which meant that leakage from the primitive drains of the houses was likely to contaminate the water. 'In one part of the village the town drain was carried only a short way into a stream which in summer became a succession of stagnant pools'.

Thanks to local inertia public health legislation only slowly effected an improvement in this situation, and as late as 1899 the Biggleswade district of Bedfordshire was described in extremely unfavourable terms by the Medical Officer of the Local Government Board: 'Water supply throughout the district generally from shallow wells, liable to be polluted. Sewerage and drainage defective; filth nuisances abundant. Public scavenging adopted for only one parish; in one other cesspools emptied by hand pumps and carts ... Practically no disinfection practised. Hospital accommodation insufficient.'[29] During the previous few years there had been, hardly surprisingly, severe outbreaks of diphtheria and enteric fever (i.e. typhoid) in the area.

Among children, measles, whooping cough, diphtheria and scarlet fever all took their toll. Evidence of outbreaks can be found in school log books – as at Steeple Aston and the nearby hamlets of Rousham and Middle Aston in Oxfordshire where scarlet fever raged during the autumn of 1863 and measles in the early part of the following year. By the end of January 1864 more than half the children were away from school with measles and one unfortunate youngster had died of it. Diphtheria was a still greater danger. Thus at Barnham Broom, Norfolk, there were sixty cases of the disease between May and September 1894 – out of a total population of just over 400; eleven of the victims died. Countless similar examples could be quoted from all parts of the country during the Victorian era. In part, the lack of effective means of isolating patients and the overcrowded and unhygienic conditions of many schools and homes encouraged the spread of illness. Dr Thursfield, a Shropshire medical officer, also considered that the long distances children had to walk to school and the fact that there was no means of drying their clothes on a wet day contributed to the problem: 'Every school in such scattered rural districts should have proper appliances for drying clothes, with supply of slippers &c ... I have repeatedly made notes of instances where during the prevalence of diphtheria, children who have had to walk long distances through muddy lanes have suffered first and most severely.'[30] One of the first things to be done in most villages when a person did die was to send to the sexton of the parish church to get him to toll the bell. As Edwin Grey recalled, in Harpenden the bell was 'tolled for about twenty minutes or half an hour, three tolls for a man, two for a woman, one for a child.' The tolling fee was a shilling. Grey also remembered that a 'certain degree of what one might call temporary importance seemed to be attained by all members of the deceased person's family during the period prior to the burial; a very marked deference being paid to them by all the cottagers round about, whilst yet the body remained unburied.' Following the death there would be a sort of 'lying-in-state', and members of the deceased person's family would, if possible, keep the coffin unclosed until the last moment so that friends could call to pay their respects.

All cottage funerals were walking funerals, the coffin being carried on men's shoulders, sometimes for as far as 2 miles. There were as a rule eight bearers, four carrying and four reliefs walking by the side. The coffin and the heads and shoulders of the bearers were covered with a black-and-white pall that smothered them and made it difficult for them to see where they were going. At Harpenden the carrier's fee was about 2s but if the family were very poor the bearers would waive all charges, so as to keep down the funeral expenses. The village carpenter would usually act as undertaker and would supply the simple coffin. The price of this varied with the quality of the wood used and the pocket of the family. The account book of Thomas Parr, a carpenter from the Newbury area, shows that in the 1860s a child's coffin could be supplied for 2s, while adults were catered for from anything between 10s and £2.[31] Similarly, the account books of the Bennett family, carpenters of Wotton-under-Edge, Gloucestershire, show that on 4 December 1858, a 'small elm coffin six handles and B[rass] P[late] for Charles French nine Months' was supplied for 5s 6d. In this case the father 'settled by Potatoes'[32] Other badly off families, too, used the barter system as a last resort to settle their debt, provided the carpenter would co-operate.

In the funeral procession the mourners walked in strict order of relationship, the near members of the deceased person's family following immediately behind the coffin. Next came more distant relatives and lastly friends and acquaintances. All would wear black and if they had none of their own, this would be borrowed. It was unthinkable not to wear black as a mark of respect – even if for the poorest this meant only a black crepe band round the arm. At most cottage funerals, bread, cheese and beer was provided for the bearers before the start of the funeral procession, and after the service had ended, a high tea was supplied to the returning mourners.

Many people belonged to a burial club, so as to avoid the disgrace of a pauper funeral – for as a west country woman declared, 'What did a poor woman work for, but in hopes she should be put out of the world in a tidy way?'[33] But where a burial did take place 'on the parish', bells would remain silent 'and coffins were not permitted to make their last sad journey on the Queen's Highway; circuitous routes on minor lanes had to be navigated by pathfinding undertakers'. Nevertheless, however humiliating this might be, many families could not afford to bury their dead out of their own resources, and application to the poor law guardians for help had to be made. In the six months ending March 1871, there were, for example, eight pauper funerals authorised in the Bletchingdon district of the Bicester Poor Law Union (covering eighteen villages) – all involving agricultural labourers or members of their families. The funeral expenses varied from 10s 6d to 24s.

Yet although the provision of such assistance was part of their statutory duty not all guardians responded favourably to the appeals. The Royal Commission on the Aged Poor was told of cases where even in the 1890s requests for aid had been rejected. In one extreme case, in the Brixworth area of Northamptonshire, a daughter who asked for help in obtaining a coffin to bury her father was told that she might get a sheet and sew the body up in that. 'The daughter came back unable to get a coffin, and a Mr Pell, at Moulton, wrote out a subscription paper and headed it himself, the man's own daughter going round from house to house collecting it.'[34] In another case, a widower was told that if he put his wife's body out into the street, then it would be regarded as a public nuisance and the sanitary authorities would do something about it. But whilst it was in the house it was a private nuisance and the authorities refused to provide help. In this case, too, charitable help was eventually forthcoming.

Happily most people managed to avoid such a degrading fate, however, either by joining a burial club or by receiving help from more sympathetic poor law authorities.

ᴘOVERTY & ᴏLD ᴀGE

The old people who were not in comfortable circumstances had no homes at all worth mentioning, for, as soon as they got past work, they had either to go to the workhouse or find accommodation in the already over-crowded cottages of their children ... The Poor Law authorities allowed old people past work a small weekly sum as outdoor relief; but it was not sufficient to live upon, and, unless they had more than usually prosperous children to help support them, there came a time when the home had to be broken up.

Flora Thompson, *Lark Rise to Candleford* (1963 ed.)

For most rural workers faced with illness or unemployment, the poor law remained as a last refuge, to be appealed to when all else had failed. In the case of the sick, poor relief applied not only to the provision of medical care, which was discussed in the last chapter, but to monetary aid as well. The sums paid out were small but at least they helped to tide the family over until the breadwinner could resume employment. In many communities they would also be supplemented by charity, while for the more fortunate who had paid into a friendly society, there would be a regular sickness benefit of a few shillings per week as an alternative to poor relief.

But for the unemployed the position was far less certain. Although the 1834 Poor Law Amendment Act was not specific on the subject, the impression was given that it was unlawful to grant relief to an able-bodied pauper in his own home. If he wanted help he must bring his family into the workhouse and submit to the rules and regulations that this entailed. In addition, the 1834 legislation enshrined the notorious 'principle of less eligibility', whereby any man in receipt of poor relief was to be placed in a worse position than an 'independent labourer of the lowest class'. Inevitably this meant that the poor law system was made so unpleasant that an appeal to parish funds was the pauper's last resort. The deterrent attitude was underlined by the issue of Special Orders explicitly banning outdoor relief in particular unions from the mid-

1830s and, still more in 1844 by a general Outdoor Relief Prohibitory Order issued by the central Poor Law Commission in London. This stated that relief to able-bodied men and women and their families was only to be given in the workhouse.

In the northern industrial areas large-scale unemployment in times of bad trade, coupled with a determined local opposition to the new poor law, prevented this ruling from being carried into full effect, but in many rural areas – despite sporadic protests – it became accepted policy during the early Victorian years. Nevertheless, among country people it aroused a sense of injustice and a deep-seated hatred of the workhouse, which epitomised all the harshness of an alien officialdom. It was 'an intrusion which a countryman reared in the more personal atmosphere of village life could never understand'. Perhaps one of the most resented aspects was the way in which families were split up inside the workhouse, so that not only were husbands and wives separated from one another but children were kept apart from their mothers.

George Edwards, who in the early twentieth century became the founder of the National Union of Agricultural and Allied Workers, was one of many mid-century labouring children who spent a part of their early life in the workhouse. In George's case this was because his father had been gaoled for stealing five turnips. Although the sentence was 'only' for fourteen days' imprisonment with hard labour, Mr Edwards was unable to obtain fresh employment before the spring and so the family went into the workhouse for the winter. As George bitterly recalled, though he was only five years of age he was not allowed to remain with his mother.[1] Others shared his experience. In 1846 a Hampshire labourer stated that during ten weeks in the workhouse, including Christmas, 'he had seen his seven children only when they passed him on the way to chapel. A husband who crossed the dining hall to talk to his wife at dinner or supper was liable to be punished both for fraternising with the opposite sex and for speaking at mealtimes.'

The treatment of children in the workhouse was a matter of particular importance since they were the largest single group of inmates. As late as the 1871 Census of Population they formed between a third and a half of the paupers in such widely separated rural workhouses as that at Kendal in Westmorland, at Blandford in Dorset, at Thame in Oxfordshire and at Wantage, then in Berkshire. And the General Report of the Census confirmed that in the nation's workhouses as a whole around one-third of the inmates were under the age of fifteen.[3] The youngsters were either orphans and abandoned children or else, like George Edwards, they had been brought in temporarily with their parents; these latter were known as the 'ins and outs'.

However, family separation was not the only hardship to be borne. In certain workhouses, like that at Andover in Hampshire during the 1830s and 1840s, the cruelty of the master and matron could make life unbearable. At Andover the paupers were kept so short of food that some of the men were reduced to gnawing old and decayed bones that they had been set to crush for fertiliser. Beatings were commonplace. When these conditions were publicised in 1845 and 1846 – with *The Times* particularly active in reporting the affair – public opinion was deeply shocked. Eventually reforms were introduced both at the workhouse itself and within the general administrative framework of poor relief. But the ill treatment of the inmates which had so horrified the general public proved difficult to eradicate, and in workhouses in many parts of the country cruelty continued in a covert form for years to come. Indeed, even at Andover itself once the publicity had died down conditions deteriorated:

> The Guardians never forgave the paupers for having complained about the bones and for having exposed them to public censure, and once the clouds had blown away they began to oppress them as brutally as ever. The pounding of bones, of course, had been stopped; throughout the country as well as in Andover. Flints were procured for the Workhouse instead which, if anything, were even worse as in extremis they could not be eaten ... The third volume of the Guardians' Minutes which opens in July, 1847 ... reveals that life inside the Workhouse was, if possible, worse than before. In the last half of this year the Porter was sacked for 'exposing his person'; the Master was accused of immorality; the Workhouse was described as 'very disorderly' and rife with measles and influenza; the diet was said to be 'not sufficient'.[4]

Of course, in almost all workhouses a few of the more determined inmates made their own protests from time to time, and there are occasional examples of men refusing to carry out the tasks assigned to them or destroying their pauper uniforms. For these acts they were normally hauled before the local petty sessional court and given a term of several days' imprisonment with hard labour. The incidence of such offences varied from one part of the country to another. At Alresford in Hampshire during 1898 there were no less than eleven cases heard under this heading out of a total of eighty-eight offences of all kinds to come before the court.[5] But defiance on that scale was rare; usually the routine and discipline of the workhouse were sufficiently stringent to smother any incipient rebellion.

Despite the *official* attitude in favour of forcing the able-bodied unemployed to accept poor law aid in the workhouse, some outdoor relief was given, even in country districts, from quite early on. As time passed, this trend increased. In East Anglia, for example, during the 1840s and 1850s the guardians periodically relieved the unemployed outside the workhouse on the ostensible grounds of sickness or accident – since these were exceptions to the official prohibition on outdoor assistance to the able-bodied. Others, as in Suffolk during the 1840s, arranged for unemployed men to be set to work on the roads and paid out of the highway rate rather than from poor law resources.[6] These developments were due not so much to an upsurge of humanitarian feelings as to the realisation that if families were taken into the workhouse they had to be fully maintained. A grant of outdoor relief, on the other hand, could be augmented by small earnings and receipts from private charity. Many boards of poor law guardians and local relieving officers openly admitted that the few shillings they gave to applicants as out relief were inadequate for maintenance; they had to be supplemented from other sources which were rarely investigated. Thus in 1860 while it cost almost 3s 6d a week to maintain a pauper in an Eastern Counties workhouse, the average per capita expenditure on outdoor assistance was only 1s 9d. In Brighton the chairman of the board of guardians frankly declared in 1895 that to 'give outdoor relief which was adequate for subsistence would double the cost of relief... All outdoor relief was relief in aid of something, either private charitable gifts or small earnings.' And as late as 1915, a Fabian Society inquiry found that widowed women field workers earning 1s a day in parts of Wiltshire were also forced to apply for poor relief in order to maintain their families.[7]

The relative cheapness of out relief was emphasised by an Outdoor Relief Regulation Order issued in August 1852, which laid down that at least half of any assistance given to the able-bodied was to be in the form of food, fuel or other necessary articles. These were purchased by the guardians on contract, with the lowest tender the one normally accepted, irrespective of the quality of the goods provided. Although the policy was modified over the years, relief in kind remained a characteristic of the poor law system. In the Essex parish of Little Dunmow as late as the 1880s, there were complaints that loaves of bread provided for out relief tasted like chaff and could only be eaten toasted. And at Chelmsford in the same county the bread supplied in one district during the mid-1890s was '"like pudding" as well as short weight ... when part was arranged to be in flour, the temporary absence of the Relieving Officer brought to light that recipients were getting 2½ instead of 3½lb of flour'.[8] No doubt the contractor and the relieving officer had been happily sharing the profits of this arrangement between them, at the expense of the poor. In 1868 even the Poor Law Board in London found it necessary to criticise rural guardians who were giving relief in kind 'by means of tickets upon shopkeepers, a course which ... is, when adopted as a general rule, obviously injurious to the real interests of the poor man as it exposes him to the danger of being supplied with inferior articles at extortionate prices or to the temptation of changing his token for money to the possible injury of his family'.[9] If the official authorisation of out relief in kind was one development of Poor Law Board policy in 1852, another was the issuing of an order in December of that year tacitly accepting the existence of out relief to the able-bodied by requiring every able-bodied man relieved out of the workhouse to be set to work by the guardians for as long as he continued to receive assistance. The work mainly took the form of chopping wood, breaking stones, digging or some other uninspiring task connected with road mending. But, despite this provision, men were still expected to maintain their families by their own independent efforts if at all possible. Any who failed to work when the opportunity offered or who deserted their wife and children, leaving them dependent on the poor law, could be summoned before the courts for this dereliction of duty. At Henley Petty Sessions in Oxfordshire during September 1866 a labourer who had allowed his two children to become chargeable was 'convicted as an idle and disorderly person' and imprisoned for fourteen days with hard labour. Similarly in October 1861 the Alcester guardians in Warwickshire offered 'a reward of £1 ... for the apprehension of Richard Maun', who had deserted his wife and family, leaving them chargeable to the poor rate. When this failed they decided to insert an advertisement 'in the Hue and Cry' to try to track him down. But all of their efforts proved in vain. The Maun family remained the responsibility of their parish.[10]

Nor were these the only problems that the system could bring. Poor relief always carried with it a social stigma. The monetary help was grudgingly given, after a careful investigation of the financial circumstances of the applicant and, as we have seen, the sums involved were totally inadequate to need. Up to 1918, receipt of poor relief also led to disfranchisement – a matter of some significance after the parliamentary franchise was extended to the rural householder in 1884. It was small wonder that many men were reluctant to apply for such aid unless they were desperate. In 1886 their feelings were recognised by Joseph Chamberlain, then President of the Local Government Board, which had assumed control of poor law matters in 1871. Chamberlain sent out a circular letter to local authorities on the unemployment issue, calling on them to provide municipal work as an alternative to poor relief. As he declared: 'The spirit of independence which leads so many of the working-classes to make great personal sacrifices rather than incur the stigma of pauperism is one which deserves the greatest sympathy and respect.' Two conditions were imposed for receipt of aid under this scheme. The first was that the man concerned should be certified by the guardians as deserving more than pauper treatment, and the second was that the wages he received should be less than those normally paid for similar work. This circular was reissued in subsequent years, and in the winter of 1893–94, for example, the poor law guardians in the Wantage and Abingdon unions of Berkshire provided employment for unemployed able-bodied labourers at daily rates for married men of 1s 4d and 1s 6d, respectively. At Abingdon the men were employed in the workhouse garden and at Wantage they were required to dig out a pond or water storage tank also on workhouse premises. Although the rates paid were pitifully small – as the *Oxford Chronicle* of 9 December 1893 put it, 'How are body and soul to be kept together on that scanty wage?' – a number of men accepted the offer.[11] The importance of Chamberlain's circular was that it acknowledged for the first time that to be workless was not synonymous with work-shy.

Yet if by the last quarter of the nineteenth century attitudes were relaxing a little as regards giving help to the unemployed rural worker, a still more significant trend in reducing the level of pauperism was the fact that men were leaving the land in growing numbers to seek employment in police forces, on the railways or in various town trades, as well as emigrating to North America and Australasia. At the same time, the real wages of those who remained behind were improving, thanks to the fall in the price of food and the comparative steadiness of money incomes.

For the able-bodied, resort to the indignities of the poor law was normally something to be endured on a short-term basis only, during temporary unemployment or illness. But for one sector of the rural population – the old – parish relief was all too often a way of life. In 1891 it was estimated that about 30 per cent of all country men and women over the age of sixty-five received some form of poor relief each year. From the beginning, outdoor relief had been paid to old people who preferred the customary allowance of one or two shillings per week to entry into the workhouse. Under the Poor Law Board's General Order of August 1852 it was further laid down that at least one-third of their relief was to be provided in the form of food, fuel or other necessaries. Although amended in detail, this policy of payment in kind remained a feature of relief to the old for the rest of the century. Furthermore, about 1870 a new deterrent school of thought sought to apply even to them the dogma of 'less eligibility'. For a time in the 1870s and 1880s poor law inspectors began to press boards of guardians to apply the workhouse test to the aged, not as a 'test of destitution' but, as one of them put it, 'to put pressure on relatives who are not legally liable' to support the man or woman concerned.[12]

From the introduction of the new poor law system in the mid-1830s members of a family who could contribute to the support of an elderly relative were required to do so. Indeed, even where poor relief was granted it was customary to place an order upon a son or daughter requiring them to remit to the authorities 1s or 2s a week, to help cover the cost. In Norfolk during the 1880s, George Edwards, for example, contributed 1s 3d a week to his mother's weekly 2s 6d poor relief. To sons who were themselves short of money, with a wife and family to provide for, this additional burden was hard to bear, even where they were anxious to perform their filial duties. Some refused to pay up, and were summoned before petty sessional courts with the offence. Others paid reluctantly and with as much delay as possible. At best such arrangements were likely to place a considerable strain on family relationships. At the same time the need to rely upon children was often seen as degrading by aged men and women who had worked hard and honestly all their lives. Flora Thompson, discussing the problem in *Lark Rise to Candleford*, wrote, 'It was a common thing to hear ageing people say that they hoped God would be pleased to take them before they got past work and became a trouble to anybody.' This situation was confirmed by the researches of Charles Booth in the early 1890s – as in the Bosmere area of Suffolk, where it was noted that 'Many sons contribute to support of aged parents only when forced by law', while in the Midlands it was reported not only that children had to be compelled to contribute, but also that they sometimes even moved away from the area 'to evade claim'. In the Eastern Counties, too, 'Quarrels frequently arise between children as regards giving the help. Parents are unwilling to ask help from children and expect little.' And from Chipping Sodbury in Gloucestershire came the comment, '[The] Aged prefer a pittance from the parish (regarded as their due) to compulsory maintenance by children; compulsion makes such aid very bitter.'[13]

The amount of parish assistance provided for old people was pathetically small. In the Bicester Poor Law Union in Oxfordshire during the 1870s people living alone were receiving only 2s a week and two loaves during the 1870s; some were even restricted to 1s a week and one loaf – an amount which must have been supplemented by the charity of friends or relatives if the recipient were to survive at all. For although children often could not afford monetary help to needy relatives, they might be able to supply vegetables from the garden or kindling for the fire. As George Edwards told the Royal Commission on the Aged Poor in April 1893, in rural Norfolk it was common for children to give their parents 'garden food; and the old lady would go and see after the children, and they would have their tea and dinner with them, so that they ... do render a large amount of assistance in kind'.[14] Elsewhere they might beg for money or goods from better-off neighbours, as was apparently the case in Caernarvonshire. Here it was said that old people often called at 'the farmers' houses, and ... seldom or [sic] ever leave without taking with them some little farm produce in the shape of potatoes, or milk, or oatmeal'.[15] In other cases even used tea leaves might be worth collecting from vicarage or manor house, together with bowls of soup in the winter months.

Yet despite such aid, it was a hard struggle to make ends meet. In South Warwickshire, 2s 6d a week out relief for single people or 5s for married couples was the norm as late as 1899. And at Great Milton in Oxfordshire, Herbert Samuel (later Viscount Samuel) recalled the poverty of many of the aged cottagers whom he met when he visited the village as an undergraduate in the early 1890s: 'All the old labourers and their wives, without exception, were "on the parish", receiving from the Poor Law 3s a week outdoor relief and some bread. The vicar, who was one of the people I saw, had confirmed this. The last entry in my note-book was: "Martha W.: 3s parish relief; 1s rent; almost starving".'[16] The sums were typical of amounts paid in most other rural unions up to 1900.

Another cause of bitterness among the aged was the attitude of relieving officers. These men were often delayed on their rounds through the villages and as a result old people waiting for their payments might have to stand about for hours, even during the winter, in order to be on hand when the relieving officer arrived at the distribution centre. If they missed him they had to wait another week before they could obtain further payment. At Southrepps in Norfolk, the distribution centre during the 1880s was a small shed. Here the poor widows and others gathered each week to receive 1s 6d in cash and a small quantity of flour. 'Sometimes a long wait in the wintry weather would have to be endured as the relieving officer came in a pony cart from Beckham [a parish a few miles away]'.[17] Yet most galling to many was the suspicion that the relieving officer kept applicants waiting not because of pressure of work but because of indifference to their plight. This treatment aroused the fury of the secretary of the Horspath Branch of the National Agricultural Labourers' Union in Oxfordshire and in March 1875 he attended the parish vestry meeting to protest that 'the poor tottering old people bent with age, were compelled to tramp to and frow for three hours on the Villege Green all weathers till the Releving Officer one of the greatest Vilens on Earth, came to Pay them the Paltry allowance. I am pleased to say regime was altred from the time I attended the Vestry Meeting.'[18] But the majority of old people were unable to find anyone to champion their cause despite the fact that one of the Poor Law Board's own medical inspectors complained of 'the brutality and insolence of relieving officers'.

Of course, certain of the more active men and women were also able to support themselves, either wholly or in part, by earning a little money at some light employment, perhaps given on charitable grounds by a farmer for whom they had previously worked. The anxiety of labourers to obtain work in old age is demonstrated by the relatively large numbers who continued in permanent employment after the age of sixty-five. In 1851 they numbered just over 72,000 or about 6½ per cent of the total male agricultural labour force; by 1901 they stood at 52,221, or about 8½ per cent of a much smaller total workforce.

And at the 1901 Census of Poulation agriculture was the only occupational group in which 20 per cent or more of its workers were aged fifty-five or over.[19] Sadly, as workers advanced in age, the level of wages paid to them was reduced. Thus in the Morpeth Union of Northumberland it was reported during the early 1890s: 'Aged men and women if strong enough, get farm work at 1s 6d a day ... shepherds and others staying for long are rarely turned off. Country work has diminished owing to less land being under the plough and less dairy work and breeding in uplands. In Morpeth women work in market gardens (1s a day), at charing (2s) or washing.' Similarly in the Brampton area of Cumberland field work or charing at 1s 6d or 2s a day were noted as customary for the older women, with 2s or 2s 6d a day paid to men for field work – turnip or potato hoeing, hedging, harvest work and stone breaking. But some earned much less, being paid according to one observer 'children's wages or food only'.[20]

A small number of the most fortunate might obtain a pension from a former employer or else be allowed to live in a rent-free cottage. Lord Valentia in Oxfordshire and the Duke of Bedford were but two employers who made these provisions, while during the 1870s and 1880s the Newdegate family in Warwickshire paid weekly pensions varying between 1s to 7s to elderly widows and other old people living on their estate.[21] There are other examples of aid provided in this way by the well-to-do, but unfortunately their help was only available to a minority of the needy.

Still more rarely, men might be able, by careful saving, to amass sufficient cash and property to give them independence in their later years. One such was John Wiggins, a labourer from Stanton Harcourt in Oxfordshire, who left nearly £800 in furniture, livestock, cash and property when he died in 1877. In his will he made provision for the rents of his properties to be paid over to his wife.[22] And J. F., a farm worker from Waterperry in the same county, was able to save up enough money to rent a 40-acre holding to run on his own account. He was in his early fifties before he was able to take the plunge, in 1888, and although he was still working as hard as he had when he was a labourer, he had the consolation of being 'his own master'.[23]

Friendly society payments or the tilling of a cottage garden or allotment were other ways in which old people managed to keep a precarious independence. Cultivation of a plot of land was a valuable boost to the food supply for as long as a man had strength enough for the digging, planting and harvesting involved. A few kept bees, chickens or a pig. But these occasional 'extras' were of themselves inadequate to support life and reluctant recourse to poor relief was also necessary, particularly during the winter months.

Nevertheless, in this manner the day of entry to the much-hated workhouse could be postponed or avoided by the aged, though they had little room for manoeuvre. Illness or the death of a partner could place the most provident in such serious financial difficulties – particularly with regard to rent – that life outside the walls of the 'House' became impossible. The attitude of many was probably summed up by the secretary of the Horspath Branch of the Labourers' Union when he wrote in the branch minute book: '... as long as Poor old Darby and Jone are alive they will manage to keep an Old Roof over their head on their out door half crown and loaf of stale Bread but if Either of the two is laid to Rest in the Parish Church yard there is no other Prospect for the [survivor?] than to end the long life of toil among Strangers and away from the Old familiar scenes and Surroundings.'[24] Sir George Crewe, in *A Word for the Poor Against the New Poor Law,* published in 1843, expressed much the same view: 'It is a melancholy sight to see the aged collected from thirty or forty parishes like a heap of cast-off, worn-out tools, to be buried alive in the solitude of a workhouse.'

Men were particularly vulnerable in this situation – as an examination of workhouse records and census returns quickly reveals. Thus at Blandford in Dorset, where men and women aged sixty-five or over formed between one-quarter and one-fifth of the total inmates at the time of the 1871 census, there were only four females recorded as opposed to fifteen males. Similarly at Kendal in Westmorland, where the aged comprised about one-sixth of all residents, the old women were outnumbered by the men in the ratio of one to five. Other country workhouses confirm the trend.

It was the unimaginative daily routine of workhouse life which old people dreaded most, plus the uninviting and stark character of the building itself. There were, indeed, many similarities between gaol and the workhouse, both in atmosphere and discipline. Thus, despite the existence of contrary legislation – passed as early as 1847 – most old married couples were still separated upon entry. In 1895 it was estimated that in the country as a whole, only about two hundred of them had 'persisted in claiming [the] bedrooms' which they were entitled to occupy jointly. Sidney and Beatrice Webb, discussing this in their *History of the English Poor Law,* concluded critically that:

> The oft-repeated excuse for noncompliance with what since 1847 had actually been the statute law – that practically no aged couples asked for or desired a separate apartment – was, we suggest, disingenuous and misleading. In some cases it seems to have been represented to the old people that they would have to live entirely in their bedroom, forfeiting their right to frequent, in the daytime, the general rooms for men and women respectively. In some cases, at least, the acceptance of a separate apartment would have entailed the giving up of smoking, as this was not permitted on the side of the workhouse in which the proposed apartment was situated.[25]

Likewise, until almost the end of the Victorian era, most paupers – like prisoners – were required to wear distinctive clothing or 'uniforms'. In 1865 it was said of one rural board of guardians that they clothed all the inmates of the Workhouse in a pronounced livery for their Sunday best, the men in white fustian and the women in blue serge, and expected them to go to Church or Chapel in procession like convicts. The Workhouse itself was not furnished much more comfortably than a farmer's barn with a load of straw in it.'[26] Indeed, at Braintree in Essex even thirty years later a uniform of corduroy suits was still worn by the men, a 'leading Guardian' remarking that he did not think 'men over sixty able to work should ... be "dressed up in fine clothes; they made a convenience of the Workhouse in the winter and went out in the spring".'[27]

Visiting times were strictly limited, while the inmates themselves were only allowed out at certain fixed intervals-perhaps once a fortnight or once a month. This restriction was a particularly bitter blow, emphasising the gaol-like ambience of the 'House'. As one labourer witness to the Royal Commission on the Aged Poor declared in February 1894, he considered that if the old people were 'allowed to go out on a Sabbath day ... to go to church or chapel where they thought proper', they would be more reconciled to their lot; 'it is the confinement that is the greatest evil'. In the following year the authorities did relax this particular rule and the 'well-behaved aged and infirm' were allowed to 'attend their own places of worship' on Sundays.

At mealtimes, except for the prayers which were read before breakfast and after supper each day, silence had to be observed. The food, although more plentiful than that available on out relief, was usually monotonous and unappetising. A typical example was the dietary authorised for the aged and infirm at Banbury workhouse in January 1892. Breakfast and supper each day consisted of bread, a little butter and weak tea (made with 1 oz of tea to ten pints of liquid and sweetened with ½ oz of sugar to 1 pint of tea). The midday dinner was, therefore, the only meal where variety was possible. On two days each week this consisted of pea soup and bread, on a further two days of meat pudding and vegetables, and on the remaining three days, cooked meat and vegetables (with 4 oz of meat for the men and 3 oz for the women). Any deviation from the set plan was frowned upon, although by the end of the century Local Government Board officials were cautiously encouraging guardians to improve the menus by offering a wider choice, including 'tea, cocoa, milk, sugar, butter, seed-cake, onions, lettuce, rhubarb or stewed fruit, sago, semolina and rice pudding'. It is not easy to decide how far their suggestions penetrated in the rural areas. The Minute Book of the Banbury Poor Law Union 28 October 1897 contains the recommendation that 'more Mutton and less Beef' be given to the aged and infirm and 'when practicable to have the meat Roasted'. 'Dough cakes with Sugar and Fruit' were to be substituted for bread and butter at 'Suppertime on Sundays and Fridays'.[28] Such alterations hardly indicate a dramatic improvement in dietary standards. Similarly in Okehampton workhouse in Devon the dishes provided in 1902 included boiled bacon, fish or meat pie and shepherd's pie to add to the usual diet of soup and boiled or stewed meat. And in order to emphasise still more clearly the 'less eligibility principle' tenders for food often drew a distinction between items intended for the inmates and those for the paid officials. In October 1899 at Banbury workhouse the cheese provided for the staff was quoted at 7½d a lb; for the inmates at 6d. Legs and shins of beef for the inmates cost 2½d per lb; 'officers' joints' were 7d per lb. It was small wonder that some of the older inmates complained of the toughness of the meat.

Unlike able-bodied paupers, old people were not usually given specific tasks to perform in the workhouse, such as stonebreaking or oakum picking or laundry work. They were merely provided with 'such light employment as would keep them from that idleness which would be much more irksome to them than light work'. This included chopping wood, gardening, cleaning the wards and yards and carrying out other domestic duties. But leisure activities to relieve the monotony of the daily routine were firmly restricted. Not until 1892 was a tobacco or snuff allowance explicitly authorised for all non-able-bodied paupers, although a circular issued by the President of the Local Government Board in the previous year had given sanction for the provision of newspapers and books for the aged. Yet reminiscences of poor law administration in late nineteenth-century Essex indicate all too clearly how sterile workhouse life still was. At Billericay in 1895 the poor law guardians were discussing their attitude towards aged inmates:

A member called attention to the aimless wanderings of old men about the grounds, and suggested the provision of garden plots to grow small salad stuff as an addition to their meals. Another member remarked that they 'had dominoes', the Chairman recalled trouble through their selling things (the trouble probably being connected with beer provided thereby), the Master would prefer not to have such plots in front of the House; and the Inspector said that if they could work it was the Master's duty to employ them for the benefit of the House and not their particular benefit ... At Chelmsford the 1895 impulse exhausted itself in the purchase of six new seats to replace broken ones in the old men's yard, nor was it until 1905 that they had seats in the grounds, though allowed, in 1901, to walk in the garden up to 5 p.m.; old people went to bed by seven at latest ... At Maldon use of the garden was obtained in 1895; the Master, probably relying on support from the Chairman, treated questions by a clerical Guardian contemptuously, saying that inmates were allowed there 'morning, noon and night', but had to admit that there were no seats; being handled gently by the cleric he thought he could find some, and did, even seats with backs, a 'funny' Guardian suggesting awnings to keep off the sun. This clerical Guardian in 1895 presented cushions for the use of old men in the day-room, who probably (as certainly at Dunmow) had only forms against a wall; the new Inspector in 1901 found the 'old fellows' so sitting in their day-room, 'bolt up-right'; in the same year he suggested purchase at Maldon of twelve Windsor chairs, on which the Board acted, and in 1906 supplied chairs for their bedrooms. Moreover, this Board, having spent £3 on replenishing the library, spent one shilling and fourpence per month on 'periodicals', for which later bound magazines, two halfpenny newspapers and a weekly local paper were substituted.[29]

At Wokingham in Berkshire, similarly, the Minute Book of the Poor Law Union reveals that a more liberal guardian proposed in December 1895 that 'overcoats be provided for all the aged men' who were fit enough to go out of the workhouse and that 'aged inmates be allowed to go out every fine day instead of being kept in during four days of the week'. After discussion both proposals were decisively rejected by the rest of the board. In this workhouse, even the newspapers and journals taken were carefully censored.

Such treatment meant that there was no consideration of inmates as *individuals;* at dinner-time each person was given 'a tin mug and tin soup-plate ... every mug and every plate exactly alike'. Just as painful to many was the breaking of the link with home – as Richard Jefferies pin-pointed when writing of an old labourer in a west country workhouse at the end of the 1870s. The old man felt cut off from all that was reassuring and familiar. Although the food was better than he had 'existed on for years ... it was not his dinner. He was not sitting in his old chair, at his own old table, round which his children had once gathered. He had not planted the cabbage, and tended it while it grew.' The dormitory in which he slept, although it was clean, was 'not his old bedroom up the worm-eaten steps, with the slanting ceiling, where as he woke in the morning he could hear the sparrows chirping, the chaffinch calling, and the lark singing aloft'. At home he was free to lift the latch of the garden gate and walk down the road when he wished. 'Here he could not go outside the boundary – it was against the regulations.'[30]

Even at Christmas and on other high days and holidays, when attempts were made to bring a little gaiety into the lives of inmates, the institutional atmosphere was difficult to eradicate. A girl who regularly spent Christmas with her grandparents, the master and matron of a small country workhouse at West Beckham in Norfolk, early in the twentieth century, provides an indication of conditions in a comparatively enlightened establishment:

Our presents duly presented and appreciated and breakfast over, it was time to go with granny on her Christmas rounds with a present for everyone – sweets for the children, tobacco for the men and tea and a cap and apron for the old ladies ... Then to the big kitchen to watch the preparations for dinner, which was served in the dining hall to all the able-bodied. Families were allowed to sit together, a great treat for them which I was too young to appreciate. The great range which cooked the great rounds of beef, and the great cauldron in which the yellow football-sized Christmas puddings were cooked, fascinated us, especially when they were hauled out of the copper on a pulley. My grandfather, father and the porter put on their aprons, sharpened their knives and carved the beef. Potatoes, greens and gravy were got ready, and then we were allowed to run backwards and forwards to the dining hall carrying loaded plates. Men and women were allowed a glass of stout or beer and the children lemonade ...

Tea for everyone in the dining hall – stacks of dripping toast made at the kitchen range, mugs of strong tea and sweet biscuits, which once again we helped to serve ... At last seven o'clock and the concert began. I loved the decorated stage, even the 'institution' smell was exciting to me ...

Many of the inmates had spent much of their lives at the House, and had their one or two songs which they always sang. They needed no asking, and grandfather would call on them in strict rotation.

Blind Jinny 'The Old Arm Chair'; Crutches Hardingham 'The Miner's Dream of Home'; Alden 'The Death of Nelson'; and so it went on, everyone singing the chorus. It seemed to me to go on for ever, but at last grandfather would say a prayer and goodnight. Everyone went to bed, the doors were locked and we returned to the back room for supper.[31]

But not all of the inmates accepted these junketings with humble gratitude; for some, bitterness at their position was the overwhelming emotion, and this other side of the coin is captured very clearly by George R. Sims in his narrative poem, 'In the Workhouse: Christmas Day', as the following verses show:

It is Christmas Day in the Workhouse,
And the cold bare walls are bright
With garlands of green and holly,
And the place is a pleasant sight;
For with clean-washed hands and faces,
In a long and hungry line
The paupers sit at the tables
For this is the hour they dine.

And the guardians and their ladies,
Although the wind is east,
Have come in their furs and wrappers,
To watch their charges feast;
To smile and be condescending,
Put pudding on pauper plates,
To be hosts at the workhouse banquet
They've paid for – with the rates.

Oh, the paupers are meek and lowly
With their 'Thank'ee kindly, mum's';
So long as they fill their stomachs,
What matter it whence it comes?
But one of the old men mutters,
And pushes his plate aside:
'Great God !' he cries; 'but it chokes me!
For this is the day *she* died.'

Sims then goes on to explain that the old man's wife had died because the parish had refused them relief. She had been 'Cruelly starved and murdered/For a loaf of the parish bread'.

Although only about 5 per cent of all old people in rural areas received poor law assistance in the form of indoor relief it was this that most of them dreaded and struggled to avoid. And it was against that background that the idea of old age pensions began to gain support. As early as 1878 the Revd William L. Blackley had put forward rather crude proposals for a contributory pensions scheme for male workers. Although his plan was investigated by a Parliamentary select committee in the mid-1880s it made little progress, foundering largely on the opposition of the friendly societies, who feared government competition, and also on general governmental indifference. It was not until 1891 that Joseph Chamberlain became the first leading politician to support the concept of a contributory pension scheme, which would provide, as he put it, for 'the veterans of industry'. Chamberlain considered that the existing relief system was unacceptable because it was 'pauperising, humiliating and deterrent'.[32] In November of that same year, the tireless social investigator, Charles Booth, also came forward with a proposal for 'universal, non-contributory, tax-supported pensions' in a paper read before the Royal Statistical Society. Although neither Chamberlain's nor Booth's ideas proved immediately acceptable, their cumulative influence, plus the growing evidence of need among the aged, meant that sooner or later something must be done. Finally, in 1906, shortly after their victory at the general election, the Liberal government promised that state pensions would be introduced. Two years later the promise was redeemed and the requisite legislation passed to bring in a system of non-contributory old age pensions.

To modern eyes the first payments appear extremely modest. The full weekly sum of 5s, payable to men and women aged seventy or over, was only available to those who had an income of up to £21 per annum (i.e. 8s per week) from other sources. For those with an additional income beyond this level, a sliding scale was introduced, reducing the pension from the basic 5s to nil for those whose income was more than £31 10s per annum (or 12s a week).

To most rural workers, however, the restrictions were matters of indifference. Very few labourers had a personal income of even £21 a year, and the vast majority, if they had anything at all, merely received a friendly society benefit of about 5s a week or a small pension paid on a free-will basis by a former employer. In such circumstances it is easy to understand the gratitude of these old men and their wives or widows when state pensions came into operation. Their reaction has been touchingly described by Flora Thompson, who as a post office clerk, was well placed to gauge the general response: 'When ... the Old Age Pensions began, life was transformed for such aged cottagers. They were relieved of anxiety. They were suddenly rich. Independent for life!

At first when they went to the Post Office to draw it, tears of gratitude would run down the cheeks of some, and they would say as they picked up their money, "God bless that Lord George!" (for they could not believe that one so powerful and munificent could be a plain "Mr") and "God bless you, miss!" and there were flowers from their gardens and apples from their trees for the girl who merely handed them the money.' This was no isolated reaction. At Rippingale in South Lincolnshire, John Holwell recalled the delight of his grandfather, a retired baker, when for the first time he 'went to draw the pension of five shillings dressed up in his Sunday best and with tears of joy'. The *Oxford Times* of 9 January 1909, published shortly after the pensions became payable on 1 January in that year, gives several similar examples. In North Oxford a pensioner 'turned to the postmaster on the receipt of his five shillings and wished to remunerate him for the trouble he had taken in seeing his application through. At least one postmistress is to be remembered in the will of a pensioner.' If such a small sum as 5s per week could be greeted in this fashion, the extent of the hardships endured by old people in pre-pension days becomes painfully clear. By 1913 three-fifths of the population over the age of seventy was in receipt of pensions, and in some agricultural counties, like Norfolk, Suffolk and Oxfordshire, the proportion was still higher. As Lloyd George himself said, this unexpectedly large demand showed how much poverty and destitution there was which was 'too proud to wear the badge of pauperism [and] would rather suffer from deprivation'.[33] But for old people in Victorian England there was no such aid, and there can be little doubt that despite the benefits of cheaper food, life for many remained harsh up to 1900. For those who failed to support themselves the workhouse – that 'dread institution' as John Holwell labels it – remained as a possible final destination[34] (see also Appendix E).

BREAKING THE LAW

From the contents of early personal diaries or journals ... it is possible
to form an impression of the kind of duties that occupied the bulk
of the rural constable's time. Most of the days consisted simply of
many hours of patrolling the long, unmade country roads, hot and
dusty in summer, muddy and wet in winter, on the chance that some
such incident as petty larceny, sheepstealing, drunkenness, or (a
common offence) 'riding without reins' might enliven the day's work.
The everyday offences were poaching, vagrancy, sheep-stealing and
drunkenness, and the supervision of public houses (which were then
open all day) constituted a great part of the daily work; and attention
had often to be given to cock-fighting or prize-fights. Vagrancy
continued well into the century to present much the kind of problem
that the Royal Commission of 1836–9 had described. A vast army of
tramps, thugs, poachers, and swindlers begged or peddled or thieved
their way from one market town to another, following the progress
of the fairs.

T. A. Critchley, *A History of Police in England
and Wales 900–1966* (1967)

It was in 1839, following the passage of the County Police Act earlier
in that year, that the first county constabularies were established. A
second rural police act, reinforcing the earlier legislation, was passed
in 1840. However, even before this, a small minority of parishes in
various parts of the country had taken action on their own account
to appoint professional policemen to supplement the work of the old
unpaid parish constables. These were areas where the crime rate was
already high and where gentry and farmers had banded together to
form protective associations. Two villages in which the initiative had
been taken in this fashion during 1833 and 1834 were Wymondham
and Ilingham in Norfolk, where four paid policemen had been recruited
from the Metropolitan force to patrol the two communities. In 1839
an acting magistrate for the area informed the Royal Commission on

a Constabulary Force of the beneficial effects: 'The sturdy mendicants, some dressed as sailors others in a disgusting state of nudity, who formerly infested the neighbourhood, have long disappeared, greatly to the comfort of the inhabitants, as many of the farmers' and labourers' wives, living in sequestered situations, have, in the absence of their husbands been obliged for safety to give these persons food or money: In the suppression of poaching, which leads man, step by step, to almost every other crime, the policemen in these two parishes have also been most useful.'[1] Similar private action had been taken at Stow-in-the-Wold, Gloucestershire, where two London policemen were also recruited to deal with mounting crime and the problem of vagrancy. The magistrates of the petty sessions at Stow informed the 1839 Royal Commission that prior to their action, sheep stealing had been so common that 'during the winter months, a sheep was stolen in the neighbourhood, on an average once a fortnight', but since the appointment of the police, only one sheep had been taken. 'Barn-breaking, house-breaking, poultry-stealing, stealing of farming implements, and the like are now of very rare occurrence.' The lodging-houses catering for vagrants had also been regulated and the result was a 'marked diminution in the number of these wanderers, by whom the neighbourhood was infested'. Even the 'disorder and robberies' which traditionally characterised the two great annual fairs held at Stow had been 'very materially' reduced.[2]

Nevertheless, the number of parishes prepared to act in this manner was always tiny, and over a large part of the country at the beginning of the Victorian era, crime stalked 'abroad with all but impunity'. Wolryche Whitmore, the high sheriff of Shropshire, was one of many who drew attention to the 'incendiarism to which large districts are exposed'; and 'the long unchecked career of the poacher, the robber of hen-roosts, and the perpetrators of those other petty thefts to which rural districts are exposed. [Many] exercise a species of tyranny over their poor neighbours.' A magistrate reporting from the Bilbury division of Gloucestershire at the end of the 1830s agreed: 'The constant depredations, such as sheep-stealing, horse-stealing, fowl-stealing, poaching, and even highway robbery, call loudly on the Legislature for interference.' In Cheshire, indeed, it was noted that 'commercial travellers and strangers who travel singly, otherwise than by public conveyances, and carry money about them, abstain from travelling after dark, for fear of robbery and violence; and ... farmers return from market in company from the like fear after dark'.[3]

Even travellers by sea were not exempt from attack, for if their boat were driven aground, people living on the coasts of Lincolnshire, Suffolk, Cornwall and Cheshire were ready to take every chance they had of plunder. A coastguard reporting from Aldburgh, Suffolk, declared that on two or three occasions when a small vessel had been wrecked 'opposite the villages of Bawdsey and Aldirton, the inhabitants came down in large numbers, and would have committed depredations, but for the protection afforded by the coastguard'.[4]

In these circumstances it might seem strange that only about half of the counties in England and Wales elected to take advantage of the first rural police legislation. But for those who declined to act, fear of the cost involved and perhaps a rather lower level of local crime proved the decisive factors. Then, too, in 1842, at a time of general political unrest associated with the Chartist movement, a new Parish Constables Act was passed, attempting, as one writer has said, 'to put new life into the old constabulary'. But this attempt to rely upon amateurs for a policing role proved unsuccessful – just as it had in the past. The calibre of men prepared to act was usually poor and since the appointment was a part-time one anyway, most of them tried to evade tasks which risked life and limb – or even the loss of a day's pay. For the small fees offered for police duty did not compensate for such risks.[5] Consequently, it was only in 1856, with the passage of a new County and Borough Police Act, that professional rural constabularies became compulsory throughout the country. Among the counties delaying their appointments to that time were Berkshire, Buckinghamshire, Derbyshire, Dorset, Kent and Somerset.

So it was not until the middle of the nineteenth century, with the appearance of efficient police forces, that the rural worker in many districts faced the likelihood of arrest and punishment for felonies or misdemeanours that he had committed. In the words of A. J. Peacock, during these earlier years he could 'steal his employer's fruit, corn or game almost with impunity. Stacks could be fired, farm buildings lit, animals maimed, fences destroyed, banks breached'.[6] Only when unrest reached a mass scale, as in the 'Swing Riots' of 1830, did public attention focus on this particular aspect of labouring life. At other times, punishments tended to be variable in their incidence though draconian in their application – for those unlucky enough to be caught. Thus it was not until 1832 that reformers succeeded in securing the abolition of capital punishment for horse, sheep and cattle stealing. Arson only ceased to be a capital offence in 1837, and even relatively minor thefts could be punished by transportation. At the Lent Assizes held at Oxford in 1840 a twenty-six-year-old labourer who stole a shovel, valued at 3s, was transported for life; it was noted that he had one previous conviction for felony. And at the Quarter Sessions held at Oxford in October of the same year, another labourer from Chinnor, charged with stealing 'five gallons of apples, one gallon of walnuts and Bergamy pears mixed, of the value of 3s.' was transported for ten years. Such cases were not isolated.

It is against this background, therefore, which also included the appointment and growing effectiveness of county police forces from the 1850s onwards, that lawbreaking in rural areas has to be considered. Throughout these years the most common offences were drunkenness, assault, poaching and petty larceny – plus in the later 1870s and early 1880s breaches of the new school attendance regulations, which were usually punished by small fines of 2s 6d or 5s per child. At Henley Petty Sessions in Oxfordshire, during the year 1880, about 22 per cent of the 150 cases heard were concerned with poaching, 18 per cent with assault, 15 per cent with petty theft, and 13 per cent with drunkenness. Breaches of the school attendance legislation accounted for around 9 per cent of the cases heard, and there was a sprinkling of other matters – such as highway offences, cruelty to animals, leaving a family chargeable on the poor rates, breaches of the contract of employment, malicious damage and one case of arson. Similarly at Ivinghoe Petty Sessions in Buckinghamshire during the same year, out of eighty-eight cases heard, 36 per cent involved breaches of the school attendance regulations, while for the rest drunkenness and poaching, including offences involving guns, each accounted for around 15 per cent of the total. Highway offences, willful damage to property, bastardy cases, the use of faulty scales by shopkeepers and petty larceny made up most of the remainder.[7] In the higher courts, on the other hand, theft was by far the most common single offence. To quote but one example, at Oxford Quarter Sessions during the year 1874, of thirty-six prisoners tried, no less than twenty-seven were charged with stealing various items, while three of the remainder were found guilty of embezzlement. And in the country as a whole by the early 1890s simple larceny formed over a quarter of all the cases reported.

Nevertheless, if these were the most usual types of crime committed in villages, there were always more serious matters arising from time to time, such as sheep stealing, maiming of animals, rioting and even murder. Certain of the crimes were committed in a desire to 'pay off' old scores against an unpopular employer or other member of the rural community. And although in the Victorian era they never reached the dramatic proportions of the early 1830s, their survival did indicate that the labourer was not entirely without means of expressing protest against unfair treatment by magistrates or farmers. Large-scale incendiarism in Essex and Suffolk in 1843, for example, was sufficiently significant for *The Times* to send a 'Special Commissioner' to visit the two counties in order to investigate the cause. He concluded that within the affected area the line of fires corresponded closely with that of low wages, and that incendiarism was being used as a protest against poverty, unemployment and the Poor Law.[8] Again, in 1851, when Caird conducted his tour of England he singled out Cambridgeshire and Huntingdonshire as infested with incendiarism, and noted that corn ricks were spaced widely apart in the fields to prevent the spread of fire. Indeed, according to the Chairman of the Quarter Sessions of the Isle of Ely, Cambridgeshire only adopted a county police force in 1851 because 'there were a great many fires, and a great deal of crime.'[9] He declared that within two years of the force's appointment things had much improved. Likewise in 1844 in East Suffolk the fact that 'Incendiary Fires were occurring almost every night' led the Chief Constable to appeal to the Home Secretary for permission to supply his police constables with firearms. That request was refused, but he was instructed instead to supply the Force with cutlasses; almost twenty years later the East Suffolk constabulary was still using these in the course of routine duties. Not until 1863 was it officially decided to withdraw them from service except 'in extreme cases', as contrary to general police regulations.[10]

Although in the second half of the nineteenth century cases of arson did diminish in East Anglia – a region where they had been especially prevalent – elsewhere the number of indictable offences known to the police did not decline. And according to the Judicial Statistics, over the five-year period 1888–92 inclusive there were, for instance, 123 persons charged with setting fire to crops, plantations and heaths, or of attempting to do so. Over the five-year period 1865–69 the comparable figure had been seventy-three, and ten years earlier, in 1855–59, the level had been only sixty-six. Many of these later fires were probably the work of vagrants or vandals rather than of labourers settling old grievances. Nevertheless, even in the 1870s fire raising was occasionally used as a form of protest. At Carlton Curlieu and Kibworth in Leicestershire during 1870 threatening letters were found tied to the hedge near to the scene of rick fires. One of them expressed the arsonist's intentions in no uncertain terms: 'If you don't raise wages this week, you won't have a chance next. If there is any Irish left here after this week they will have to have a fresh gaffer. This is the last week of low wages.' Clearly the crime was motivated both by resentment at the competition of migratory Irish workers, whose employment in the village was undermining the bargaining position of the regular labourers, and by low wages. Despite the offering of rewards the perpetrators were never discovered.[11] In December of the following year, the *Leicester Chronicle and Leicester Mercury* carried a report of stack fires at Hathern in the same county, which were also supposed 'to have been the work of an incendiary'. Shortage of water had made the tackling of the blaze difficult and it had been visible for 'miles around'. Once again, the culprits were not discovered. And in Dorset during the depressed years of the 1880s and 1890s there were accounts of fires started by men concerned with getting their own back on a way of life that offered them no prospects – 'assailed by a misfortune they cannot resist' – while as late as 1914 in two North Essex villages stacks built by black-leg labour during a dispute were set alight.[12]

Arson was one crime which could be used as a social protest. Sheep stealing with, more rarely, sheep and cattle maiming, formed yet another. Of course, sheep stealing also had the advantage of providing meat for the family or, if suitable contacts were available, for sale. At Ampthill in Bedfordshire, where sheep stealing was particularly prevalent in 1834, it was thought to be the work of a gang aiming to sell in the London market. The Eastern Counties, notably the marshlands of Norfolk were justly famous for their fine flocks and it was here that the crime reached a peak, although virtually every country district felt its effects at one time or another. It had its 'high season' during the winter months when the sheep were full grown and nights were long. The East Anglian press contained numerous accounts of the offences committed, as on 30 May 1834, when the *Cambridge Chronicle* reported that despite the offering of rewards, the crime was increasing 'both in extent and audacity', while on 7 November of the same year, it was observed of the Wisbech area: 'The system of thieving in this neighbourhood seems to be so well organised that nothing comes amiss or to have [*sic*] any apprehension of detection.' By the 1840s the crime had become common all through the Eastern Counties, including Huntingdonshire, Cambridgeshire, Suffolk and Bedfordshire. At the Cambridgeshire Assizes of March 1846 no less than twelve men were charged with sheep stealing, receiving sentences ranging from ten years' transportation to six months' hard labour.[13] But even Oxfordshire, a county not particularly noted for this crime, had its share of offenders. At the Summer Assizes in 1840, six men were so charged, of whom four were acquitted. One of the two found guilty, a man of fifty-nine, was sentenced to fifteen years' transportation, while the other, aged twenty-two, received ten years' transportation. At the Assizes held in the previous spring there had been four sheep stealing cases heard at Oxford, in one of which the defendant was acquitted, in another he could not be traced, in a third the prosecution was not proceeded with, and in the fourth a sentence of fifteen years' transportation was imposed.

But where sheep stealing stepped undeniably into the realms of social protest was when it was accompanied by acts of wanton destruction and defiance, as at Heckington, Lincolnshire, where the thieves nailed their trophies' heads to the church door 'for bravado', and at Tempsford in Bedfordshire, where in 1836 sheep were taken and a note left affixed to the gate:

> Sir, your mutton's very good
> And we are very poor,
> When we have eaten this all up
> We'll then come and fetch some more.[14]

Nevertheless, most cases of sheep stealing were inspired not by vengeful or defiant motives – or at least not by these alone – but by hunger and poverty. Hunger made people reckless even when, as was the case up to 1832, sheep stealing was a capital offence. In any case, transportation, a sentence imposed for this crime until 1853 (when transportation was replaced by penal servitude in most cases) was almost as big a wrench as death for uneducated people who had no way of communicating with loved ones overseas.

One Wiltshire farm worker, named Shergold, who had killed a sheep for food despite the risks involved is described by W. H. Hudson in *A Shepherd's Life*. It was in mid-December and the man was helping to drive a flock from Chitterne on the Salisbury Plain to the nearby village of Tilshead.

> It was a cold, cloudy night, threatening snow, and so dark that he could hardly distinguish the dim forms of even the hindmost sheep, and by and by the temptation to steal one assailed him. For how easy it would be for him to do it! ... And he thought of what a sheep would be to him and to his hungry ones at home until the temptation was too strong, and suddenly lifting his big, heavy stick he brought it down with such force on the head of a sheep as to drop it with its skull crushed, dead as a stone. Hastily picking it up he ran a few yards away, and placed it among the furze-bushes, intending to take it home on his way back, and then returned to the flock.[15]

Shergold and the rest of the sheep arrived at Tilshead in the small hours, and after receiving his pay for the drive, he walked quickly to the place where he had hidden the sheep. But by then day was breaking and he realised that if he walked into Chitterne with a heavy burden on his back people would wonder what he was carrying. Consequently he dragged the carcase to a small hollow in the downs and covered it with dead bracken and herbage, intending to collect it later. But that afternoon snow began to fall and he dared not go to recover his sheep, since his footprints might betray him. As he waited during the next hungry days for the thaw to come, his feelings can be imagined: 'even that poor comfort of sleeping or dozing away the time was denied him, for the danger of discovery was ever present to his mind, and ... it was his first crime, and he loved his own life and his wife and children, crying to him for food ... Roast mutton, boiled mutton – mutton in a dozen delicious forms – the thought of it was as distressing, as maddening, as that of the peril he was in.' Eventually, after a fortnight, a thaw set in but when he went with some trepidation to look for the carcase he found it had been pulled to pieces and the flesh devoured by dogs and foxes.

In Dorset, too, sheep stealing was a major problem in the 1840s, with at least sixty to seventy sheep stolen each year, while in Hampshire there were seventy-two cases of sheep stealing in 1847 and eighty-three in 1848. However, in the case of this latter county, the appointment of the county constabulary was felt to be improving the situation by the beginning of the next decade. A similar point was made with regard to Essex, where the Chief Constable declared in 1853 that in the year before the police force was established in 1840 'in two divisions out of 14 in the county ... 140 sheep were stolen in the year ... that number has never been taken in the whole county subsequently'.[16]

The national statistics for the crime bear out this trend. In the twelve months ending 29 September 1857, 649 offences of sheep stealing were reported by the police; by 1874 the figure had fallen to 210 and in 1892 to 119. Similarly, sentences had eased; in the late 1830s around three-quarters of those convicted were sentenced to transportation, whereas by the mid-1870s less than one-quarter were being sent to penal servitude.[17]

Cattle maiming was a rarer but more hideous form of social protest, and one which, like sheep stealing, declined during the period. The judicial statistics suggest that in 1874 thirty-nine cases of killing and maiming cattle were reported; but by the twelve months ending 29 September 1892 the number had fallen to twenty-eight. This crime, when it occurred, was particularly characteristic of the marshlands of the eastern counties. The *Cambridge Chronicle,* for example, spoke in November 1834 of the 'diabolical practice of cutting and maiming cattle', which it claimed had in western Norfolk 'in some degree taken the place of incendiarism'. And in February 1841 the tails were cut off two cows belonging to a farmer at Outwell, while the leg of another was 'nearly severed'.[18] Most of the cases reported followed the same pattern.

Rioting and similar forms of violent opposition, on the other hand, never reached the proportions of 1830 during the Victorian years – despite the alarm felt by some magistrates during the Chartist agitation of the 1840s. At Trowbridge, Wiltshire, during January 1840, for example, there were fears that 'upwards of *ten thousand* persons' were planning to hold a rally to petition for clemency for three Chartist leaders who had been sentenced to death for high treason, and that some of those present would 'take large sticks, staves, Bludgeons, and more than probable even Fire Arms'. And on 11 February in the same year the Chief Constable of Wiltshire wrote to the Home Secretary to inform him that 'the Chartists attempted to hold a Meeting at 1 o'clock yesterday at Bradford[-on-Avon] but on one of the Constabulary force approaching the Speaker (a person named Potts) he ran off and the people quietly dispersed'.[19] In the event, Chartism in the rural areas never assumed the threatening aspect that it did in the larger towns, and the much-feared riots did not occur. However, there were other sporadic disturbances – as at Folksworth in the eastern counties during 1844, when fences were thrown down in an anti-enclosure action, while the implementation of the 1834 Poor Law Amendment Act caused revolt in some quarters. Indeed, as late as 1853 Sir John Walsham, a poor law inspector, informed the Select Committee on the Police that the rural police had played a valuable part in dealing with unrest in Essex and Suffolk workhouses: 'My firm persuasion is, that these workhouses might have been pulled down or nearly destroyed, if we had not had the assistance of the police.'[20]

Yet if the offences discussed above aroused alarm among well-to-do members of rural society, it was the game laws which caused the greatest friction between them and their poorer fellow villagers. Although the Game Act of 1831 had eased and simplified earlier punishments for daytime poaching, night poaching still carried with it imprisonment or transportation 'without the option of a fine'. As a result of the 1831 Act, there were two basic daytime poaching offences. The first was killing game (not rabbits) without a certificate, which was punishable by a fine of £5. The second was trespass in search of game, rabbits, snipe, woodcock, quail or landrail, for which there was a maximum fine of £2. 'The fine could be increased to £5 for poaching in an armed gang of five or more, or for refusing to give one's correct name and address.'[21] Yet despite the changes, the game laws were bitterly resented by virtually all ordinary country men and women. As Sidney Smith wrote, 'It is utterly impossible to teach the common people to respect property in animals bred the possessor knows not where – which he cannot recognise by any mark, which may leave him the next moment.' And he added, 'The same man who would respect an orchard, a garden, or a hen-roost scarcely thinks .he is committing any fault at all in invading the game covers of his richer neighbour.'[22]

Similarly, the Select Committee on the Game Laws of 1873 noted that 'whereas little or no sympathy is given by any class to the night poacher, the man who kills a hare or a rabbit in the daytime is not looked upon with any disfavour by his equals, or by society in general'.

Concern for the preservation of game extended, in the case of some landowners, to *general* prohibitions against trespass for any purpose. Typical of the notices issued in this fashion was one produced in respect of Hackwood Park, Hampshire, in August 1845, which warned that 'all Persons found trespassing in any of the Woods, Plantations, Coppices, or Grounds belonging to the Right Honourable Lord Bolton, whether for NUTTING, or any other Purpose, will be prosecuted with the utmost Rigour of the Law'.[23] But even more disturbing was the discovery by the Home Office in 1844 that in many rural areas 'so much irregularity' had been found in the trial of game law offences before country magistrates that 'a number of pardons and mitigations of sentences' had to be issued.[24] Samuel Phillipps, an Under Secretary of State at the Home Department, informed the Select Committee on the Game Laws in 1845 that in Bedfordshire 'there were four game cases in which there had been illegal sentences, the prisoner having been committed for three months when the maximum of imprisonment could only have been two'. In other cases 'too great a penalty [was] imposed. For instance, under the trespass clause in the Game Act, where 40s is the maximum of penalty, £3 have been imposed. In other cases the imprisonment has been too long with reference to the penalty.' In all, Phillipps claimed there had been '40 discharges out of prison, under illegal sentences, and 14 commutations of sentences besides' as a result of the Home Office's investigations.[25]

Popular hostility to the game laws was, however, aggravated in 1862 by the passage of the Poaching Prevention Act, which allowed the police to search any person on the road or in a public place whom they suspected of poaching or of having in their possession a gun, nets, or snares for the purpose of killing or taking game. Magistrates could order the confiscation of a convicted poacher's nets, snares and gun. But what most villagers disliked was the increased right of search the Act gave to the police and also the way the legislation could be turned to obtain convictions for minor thefts, such as the taking of pieces of wood for firing or even of traditional perquisites like turnips, carried away by men and women who had been cutting them to feed to the sheep. The bitter feelings to which this measure gave rise were expressed by the agricultural trade union leader, Joseph Arch, in evidence before the Select Committee on the Game Laws in 1873, when he declared:

The day that the Poaching Prevention Act of 1862 became law was a black day for the labourer; from that time onwards he might at any hour be subjected to the indignity of being assailed and searched by the police officer ... Before this Act passed a working man might trudge home at night in peace, carrying his little basket or his bundle of perquisites; but after it became law the insulting hand of the policeman was hard and heavy upon him. 'Twas as if so many Jacksin-the-Box had been set free to spring out on the labourer, from the hedge, or the ditch, or the copse, or the field.[26]

Arch also added that if he saw a hare or rabbit on the high road he would feel quite free to kill it, since it did not belong to anyone in particular: 'To see hares and rabbits running across his path is a very great temptation to many a man who has a family to feed ... If a man sees unstamped temptation running along before him on four legs he'll run after it on his two, and will knock it over if he can, and take it home and make a feast of it. I should not consider him a guilty person if he did, but he would be run in to prison and run up before the bench in no time, if the police officers or the gamekeeper caught him.'

Arch's complaints about the way the 1862 Act was applied were supported by other witnesses to the 1873 Select Committee, including Mr W. S. Walpole, an attorney from Beyton near Bury St Edmunds, who quoted several cases where labourers had been stopped by the police without justification. He concluded that 'the police very frequently stop and search without reasonable and probable cause to suspect', and also called for game law cases to be transferred from the magistrates in petty sessions to stipendiary magistrates. For one of the complaints of labourers was that if they were brought before the courts their case was likely to be heard by magistrates who were themselves, as major landowners, interested in the preservation of game. Yet, despite the appeals for change, nothing happened and the 1862 Act remained on the statute book in the later twentieth century.

There is little doubt that the character of the men charged with poaching also had a role to play in the punishment they received – as an examination of petty sessions minute books soon indicates. Thus at Henley Petty Sessions in October 1880, three men were charged with game offences – two with 'unlawfully' using a wire to snare hares, and the third with 'trespassing in search of game and conies'. One of the men was fined £5 with 13s costs and in default two calendar months' imprisonment with hard labour. A second was fined £1, including costs, and in default fourteen days' hard labour, and the third, who was charged with the trespass, was fined only 2s, with 8s costs or in default seven days' hard labour. But many of those convicted particularly in the 1850s and 1860s, preferred to go to prison rather than pay a fine. Indeed, given the low level of farm wages at this time, it is doubtful whether they had enough money to pay a fine anyway. Typical of those making that choice was Thomas Buckett of Henley-upon-Thames, who was fined 3s with 12s costs for committing 'a trespass by being in the daytime ... upon a certain piece of land in the occupation of Robert Outhwaite there in search of Game'. Instead of paying up, Buckett preferred the alternative of fourteen days' imprisonment with hard labour. But his brushes with the Henley magistrates at this time seem to have been generally unfortunate, for on 3 January of the following year he was charged with breaking 'down a piece of ivy to the value of 1d' on 21 December – no doubt for Christmas decorations. For this tiny 'theft' he was again sentenced to fourteen days' imprisonment with hard labour.[27]

Yet if men like Buckett were casual poachers who were driven to the action by a desire to feed their families, there were always a few who were attracted by the excitement of the chase and perhaps by the money that

could be earned by illicit sales. Such men became professionals – like a
Filkins horse dealer named Thatcher whom George Swinford knew: 'Mr
Thatcher was also a noted poacher. He always kept some good dogs which
used to lie in the bed of his trap as he was going around the countryside,
and if he saw a hare in a field, he would send them after it.'[28] It was this kind
of 'professional' who was usually involved in night poaching – an offence
which even at the end of the century carried with it severe punishments.
Thus two men charged at Ivinghoe Petty Sessions in Buckinghamshire
with night poaching in May 1888 were each committed to gaol for three
calendar months' imprisonment with hard labour and 'at the expiration to
find two sureties in £5 with themselves each in £10 that they will not so
offend again for a year and in default of finding such sureties to be further
imprisoned for six cal. months each'.[29] Nevertheless, despite the severity
of the penalties a minority of men were clearly not discouraged. In 1862
there were 888 prosecutions for night poaching and destroying game in
England and Wales – out of a total of 10,187 game law prosecutions; in
1870 the totals were 522 and 10,580 respectively. At the later date the
1862 Poaching Prevention Act had also accounted for 904 prosecutions
– but in both years 'trespassing in daytime in pursuit of game' was the
major category, accounting for 9,144 prosecutions in 1862 and 9,084 in
1870.[30] Even in 1892, when the number of game law prosecutions had
fallen to around 8,500, nearly seven-eighths of them were for the daytime
pursuit of game.[31]

Some of the 'professional' poachers prided themselves on their skills,
like 'Blacky' Tapper, who was said to be one of the best poachers in the
south of England. He was able to walk innocently across a field setting a
dozen hare snares without any spectator being able to detect the operation.
Perhaps appropriately, he was described as 'a small, bent man with keen
eyes and abnormally long arms: holding the snare, complete with "tealer"
or "pricker" arranged in his hand he would drop it on a run and, with
almost unnoticeable stoop, place the peg and tread it in as he walked
along'. Every snare that he set would be exactly right. 'He used to say that
hares ran better in the Kennet Valley than anywhere between Lincolnshire
and Brighton. With the aid of several bystanders on whom they called in
the Queen's name, four policemen managed to arrest him at Ilsley Sheep
Fair, handcuff him and load him into a tip-up dung cart.' But Blacky refused
to go quietly and dragged the chain of his handcuffs down the sergeant's
face, skinning it from forehead to chin.[32]

Occasionally this sort of violence spilled over into battles between
gamekeepers and poachers – as on the estate of Mr C. S. Hope near
Canterbury, where in December 1886 the head keeper was shot and
killed by a gang of poachers. Again in July 1891, seven of the Duke of
Devonshire's keepers came upon a gang of eight poachers at work with

nets. A desperate struggle took place. 'One keeper was fearfully battered about the head, and three others were severely injured. One poacher was left insensible on the field. The others retreated taking their nets with them.' In all, over the period November 1880 to July 1896 there were at least thirty serious affrays involving poachers and keepers in various parts of the country. In seventeen of the cases either poachers or keepers were killed and in the remaining thirteen severe injuries were sustained. It was this kind of situation which caused one anti-Game Law writer to speak of 'The Blood Tribute' of game preservation.[33]

Another 'professional' who was, at least in his own estimation, the 'King of the Norfolk Poachers', had as deep an attachment to the poaching life as had 'Blacky' Tapper: 'Poaching is something like drug taking – once begun no goen back, it get hold of you. The life of a Poacher is any thing but a happy one, still it is exciting at times, and the excitement go a long way to sothe his conscience if it trubble him … I loved the excitement of the Job. Beside you had the satafaction of knowen that you had got Keepers and Police beat, and that went a long way towards recompence for the danger and risk run.' This man began his poaching career whilst still a boy, snaring rabbits for sale to a local fish hawker. Eventually he was caught and sentenced to a month's imprisonment in Norwich Gaol – an event which served more to confirm him in his path of crime than to divert him from it. After almost sixty years he described his emotions as he was escorted by a policeman from his home village to the gaol: 'I shall never forget what I felt when I first saw that gloomy Place, and I was just fit to cry, but held back my tears some how.'

Once inside he was made to take a bath before being dressed in a prison uniform 'covered all over with the broad Arrow and a number to wear on my Jacket'. He was then taken to his small, stone-flagged cell and settled in for the night with bread and water for his first meal. The next morning and each succeeding day he had to rise at 6 a.m., dress, make up his bed and then scrub the floor and table of his cell. Breakfast lasted from 7.30 a.m. to 8 a.m. and was followed by half-an-hour in the chapel.

'Nine o'clock we were marched off to the Weel room.' Working on the tread wheel was exhausting. 'It was like walking up steps and never getting any higher, but very hard work and we was kept at it from nine till twelve. Then came diner, which was one pint and a half of stirabout, composed of one pint of oatmeal, and half a pint of maze meal put in the oven and baked. We were put on the Weel again from one o'clock till four of the afternoon, then we were set to pick okum till eight, wen we went to bed.'

The young prisoner's days continued to be spent in much the same fashion for the remainder of his sentence, except that after the first fortnight the food at least was improved, as he received a little cooked beef or bacon to supplement the earlier monotonous diet. From time to time, too, the chaplain visited him and left religious tracts: 'He would some times come and se you, to tell you the enormity of your crime ... I used to hate the sight of him.'[34]

Yet if offences against the game laws were a fairly common cause of imprisonment for countrymen, petty theft was a still more frequent reason. Throughout the nineteenth century punishments for larceny were severe. Nevertheless, as with the Game Law cases mentioned earlier, variations did occur and it would seem that the character and personality of the individual charged had some influence on the punishment received. At Oxford Quarter Sessions in April 1840 one farm worker who was found guilty of stealing 'four tame fowls' valued at 4s, was sentenced to three months' hard labour in the house of correction. A second man found guilty of stealing a pair of stockings was imprisoned for six months with hard labour; and a third, who had an earlier conviction for housebreaking, was sentenced to seven years' transportation for taking 'one peck of barley of the value of one shilling'. Nor was it only in the earlier Victorian years that such sentences were handed out. At the Quarter Sessions held in April 1874 at Oxford a female labourer who had stolen a bushel of oats and two pecks of barley was sentenced to four calendar months' hard labour, and later in the year the same Quarter Sessions sentenced a forty-eight-year-old labourer, with one previous conviction to '9 calendar months at hard labour' for stealing coconut matting of unspecified value. Countless similar examples could be provided from the records of courts at all levels throughout the country.

Not even children were exempt from the spasmodic severity of the British judicial system. Thus on 21 July 1864 two boy labourers from the village of Northstoke, Oxfordshire, were convicted of stealing 'four pounds of Bacon and one four pound loaf of Bread of the value of three shillings and sixpence' and were sentenced by the Henley bench to twenty-one days' imprisonment with hard labour. And at Great Marlow Petty Sessions in Buckinghamshire two boys found guilty of stealing turnip tops valued at 1s were each given the alternative either of paying a fine, costs and compensation, amounting to £1 9s 3d, or of facing one calendar month's imprisonment with hard labour. The sentences were imposed in April 1871 and in the event only one of the boys was able to pay his fine. The other – as was hardly surprising for a farm labourer's son – could not raise such a substantial sum of money and so presumably was forced to serve a term in prison.

Other frequent causes of country people appearing before the courts were drunkenness and assault. For excessive drinking was common among most labouring men in the nineteenth century. A few committed one or other of the varied minor offences that are carefully noted in the petty sessions records. Perhaps there was a failure on the part of small shopkeepers to have carts marked with a legible nameplate or they may have been found in possession of scales that did not register the correct weight. This particular offence was, in fact, so common that *Punch* ironically remarked: 'Highwaymen are extinct, and indeed where is the fun of risking your life when you can rob as you please simply by opening a shop and using false weights and measures'.[35] In some instances there were breaches of the highway regulations – as at Ivinghoe in January 1881, when James Harrowell was fined 1s with 9s costs, or in default seven days' imprisonment, for 'being asleep while in charge of a cart'.[36] Then there was the small boy charged before Moreton Petty Sessions in Berkshire during May 1869 with allowing two horses to graze illegally on the side of the road. The police sergeant who caught the youngster admitted that he had observed the scene of the 'crime' for over twenty minutes before approaching the boy to ask him the name of the owner of the horses. The leisurely nature of this piece of policework indicates that in that part of rural Berkshire at least, mid-Victorian crime was at a low level. The case ended with the imposition of a 1s fine, plus costs of 14s 6d.[37]

Finally, for the annually hired farm worker there was the possibility of being charged with a breach of the contract of employment if he absconded from his job before the term was up. And in the years before the passage of the Master and Servant Act in 1867, a prison sentence could be given for this offence. Even after that date in 'aggravated cases' imprisonment could be imposed – as for example, at Salisbury, Wiltshire, where a Coombe Bassett labourer who absconded from his employment in April 1870 was sentenced to two calendar months' imprisonment with hard labour.[38] Not until the 1875 Employer and Workmen Act was a breach of the contract of employment made a civil offence for both of the parties, although a breach by the master had always been treated as a civil matter.

Yet, despite the range and variety of crimes discussed, most villages were peaceful places, especially in the second half of the nineteenth century, when the county police forces had become established. In such small communities the 'retreats and opportunities for delinquency' were few and limited, while the pursuits and character of the inhabitants were 'matters of notoriety and interest; not to be known is to be an object of inquiry or suspicion; in a word, every one is the police of his neighbour, and unconsciously exercises over him its most essential duties'.[39] The hierarchical character of village society reinforced this trend. Edwin Grey, writing of Harpenden in the 1860s and 1870s, describes the typical picture as regards rural lawbreaking in mid- and later Victorian England:

I should say that the village, and indeed the whole of the parish, was, in the days of my boyhood and youth, free from any serious crime, for I can remember nothing more startling than an occasional poaching affray, or fowl-stealing case, a public-house fight, a neighbour's squabble, or maybe a few cases of petty theft, principally of fruit from some nearby orchard ... Our police force at this time consisted of one man – PC Best – the whole of the parish being under his jurisdiction. As far as I can remember him 'George Best the Bobby' was a very pleasant personage, seemingly by no means depressed or worried by the responsibility of his office, and when on his beat, attired in his official 'Top Hat', and with staff dangling at his side, he would, as he perambulated the various parts of his wide and scattered parish, be met with many a cheery greeting, not much signs of fear being evinced. Where 'Mister Best' detained his prisoners, or how he managed when he had arrested anyone, I cannot recollect. Probably he commandeered some conveyance and took them handcuffed straight off to St Albans gaol; anyhow, there was no Police Station, neither was there a detention room in his own little dwelling.[40]

The vast majority of country policemen, then, had nothing worse to fear than long hours of toil and tedium, with aching feet, boredom and blisters, and with the odd recalcitrant poacher or 'highway offender' to break the monotony. Or perhaps, as at Filkins in Oxfordshire, it would be checking up on the boys' cricket-playing activities that would help to fill in the day.[41] But none of these matters assumed serious proportions likely to disturb the even tenor of day-to-day life. In return for his labours. the constable received, in mid-Victorian times, a weekly wage of between 16s and 21s, plus a free uniform and, from 1873, a boot allowance as well. He was subjected to strict personal regulation by his superiors – including compulsory attendance at church on Sundays, and discouragement from entering public houses and beer-houses even during his brief leisure time. Nevertheless, despite these restrictions many young country workers found the career of policeman an attractive alternative to labouring on the land, and both urban and rural police forces burgeoned in consequence.

THE CHANGING SCENE: A CONCLUSION

Cynics may say that it was the parliamentary vote which gave the labourer his first real step upwards. It made him the most important of the three classes which constitute the agricultural interest, and, from that moment politicians have tumbled over, one another in their eagerness to secure his support. Be this as it may, there can be no doubt of his substantial progress since 1884. Most men of the class are still poorly paid; many are precariously employed and poorly housed; among all, poverty is chronic, and, though destitution is certainly rare, the dread of it is seldom absent. But, speaking generally, labourers in 1912 are better paid, more regularly employed, better housed, better fed, better clothed. They are better educated and more sober. Their hours of labour are shorter. They are secure of a pension for themselves and their wives in their old age. They can, if they choose, make their influence felt in the government of their parish, the administration of their county … Their wives and children are no longer driven by necessity to labour in the fields.

R. E. Prothero (later Lord Ernle),
English Farming: Past and Present (1912)

Although Lord Ernie wrote these words in the early years of the twentieth century, most of his observations were equally applicable to the late Victorian era. Despite the continued lack of amenity and opportunity in the lives of many country people – the deplorable housing and the still low wages – much had been achieved as compared to the first years of the Queen's reign, even on the thorny questions of poor relief and help for the aged. Indeed, the very structure of rural society was itself changing, with the decline in the numbers of rural craftsmen and the massive outflow of labourers from the land during the second half of the nineteenth century. By 1900 country dwellers were a minority of the population of England and Wales rather than the majority they had been in 1837. In the new century these trends were to be intensified, especially as the ravages of the First World War undermined still further the traditional values of the old deferential rural society.

Already, by the closing years of the nineteenth century, men with ambition had grown to despise farm work and had begun to look instead to the wider opportunities of employment in the factories, on the railways and docks, and in the urban police forces. Although when they reached their new homes many found that the higher wages to be earned were counterbalanced by poor living accommodation and, for the unskilled, periodic unemployment, few chose to go back. They preferred the greater social freedom and the bright lights to their former way of life.

Some observers blamed the improvement in school provision for this attitude – like the Northamptonshire landowner, Sir Hereward Wake, who in about 1911 complained bitterly of the reluctance of women to undertake work on the land: 'Nowadays, with their high heels and pretty hats and hobble skirts ... they are not at all anxious to do any manual labour in the fields, or their own allotment gardens for that matter ... I think we have to thank the Education Acts for this alteration in the character of the rising generation of our rustic females. The teachers are town and city bred for the most part, and look upon manual labour, any work in fact which causes the worker to perspire, as beneath the dignity of a twentieth century "laidy".'[1] And in Lincolnshire a former schoolmaster remembered that 'When the children got a little education, they began to look down on their parents' condition, and I have often heard boys say: "I'll never be a farmer's drudge if I can help it." In this man's experience, 'the smartest and best of the young men found employment upon the Railways; a few in the Post Office; and many in the Rural Police ... I taught a village school myself several years and nearly all the boys passing through that school were lost to agriculture.'[2]

Equally, those young men who chose to stay on the land were more interested in the new possibilities of a better house, an adequate water supply, or higher pay than in the preservation of the old ways. 'Candles and thatch had never gone well together; in a dry summer, when it was impossible to collect rainwater, some villages, especially those on high chalk, suffered severely ... Picturesque old cottages had no charm for the young farm workers and they moved out, if they could, abandoning the home of their forbears.'[3]

Conditions were, of course, by no means uniform throughout the country and in a few cases villages near to large towns increased their populations from the end of the century, as they were turned into dormitories for urban workers. Even the smaller towns developed suburbs, while thanks to the new cheap bicycle, country people had a readier access to market towns for shopping. Loyalty to the village shop was undermined as women took advantage of the wider choice and lower prices available a few miles away. Flora Thompson described this subtle process of change in the small town of Buckingham – or Candleford as she preferred to name it: 'Candleford Green was at that time a separate village. In a few years it was to become part of Candleford. Already the rows of villas were stretching out towards it; but as yet the green with its spreading oak with the white-painted seats, its roofed-in well with the chained bucket, its church spire soaring out of trees, and its clusters of old cottages, was untouched by change.'[4] But that situation was not long to persist. Even in Candleford Green demand for the old solid, handmade productions 'into which good materials and many hours of patient skilled craftsmanship had been put' was to decline. They were replaced by new and cheaper machine-made goods which were also fashionable 'and most people preferred them on that account'. Some of the more perceptive craftsmen moved with the times, like the blacksmiths mentioned by Mrs Thompson who painted above their shop door 'Motor Repairs a Speciality', but most were helpless before the mechanised production of urban industries. And this, writ large, was to be the history of the twentieth century-the relentless progress of the machine at the expense of traditional methods and craftsmanship. Yet it was through such mechanisation that the material living standards of the vast majority of the population of England and Wales were to be raised so dramatically after 1900. Among those benefiting were the people of the countryside. And although in the process of change they may have lost some of the warmth, good humour, fellowship and pride in individual skills which characterised life in the earlier rural communities, it is unlikely that many present-day villagers would wish to change places with their Victorian forebears.

APPENDICES

Appendix A
Budgets

From: *The Royal Commission on Labour: The Agricultural Labourer,*
Parliamentary Papers 1893–94, XXXV.
(a) Edward Wood, Foreman of Farm Labourers, Bromyard, Herefordshire,
November 1892.

Budget
Family consists of man, wife, one boy working on farm, and four
children aged 9, 7, 5, 2. One lad at service in gentleman's stable.
Two girls in domestic service.

Wages			
Self		16s.	0d.
Boy		6s.	0d.
	£1	2s.	0d.
One Week's Expenditure			
11 loaves of bread at 5d.		4s.	7d.
1 quarter flour			5d.
7 lb meat at 7d.		4s.	1d.
3½ lb cheese at 6d.		1s.	9d.
2 lb butter at 1s. 3d.		2s.	6d.
½ lb tea		1s.	0d.
6 lb sugar at 2d.		1s.	0d.
4 packets cocoa at 2d.			8d.
2 lb rice at 2d.			4d.
1 lb candles			5d.
2 quarts lamp oil			4½d.
Club money			11½d.
		18s.	1d.

One Year's Clothing &c.

7 pairs boots	£2	12s.	od.
Clothing	£3	os.	od.
4 tons coal at 20s.	£4	os.	od.
200 faggots		14s.	od.

£10 6s. od. (averaging 4s. od. a week).

Rent free.
Gets coat from employer every alternate Christmas.
Gets pair trousers from employer every alternate Christmas.
Gets blanket and flannel every alternate Christmas.
Cast-off dress for gowns for children.

(b) Family of two parents and five children from Child Okeford, Dorset.

Wages	15s.	od. a week
One Week's Expenditure		
Rent	2s.	6d.
Ten loaves at 5d.	4s.	2d.
¼ lb of tea		6½d.
2 lb of sugar		6d.
½ lb of butter		7d.
2 lb of cheese		9d.
½ gallon of oil		4d.
Soap		3d.
Soda		2d.
Meat	1s.	6d.
Coal		7d.
Clothing club		6d.
Slate and loan club		6d.
Salt &c.		1d.
Sundries		3d.
Total	13s.	2½d.

Appendix B
Condition of the Peasantry in
Dorset in 1846

From the reports of *The Times* Special Correspondent.

25 June 1846 (p. 3)
'In pursuance of the duty assigned me, I shall today lay before you the
result of my inquiries in Stourpain, a parish about two miles distant from
Blandford, and forming part of the district to which public attention has
been drawn.

'The first feature which attracts the attention of a stranger on entering the
village, is the total want of cleanliness which pervades it. A stream, composed
of the matter which constantly escapes from pigsties and other receptacles
of filth, meanders down each street, being here and there collected into
standing pools, which lie festering and rotting in the sun so as to create
wonder that the place is not the continual abode of pestilence – indeed the
worst malignant fevers have raged here at different times ...

'Another fruitful source of misery as well as immorality, is the great
inadequacy of the number and size of the houses to the number of the
population, and the consequently crowded state of their habitations, which
in Dorsetshire generally, and in Stourpain particularly, afford the most limited
accommodation. It is by no means an uncommon thing for the whole family
to sleep in the same room, without the slightest regard to age or sex, and
without a curtain or the slightest attempt at separation between the beds.
In one instance which came under my notice, a family, consisting of nine
persons, occupied three beds in the same bedroom, which was the only one the
house afforded. The eldest daughter is twenty-three years of age, the eldest son
twenty-one. I am enabled to give you the dimensions of the room into which
these nine persons are nightly crammed. It is 10 feet square, not reckoning two
small recesses by the sides of the chimney, about 18 inches deep ...

'The rents of these hovels vary, with few exceptions from 1s a week up
to £3 and even £4 per annum; but it should here be stated that the rents
of all cottages belonging to the chief landed proprietor have lately been
considerably reduced ...

'The want of proper ventilation in these houses must be to the last degree
detrimental to the health of the inhabitants; the atmosphere, especially to
an unpractised nose is almost insupportable. It is perhaps worthy of remark
that dishes, plates, and other articles of crockery, seem almost unknown;
there is, however, the less need for them, as grist bread forms the principal,
and I believe only kind of food which falls to the labourer's lot. In no single
instance did I observe meat of any kind during my progress through the
parish. The furniture is such as may be expected from the description I

have given of the place – a rickety table and two or three foundered chairs generally forming the extent of the upholstery. Want, famine, and misery are the features of the village ...

2 *July 1846 (p. 6)*

'Perhaps the most effectual way of laying before your readers the real condition of the district will be to give the usual amount of the labourer's wages, the rent he pays for his cottage, and other such information as I have been enabled to collect throughout those parishes I have visited. I will commence the dreary list with Spetisbury, a parish situate about three miles from Blandford ... In this parish the wages have lately been raised from 7s to 8s; out of this sum, however, 1s per week is deducted for rent, so that 7s in money is all that finds its way to the pocket of the labourer. Here the cottages are for the most part let with the farms, so that, with respect to the labourer the farmer may be considered as a kind of "middleman". This, in a district where house accommodation is so scarce, gives the farmer a most undue advantage over his servant, as it is in his power upon the slightest disagreement between them, either on the score of wages or any other subject, at once to deprive him of the shelter of a roof, thus compelling him to seek refuge in the nearest town, and perhaps forcing upon him the necessity of walking two, four, and even six miles to and from his work each day. In the back streets of Blandford, I am credibly informed that there are living at this present time as many as 90 labouring families, who have been driven into the town by reason of the impossibility of procuring dwellings in the country ...

'In the parish of Sturminster Marshall, things wear a worse aspect. Here wages do not exceed 7s, and out of this [the labourer] has often to pay £3 or £4 [per annum], and sometimes even more, for his rent. The truck system also prevails here to a most shameful extent. In one instance a farmer, who occupies a considerable number of acres in the parish, at the end of the week, instead of paying his men in money, gives to each man a ticket, which is taken to the shop of his (the farmer's) mother, and then exchanged for provisions and other such necessaries as the labourer stands in need of. To use his own phrase, "he is paid across the counter." In some instances here the labourer has a small allotment of potato ground, for which I think the general price 1s 6d per "lug" ... In Winterbourne Zelston the labourer's wages are 7s, out of which he has to pay rent, the amount of which varies from 1s per week up to £3 10s per annum. Here "grist" is generally 6s per bushel, and it is a privilege of the carter to be allowed to take it at 5s In some instances the labourer has his potato ground rent-free; in some other cases he is allowed a certain number of "lug" provided he will agree to take a like quantity at the rent of 1s per lug, or £8 per acre ...'

Appendix C
The Labourer's Daily Life

From: Richard Jefferies, *The Toilers of the Field* (London 1892), 80–92.

'In the villages there is almost sure to be one or more cottages which carries one's idea of Lilliputian dwellings to the extreme. These are generally sheds or outhouses which have been converted into cottages. I entered one not long since which consisted of two rooms one above and one below, and each of these rooms could not have measured, at a guess, more than six feet across. I had heard of this place, and expected to find it a perfect den of misery and wretchedness. No such thing. To my surprise the woman who opened the door was neatly clad, clean, and bright. The floor of the cottage was of ordinary flag-stones, but there was a ceiling whitewashed and clean. A good fire was burning in the grate – it was the middle of winter – and the room felt warm and comfortable. The walls were completely covered with engravings from the *Illustrated London News*. The furniture was equal to the furniture of the best cottages, and everything was extremely clean …

'The ordinary adult farm labourer commonly rises at from four to five o'clock; if he is a milker, and has to walk some little distance to his work, even as early as half-past three … At six he goes to breakfast, which consists of a hunch of bread and cheese as the rule, with now and then a piece of bacon, and as a milker he receives his quart of beer. At breakfast there is no hurry for half an hour or so; but some time before seven he is on at the ordinary work of the day …

'The time of leaving off work varies from half-past five to half-past six. At ordinary seasons the men leave at six; but in haymaking or harvest time they are expected to remain till the job in hand that day is finished, often till eight or half-past. This is compensated for by a hearty supper and almost unlimited beer. The women employed in field labour generally leave at four, and hasten home to prepare the evening meal. The evening meal is the great event of the day. Like the independent gentleman in this one thing, the labourer dines late in the day. His midday meal; which is the farmer's dinner, is his luncheon. The labourer's dinner is taken at half-past six to seven in the evening, after he has got home, unlaced his heavy and cumbrous boots, combed his hair, and washed himself. His table is always well supplied with vegetables, potatoes, and particularly greens, of which he is peculiarly fond. The staple dish is, of course, a piece of bacon, and large quantities of bread are eaten. It is a common thing now, once or twice in the week, for a labourer to have a small joint of mutton, not a prime joint, of course, but still good and wholesome meat … Instead of beer, the agricultural labourer frequently drinks tea with his dinner – weak tea in large quantities. After the more solid parts comes a salad of onions or lettuce ... After dinner, if it is the season of the year, they go out to the allotment and do a little work for themselves, and then, unless the alehouse offers irresistible attractions, to bed. The genuine agricultural labourer goes early to bed. It is necessary for him, after the long toil of the day, on account of the hour at which he has to rise in the morning ...

'Some of the cottagers who show a little talent for music combine under the leadership of the parish clerk and the patronage of the clergyman, and form a small brass band which parades the village at the head of the Oddfellows or other benefit club once a year. In the early summer, before the earnest work of harvest begins, and while the evenings begin to grow long, it is not unusual to see a number of the younger men at play at cricket in the meadow with the more active of the farmers. Most populous villages have their cricket club, which even the richest farmers do not disdain to join, and their sons stand at the wicket.

'The summer is the labourer's good season. Then he can make money and enjoy himself. In the summer three or four men will often join together and leave their native parish for a ramble. They walk off perhaps some forty or fifty miles, take a job of mowing or harvesting, and after a change of scenery and associates, return in the later part of the autumn, full of the things they have seen, and eager to relate them to the groups at the crossroads or the alehouse. The winter is under the best circumstances a hard time for the labourer. It is not altogether that coals are dear and firewood growing scarcer year by year, but every condition of his daily life has a harshness about it. In the summer the warm sunshine cast a glamour over the rude walls, the decaying thatch, and the ivy-covered window ... Mud floors are not so bad in the summer; holes in the thatch do not matter so much; an ill-fitting window-sash gives no concern. But with the cold blasts and ceaseless rain of winter all this is changed ... The rain comes through the hole in the thatch (we are speaking of the large class of poor cottages), the mud floor is damp and perhaps sticky. If the floor is of uneven stones, these grow damp and slimy. The cold wind comes through the ill-fitting sash, and drives with terrible force under the door. Very often the floor is one step lower than the ground outside, and consequently there is a constant tendency in rainy weather for the water to run or soak in ... Inside the draught is only one degree better than the smoke. These low chimneys, overshadowed with trees, smoke incessantly, and fill the room with smother. To avoid the draught, many of the cottages are fitted with wooden screens, which divide the room, small enough before, into two parts, the outer of which, towards the door, is a howling wilderness of draught and wet from under the door; and the inner part close, stuffy, and dim with smoke driven down the chimney by the shifting wind.

Here the family are all huddled up together close over the embers. Here the cooking is done, such as it is. Here they sit in the dark, or in such light as is supplied by the carefully hoarded stock of fuel, till it is time to go to bed, and that is generally early enough. So rigid is the economy practised in many of these cottages that a candle is rarely if ever used. The light of the fire suffices, and they find their beds in the dark.'

Appendix D
Calendar of Farm Labour:
Monthly Operations on the Farm

From: John C. Morton, *Handbook of Farm Labour*, London 1861.

'*January*: Drainage operations; carriage of manure to heaps in fields, also of lime and marl, also of grain to market; threshing grain for sale; ploughing, probably the last of the stubbles for root crops; applying clay and marl, carrying lime, &c.; attendance on cattle and sheep; road and fence mending; top-dressing pastures.

'*February*: Preparing for and sowing spring wheat, beans, and peas towards the end of the month; continuance of all works of carriage, viz. manures, lime, &c.; purchase of manure and seeds, and carriage home; marketing of grain and fat stock; attendance on feeding and breeding cattle, sheep, and swine; gathering stones off the meadows which are to be mown.

'*March*: Finishing sowing wheat, peas, beans; preparation of land for and sowing oats, barley, carrots, grass, clover, vetches; potato cultivation and planting; preparation of land for mangold-wurzel, turnips, cabbage, flax; turning manure heaps in the field and yard, for use in the cabbage or mangold-wurzel field; threshing, if necessary, for marketing or for straw; attendance on fatting and breeding stock of all kinds; marketing; mowing-fields to be cleaned, harrowed, rolled, and shut up.

'*April*: Finishing sowing oats, barley, carrots, grass, and clover seeds; also potato planting, and, if possible, mangold-wurzel sowing; sowing sainfoin, vetches, flax; cleaning out yard and carrying to field all the manure for turnip fields; horse hoeing wheat, and possibly beans and peas; attendance on breeding and feeding stock of all kinds.

'*May*: Finishing sowing of mangold-wurzel; transplanting cabbage; preparation of land for turnips; horse and hand hoeing grain crops; also carrots and parsnips and early-planted potatoes; cutting and carrying green rye and vetches. Cattle fed in houses or turned out to pasture; sheep in pastures; sheep-shearing.

'*June*: Sowing turnips; horse and hand hoeing mangold-wurzel, carrots, parsnips, beans, cabbages, potatoes; preparing land still for turnips, rape, &c. Attendance on cattle and sheep in pastures; sheep-shearing; haymaking.

'*July*: A last horse hoeing of carrots and parsnips; finishing sowing turnips as a main crop; sowing rape and mustard; mowing clovers and meadows; haymaking; harvesting peas and winter beans; ploughing and sowing turnips and rape, after rye and vetches; pulling flax when ripe enough; horse and hand hoeing turnips and mangold-wurzel; carriage of tiles, road material, &c. for autumn and winter use; also of lime for use on either clover or corn stubble.

'*August*: Wheat, barley, oat, bean harvest; finishing haymaking; horse hoeing turnips and mangold-wurzel; ploughing and scarifying stubbles; finishing sowing turnip and rape after vetches or corn crop.

'*September*: Corn harvest; autumn cultivation; ploughing clovers (after in some cases carrying manure on them) for wheat; sowing trifolium on com stubbles.

'*October*: Finishing corn harvest; preparation for and sowing wheat, rye, winter beans, winter vetches; harvesting potatoes, swedes, and mangold-wurzel; autumn cultivation of stubbles; carrying and application of lime, also of manure, on fields for root crops. Folding sheep on turnips.

'*November*: Wheat sowing; finish harvesting swedes, mangold wurzel, carrots, potatoes; continue carrying manure on to stubbles and ploughing them in; also ploughing clover and grass lands for oats; threshing grain for market and for straw. Attendance on cattle in stalls, and sheep on turnips in the field. Road mending, draining, chalking, marling.

'*December*: Wheat sowing in favourable weather. Continuing ploughing stubbles, and finishing ploughing lea for oats; threshing and marketing; carriage of manure to field. Attendance on fattening stock in stalls, yards, and fields.'

Appendix E
Workhouse Life in the Country

From: Mrs Brewer, 'Workhouse Life in Town and Country' in *Sunday at Home,* August 1890.

'The agricultural unions are a striking contrast to those in the metropolitan and manufacturing districts – the numbers are far less, while the space for each person is often greater. The views from the windows, instead of miles of roofs and chimney-pots, are often quite beautiful. Most of them too have large gardens of flowers, vegetables and fruit, and these mean a great deal to the inmates – pure air, and a variety of vegetables for the midday meal, stewed fruit for the children, and plenty of flowers in the day and workrooms, in the school-rooms and in the wards – turning what would be otherwise bare and cheerless into an atmosphere of perfume and brightness.

'The gardens mean also better employment than oakum picking for the men, and pleasanter walks for the old women than the crowded hot streets of our towns.

'Of course, in a certain way, all workhouses are much alike, and the inmates live much in the same fashion, but as one gets accustomed to the life within their walls it is easy to note a vast improvement in the comfort and happiness of the poor people where the master and matron are kind and sympathetic, and where they interpret the law on the side of gentleness rather than severity.

'First, then, to Cirencester Union, which occupies seven acres of land on the outskirts of the town, half a mile from the railway station, and stands in the midst of gardens.

'We found ourselves at the gate at half-past ten in the morning, and while waiting for admission noted the printed order that the inmates are allowed to see their friends on Mondays and Fridays, from one o'clock till four, and on no other occasions, except under special circumstances ...

'As the district is purely agricultural, the inmates are chiefly of that class. The average wage of the day labourer is nine shillings a week; and as it is a matter of impossibility that the man and wife can bring up a family and save out of this for old age, even if they do get a nice little cottage and bit of garden for five pounds a year, it is but natural that they should end their days here, when work fails them through old age or sickness.

'There were many more old men than women in the house the day we were there; and we heard from the matron that the old women can postpone their coming in for weeks or even months by the variety of work they can put their hands to – whereas the men can do but one kind of work, and when that fails all is over with them. Those, not agricultural labourers, who find themselves paupers, have as a rule arrived at this condition through drink.

'The children here, as at other workhouses, are almost all illegitimate. The orphans, twelve at present, are boarded out in the villages round about ...

'We found everything spotlessly clean but very bare. Take the boys' day-room for example, which had stone floor, bare walls and two forms for furniture, their play-yard outside being equally bare; there was an absence of pictures and games, or of anything that would afford the slightest amusement.

'We were exceedingly pleased with the schoolroom, its thirty scholars and gentle little schoolmistress, the daughter of the master and matron. The children looked happy and industrious; their sewing, writing, and spelling were good. The chaplain who lives in the town comes once a month to give religious instruction.

'As a rule, the children are docile and easily managed.

'For the infirmary there is a trained nurse under the authority of the matron; she has a sitting-room and bedroom, and a bell communicating with her apartments hangs in each sick ward ...

'The old people breakfast on porridge and bread, while the infirm, the laundry women and the wardswomen have bread, butter, tea, milk and sugar and at night, all except the children, have tea.

'In the kitchen the inevitable pea-soup was being prepared for dinner for all the inmates, except the children, who were going to have rice and milk. A pound and a half of meat goes to the gallon of water; but it so happens that now and then they boil a large quantity of beef, and then the liquor is used instead of water, and with the addition of vegetables an exceedingly good soup is made.

'The dining hall is of fair size, and here all take food together in the presence of a superintendent; and here on Sundays the chaplain holds service.

'I think the food is very good and varied and well cooked. Two days in the week they have boiled bacon and two vegetables, two days meat and two vegetables, two days pea-soup, and another day beef and potatoes. The average cost per head for maintenance and clothing is 3s 8½d a week.

'They deal with the casuals on the Berkshire system, which is that the tramp obtains from the police a pass with his name and age written on it together with his destination. This he takes to the union, and on his leaving the master fills in the name of the next union on the direct route to his destination, and also the places on the road where he may get bread. So, if a man comes with a brand new ticket, or one showing he is out of his proper route, he is deprived of his liberty for a day and made to work, as he is considered a loafer. Of course the men do what they can to circumvent this, tearing up their tickets whenever they get a chance, and sometimes the lane outside is strewn with torn-up tickets.

'The employment given is stone-breaking, oakum-picking, and gardening.

'The casuals are lodged in cells, each of which has a bell, and on its being rung a red indicator outside the door falls down, and is at once clearly seen by the person in charge.'

Appendix F
Female Labourers:
The Bondagers of Northumberland

From: Vol. 21 of the Munby Diaries at Trinity College Cambridge and quoted by permission of the Master and Fellows of Trinity College.

August 1863
'*Area of Employment*. Bondagers are in general use all over Northumberland, and in parts of Cumberland also. They are fewest

about Newcastle; they increase and become universal as you go north and west from thence: they are most numerous in the country about *Wooler.* They are to be seen all down the vale of the Tweed, on the Scotch side as well as the English; and that is their northern limit. The line of country from Hexham by Morpeth and Alnwick to Wooler is said to be about the best for seeing them, especially if you take the cross roads. There are many of them at the farms along the coast.

'*Sex and Age.* Bondagers are always *women:* there seems to be no such thing as a male bondager. And they are all young, & unwed: a girl may be bondaged at ten years old, and there are stout strapping bondagers of thirty: but a married woman, apparently, is hardly ever a bondager; unless the hind's wife may sometimes act as one.

'*Hiring and Wages.* The hind is the farmer's servant, and the bondager is the servant of the hind, which he is bound to keep for his master's use. She is hired by him at the statute fairs, yearly or half-yearly: is fed and housed by him, and paid wages at the rate of eightpence a day or £12 a year; though she has more in harvest time. But often she is his own daughter; and then he saves her wages. If not, she is the daughter of labouring parents living in some neighbour village.

'*Kinds of Work.* The bondager is strictly a servant in husbandry: she is hired to do outdoor work, and that only. If there is nothing to do in the fields, she often helps to do the dirty work of her master's house or her master's master's; just as at Halton I saw the bondager busy at the washtub: but she is not bound to such trivial tasks: she may lounge about like a lad & whistle or snooze, until she be ordered afield. Once afield she is put to any thing, except ploughing and ditching. She takes up potatoes: she hoes turnips: she cleans the land of weeds and stones: she harrows at times: she leads the team and drives the cart: she spreads muck in the furrows and stands on the midden and loads the dung cart: she cleans out the byre and the pig stye, aided sometimes by a boy: she makes hay of course: she binds corn, and she reaps with the sickle, three women reaping down an acre per diem. But reaping machines are coming in fast; and then she tents the machine.

'*Times of appearing.* The best times of year for seeing bondagers are, the statute fairs at *Whitsuntide* and *Martinmas* in the market towns; and, to see them at work, *June* and *July,* when they are all out hoeing turnips, especially in the district about Wooler; and late *August* or early *September,* when harvest is going on. I indeed saw very few: but that was owing to the weather. Constantly I asked, whether the bondagers would be out harvesting today? and constantly was told that it was "too wet". This however did not mean that it was too wet for the girls to be at work, but simply that the corn was not dry enough to be meddled with. And it was explained to me that a farmer likes to have his wenches under bondage, because then he can send them afield to hoe or dig in all weathers, and they can't shirk it.

'*Numbers*. On the small farms, about the Wall, there is often but a single hind, who has one or two bondagers. The large farms of the Wooler country employ, I am told, six or eight hinds apiece, so that one farm may have sixteen or twenty bondagers. In any case the bondagers work in gangs, either by themselves or under a male overseer. Every farm seems to have besides its bondager, an ordinary farm maidservant, who sometimes works in the fields as well as about the house.

'*Dress*. The bondager wears a rough straw bonnet tilted over her eyes, with sometimes a kerchief underneath; a short cotton frock; a big apron of sackcloth, or a smock; and stout hobnailed boots and woollen stockings.

'*Education*. They tell me that bondagers can generally read a bit, but cannot write. As to this however I can yet form no opinion.

'*Generally*. Every one has told me, that although on the large farms it is often hard to find as many girls for bondagers as you want, the system is in full vigour, & is approved. "And the wenches like it, bless you Sir: they know they're a deal better off than in a town-place. It's healthier for 'em, & freer, and they earn more money, too,"… it has at least three advantages; it leaves the married women to their home duties; it trains up the wenches to be hardy and lusty and familiar with outdoor ways; and it keeps up a wholesome protest against the molly coddlers, to see a whole countryful of stout lasses devoted to field-labour only; not taking it as a parergon in the intervals of housework …'

Appendix G
Rates of Weekly Cash Wages of Agricultural Labourers*

Authority	year	1 s. d.	2 s. d.	3 s. d.	4 s. d.	5 s. d.	6 s. d.	7 s. d.	average s. d.
Commission on Wages and Poor Rates, 1824. Poor Law Commissioners, 1834.	1824	11 6	10 3	8 10	7 8	8 4	10 1	8 11	9 6
Purdy, 'Earnings of Agricultural Labourers', Journal of the Royal Statistical Society, 1861.	1833	11 1	12 3	9 8	8 9	10 4	11 10	10 4	10 8
Caird, English Agriculture in 1850–51. 'Returns of Wages, 1830–36' and 'Returns of Agricultural Wages, 1860–61 and 1869'.	1837	12 2	11 6	9 7	8 1	9 3	10 8	10 4	10 3
	1850–51	12 2	10 1	8 4	7 9	8 8	9 1	7 10	9 7
Hasbach, English Agricultural Labourer.	1860–61	12 3	12 6	10 4	9 7	10 7	11 10	11 1	11 7
See preceding entry. Commission on the Employment of Women and Children in Agriculture, 1867–9. T. Kebbel, The Agricultural Labourer (2nd ed. 1893).	1867–71	15 1	13 4	11 4	10 6	11 7	11 8	11 0	12 5
Little, Royal Commission on Labour: The Agricultural Labourer, Vol 5, Pt I, 1894.	1879–81	16 2	14 5	13 4	12 4	13 0	13 10	12 6	13 9
Wilson Fox, First Report on Wages, Earnings and Conditions of the Agricultural Labourers, 1898.	1892–93	16 5	15 2	12 6	11 8	12 4	12 10	11 10	13 4
	1898	16 10	16 2	13 10	12 7	13 0	14 10	11 11	14 5

Divisions

1 Cumberland, Westmorland, Northumberland, Durham, Yorkshire, Lancashire, Cheshire.
2 Derby, Nottingham, Lincolnshire, Rutland, Leicester.
3 Warwick, Worcester, Stafford, Shropshire, Hereford, Gloucester.
4 Somerset, Cornwall, Devon, Dorset, Wiltshire.
5 Cambridge, Bedford, Huntingdon, Northampton, Hertford, Buckingham, Oxford.
6 Hampshire, Sussex, Kent, Surrey, Middlesex, Berkshire.
7 Essex, Suffolk, Norfolk.

*Adapted from: C. S. Orwin and B. I. Felton, 'A Century of Wages and Earnings in Agriculture' in Journal of the Royal Statistical Society of England, Vol. 92 (1931), 233.

NOTES

Chapter 1

1. Evans, *Ask the Fellows*, 239.
2. Mr D. Thomas of Lambourn, Berkshire, in correspondence with the author, January 1975.
3. Hobsbawm and Rudé, *Captain Swing*, 117.
4. Hobsbawm and Rudé, *Captain Swing*, 262–3.
5. Howitt, *Rural Life*, I, 286.
6. *Reports of Special Assistant Poor Law Commissioners on the Employment of Women and Children in Agriculture*, 20–21.
7. Savage, *Rural Housing*, 56–7.
8. Thirsk, *English Peasant Farming*, 333.
9. Evans, *Where Beards Wag*, 124.
10. Hertford MSS. *re.* Agricultural Children Act, 1873, at Warwickshire Record Office, CR.114A/765.
11. Fremantle MSS. D/FR. 133/13, at Buckinghamshire Record Office.
12. Thompson, *Lark Rise*, 46. The Rules for Servants at Chesterton Farm are at the Museum of English Rural Life, Reading, D.67/34.
13. *First Report of the Royal Commission on the Employment of Children, Young Persons and Women in Agriculture*, Report by the Hon. E. Stanhope on Lincolnshire, Nottinghamshire and Leicestershire, 74.
14. 'Bourne', *Change in the Village*, 82–3.
15. Thirsk, *Peasant Farming*, 315–16.
16. Census Return for Epworth for 1871, at National Archives, RG.10.4725.
17. Howell, 'Agricultural Labourer in Nineteenth Century Wales', 262.
18. Census Returns for Kidland and Linbridge for 1871, at National Archives, RG.10.5196.
19. Emery, *Oxfordshire Landscape*, 172.
20. Verinder, 'Agricultural Labourer', in Galton, ed., *Workers on their Industries*, 170–71. Verinder noted that in Wiltshire 'out of 2,958 cottages in 45 parishes, 1,660 were found to be tied, and the case of Norfolk is probably nearly as bad.'
21. Evans, *Where Beards Wag*, 116.
22. Census Return for Kingham for 1871, at National Archives, RG.10. 1456.
23. Everitt, *Rural Dissent*, 20–36. For details of life at Ardington and Lockinge see M. A. Havinden, *Estate Villages*, Reading 1966, 70.
24. Reminiscences of Mr Wilkinson are preserved at Oxfordshire Record Office. The Essex example is derived from the Reminiscences of Old People preserved at Essex Record Office, T/Z 25/ 172.

25. Reminiscences of Mr Fred Green of Sibford, Museum of English Rural Life, D.68/53.
26. *First Report of the Royal Commission on the Employment of Children, etc. in Agriculture*, Report by Henry Tremenheere on Cumberland and Westmorland, 141.
27. Rose, *Good Neighbours*, 129–30.

Chapter 2
 1. *Royal Commission on Labour: The Agricultural Labourer*, Report by Mr C. Chapman on the Thame Union of Oxfordshire/ Buckinghamshire, 55; Sun Insurance Records at Guildhall Library, MS, 11,937, Vols. 272,490 and 527; Horn, *Victorian Country Child*, 200.
 2. See, for example, Thresh, *Housing of the Working Classes* 8, at Essex Record Office; and *Royal Commission on Labour*, Mr A. J. Spencer's Summary Report, 15.
 3. Thresh, *Housing of the Working Classes*, 9.
 4. Purser, *Our Ilmington*, 9.
 5. *Royal Commission on Labour*, Report by Mr C. Chapman on the Atcham Union of Shropshire, 136.
 6. Mrs M. N. Dowrick of Coombe, St Austell, Cornwall, in correspondence with the author, January/February 1975.
 7. *Within Living Memory*, 22.
 8. 'Bourne', *Change in the Village*, 22.
 9. *Cheshire Village Memories*, 56, 108.
10. Heath, *English Peasantry*, 65.
11. Old People's Reminiscences, at Essex Record Office, T /Z 25/508.
12. Rider Haggard, *Rural England*, I, 282–3.
13. *Reports of Special Assistant Poor Law Commissioners on the Employment of Women and Children in Agriculture*, 242.
14. *Sixth Report of the Medical Officer of the Privy Council*, 245, 249.
15. Memories of John Boaden (1828–1904) of Cury, written in 1902. I am indebted to Mr John Boaden of North Harrow for allowing me to use these.
16. Morris, *British Workman*, 17. The reminiscence concerns William Blades, born in 1839 at Nafferton in Yorkshire, who was hired out as a farm servant at the age of eight.
17. Information provided by Mr Hare's grandnephew, Mr Edmund Esdaile, in correspondence with the author, January 1975.
18. Fox, 'Agricultural Wages in England and Wales', 142.
19. Reminiscences of Old People, at Essex Record Office, T/Z 25/930.
20. Labour Books of Mr John Butler, in Museum of English Rural Life, Reading, DOR. 5/3/1–2.
21. Farm Labour Accounts of G. Hyatt of Snowshill, at Gloucestershire Record Office, D.2267. A.8.
22. *Within Living Memory*, 14–15.
23. *Life and Experiences of a Warwickshire Labourer*, 9, at Warwickshire Record Office.
24. *Within Living Memory*, 16–17.
25. Evans, *Horse in the Furrow*, 75.
26. Thompson, *Lark Rise*, 19; see also *Royal Commission on Labour*, Report by Mr Wilson Fox on the Glendale Union, 104.
27. Reminiscences of Old People, at Essex Record Office, T/Z 25/930.
28. Martin, *Shearers and Shorn*, 92.

29. The Minute Books of the Long Buckby Co-operative Society are preserved at Northamptonshire Record Office, SL. 396.

30. *Within Living Memory*, 27. Both pedlars and hawkers had to be duly licensed, and those who omitted this formality could be convicted for the offence before the petty sessional courts. For the pedlar a licence cost £1 a year in the earlier Victorian years but only 5s from 1871, while the hawker's licence of £4 a year was reduced in 1888 to £2.

31. Swinford, 'History of Filkins', 15–16.

32. *Life in Our Villages*, 147.

Chapter 3

1. Horn, *Victorian Country Child*, 56–61 for a detailed examination of the school attendance laws. See also Horn, 'Agricultural Children Act of 1873', 34–5.

2. Pershore School Attendance Committee Minute Book at Worcester Record Office, 409:251:22.

3. *First Report of the Royal Commission on the State of Popular Education in England*, Pt I, 175. Hereafter cited as *Newcastle Report*.

4. *Newcastle Report*, Pt II, 57.

5. Sellman, *Devon Village Schools*, 121.

6. Calculated from *Clergy Visitation Returns for the Archdeaconry of Oxford in the Year* 1854, Oxfordshire Record Society, Vol. XXXV, 1954.

7. Reminiscences of Old People, at Essex Record Office, T /Z, 25/21 3.

8. Atkinson, *Forty Years in a Moorland Parish*, 46–7.

9. Memories of John Boaden of Cury (1828–1904) consulted by permission of Mr John Boaden.

10. *Reports of Special Assistant Poor Law Commissioners on the Employment of Women and Children in Agriculture*, 153.

11. *First Report of the Royal Commission on the Employment of Children, Young Persons and Women in Agriculture* evidence submitted by the Revd James Fraser, 197.

12. Spelsbury School Log Book at Oxfordshire Record Office T/Sl.48/i.

13. *Newcastle Report*, Pt. I, 258.

14. Sellman, *Devon Village Schools*, 110–11.

15. Sneyd-Kynnersley, HMI, 56–9.

16. *Report of the Board of Education for 1900–01*, Report by HMI Henderson on small rural schools.

17. Johnson, *Derbyshire Village Schools*, 174.

18. Rose, *Good Neighbours*, 115–16.

19. Minutes of the Committee of Council on Education 1843–44, report by the Revd H. W. Bellairs on schools in the Western District 111. The Report was written in February 1845.

20. Bromsberrow School Log Book, at Gloucestershire Record Office, S.62.

21. Rose, *Good Neighbours*, 116–17.

22. Ashby, *Changing English Village*, 352.

23. *Newcastle Report*, Pt II, 99.

24. Simon, Education *and Labour Movement*, 141.

25. Finedon Boys School Log Book, at Northamptonshire Record Office: see, for example, entry for 18 January 1881.

26. Sellman, *Devon Village Schools*, 63–4.

27. *Within Living Memory*, 107.

28. Ashby, *Joseph Ashby*, 20–21.

29. Ashby, *Joseph Ashby*, 23.
30. Sellman, *Devon Village Schools*, 5.
31. Tweedy, 'Recollections of a Farm Worker', 3.

Chapter 4
   1. Howitt, *Rural Life in England*, I, 157.
   2. *Royal Commission on Labour: Report on the Swaffham Union*, 69, and *Report on the Wantage Union*, 66.
   3. *Reminiscences of William Clift*, 26.
   4. Evans, *Farm and Village*, 110-11.
   5. *First Report of the Royal Commission on the Employment of Children, Young Persons and Women in Agriculture*, Evidence attached to the Revd James Fraser's Report, 202.
   6. Morris, *British Workman*, 17.
   7. Weekly Labour Account Book of Audley End Park Farm, Essex, at Essex Record Office, D/DBy a.303.
   8. *Royal Commission on Labour: Report on Pewsey Union, Wiltshire*, 38.
   9. Rose, *Good Neighbours*, 17-18.
  10. Jefferies, *Toilers of the Field*, 93.
  11. Labour Book of Mr John Butler of Launceston, Blandford, at Museum of English Rural Life, Reading, DOR. 5.3.
  12. Dairy agreement, at Dorset Record Office, MK/29.
  13. Kitchen, *Brother to the Ox*, 125.
  14. Evans, *Farm and Village*, 99.
  15. Labour books of John Butler, at Reading, DOR. 5.3.1.
  16. Reminiscences of F. W. Brocklehurst, at the Museum of English Rural Life, D. 72/1/1–6.
  17. *Royal Commission on Labour: Report on the Glendale Union*, 120.
  18. *Royal Commission on the Employment of Children, etc. in Agriculture*, Report by Mr Henley on Northumberland, 53–4.
  19. Munby Diaries, Vol. 16, entry for 7 October 1862, 123-4. The Munby Diaries have been quoted by kind permission of the Master and Fellows of Trinity College, Cambridge, where they are preserved.
  20. Munby Diaries, Vol. 16, entry for I October 1862, 74.
  21. Reminiscences of Mrs Florence Davies (nee Stowe) at the Bodleian Library, Oxford.
  22. Randell, *Sixty Years a Fenman*, ed. Porter, 23.
  23. *Reminiscences of William Clift*, 64.
  24. Swinford, 'History of Filkins', and Evans, *Where Beards Wag All*, 237.
  25. The Hall Farm Harvest Agreement is preserved at Museum of English Rural Life, Reading, CAM. 1.1.1.
  26. Collins, *Sickle to Combine*, 7.
  27. Mr Frank Wensley in correspondence with the author January 1975.
  28. Thompson, *Lark Rise*, 258-9.
  29. Donovan Thomas in correspondence with the author January 1975.
  30. Morgan, 'Place of Harvesters' in Samuel, ed., *Village Life and Labour*, 58.
  31. Day, *Glimpses of Rural Life*, 25.
  32. Munby Diaries, Vol. 25, entry for 3 July 1864, 261.
  33. *Reports of Special Assistant Poor Law Commissioners on the Employment of Women and Children in Agriculture*, 134.
  34. Lewis, ed., *Old Days in Kent Hop Gardens*, 22–4.
  35. Quoted in *Pershore: A Short History* (Anon.), 74.

36. The Log Books of Pershore National School and Pinvin School are preserved at Worcestershire Record Office, WR.10.IDF and WR.10.2ER, respectively.
37. 'Agricultural Gangs', 174.
38. *Sixth Report of the Children's Employment Commission*, Report by Mr F. D. Longe, 2.
39. 'Agricultural Gangs', 179.
40. 'Agricultural Gangs', 180.
41. *Sixth Report of the Children's Employment Commission*, 103.
42. 'Agricultural Gangs', 182–3.
43. Reminiscences of Old People, at Essex Record Office, T/Z. 25/311.
44. Tweedy, 'Recollections of a Farm Worker', 2.
45. Rules of Service on Chesterton Farm, preserved at the Museum of English Rural Life, Reading, D.67/34.
46. Verinder, 'Agricultural Labourer', in Galton, ed., *Workers on their Industries*, 161–2; and 'Among the Agricultural Labourers with the "Red Vans"', *English Land Restoration League Report*, 1894 (at Bodleian Library Oxford), 16–17.
47. Rider Haggard, *Rural England*, I, 113–14.
48. *Royal Commission on Labour*, Report on the Swaffham Union, 85.

Chapter 5

1. The Census Return for Mapledurham for 1851 is preserved at the National Archives, H.O. 107. 1691. The craftsmen in Halwell are listed in Saville, *Rural Depopulation*, 23.
2. *Report of the 1871 Census of Population*, Pt I, and *Report of the 1901 Census*.
3. Rose, *Good Neighbours*, 91–2.
4. Arch, *Story of His Life*, 63.
5. Evans, *Where Beards Wag All*, 236; see also Ready, *Countryman on the Broads*, 72.
6. *Royal Commission on Labour*, Report by Roger C. Richards on the Bromyard Union in Herefordshire, 77, 80.
7. Samuel, 'Village Labour', in Samuel, ed., *Village Life and Labour*, 5.
8. Horn, 'Child Workers in the Pillow Lace and Straw Plait Trades', 799.
9. Sun Insurance Company Records at Guildhall Library, London, MS.11,937, Vol. 272. For an example of a tradesman borrowing from neighbours there is Isaac Besley of East Hendred in Berkshire who borrowed £400 from a farmer in the nearby village of Milton at rate of interest of 5 per cent, in 1834. In 1835 the mortgage was assigned to a Wantage draper. Besley's property included paintshops, a smith's forge, etc. I am indebted to the late Mr Harrison of East Hendred for a sight of these documents.
10. Ashby, *Changing English Village*, 226.
11. *Cheshire Village Memories*, 96.
12. Accounts of F. Robbins with George Amos, blacksmith, of Weston-sub-Edge, at Gloucestershire Record Office, D.2267A/2.
13. Accounts of J. Gabb, blacksmith, of Falfield, at Gloucestershire Record Office, D.2708.
14. Steer, ed., *Memoirs of Gaius Carley*, 20.
15. Evans, *Horse in Furrow*, 203.
16. Reminiscences of the Pitstone blacksmith from my late husband's family, who lived at nearby Ivinghoe. See also Pierce, 'Village Life in Hampshire, 23.
17. Rose, *Good Neighbours*, 41–2.
18. Evans, *Horse in Furrow*, 209.

19. Brill, *Life and Tradition in Cotswolds*, 54.

20. Sturt, *Wheelwright's Shop*, 17–19.

21. *Within Living Memory*, 99.

22. Records of the Fleming family of Gaydon, 1826–1863, at Warwickshire Record Office, CR 1088/1.

23. Reminiscences of Alec Walter, plowright, from Shalbourne, Wiltshire, at Museum of English Rural Life, D.68/82, 8.

24. Rose, *Village Carpenter*, 36–7.

25. Account books of the Bennett family, carpenters, of Wortley, Gloucestershire, D.689/ 4.

26. Day, *Glimpses of Rural Life*, 25.

27. Sun Insurance Company Records at the Guildhall, MS.11,937, Vols, 272 and 527; and Wray, *Pitstone Windmill*, 4.

28. Evans, *Farm and Village*, 131.

29. Horn, *Victorian Country Child*, 24.

30. Reminiscences of Mr A Gardner sent to me by Mr G. Gardner of Wellesbourne, December 1974; and Allwood, *Third and Fourth Generation*, 4–5.

31. Census Return for Earl's Barton, at National Archives, RG.9.951; and for Grendon, RG.9.951. For comments on the shoemakers see Wright, *Romance of Shoe*, 292, and *British Almanac and Companion*, 1861, 18.

32. *Fourth Report of the Children's Employment Commission*, Evidence, 135–6.

33. Wright, *Romance of Shoe*, 172–3. For an account of the various production processes see also P. Head, 'Boots and Shoes', in Aldcroft, ed., *Development of British Industry*, 163, 166.

34. Census Return for Finedon, at National Archives, RG.10.1500; and Finedon Girls' School Log Book entries, at Northamptonshire Record Office.

35. *Fourth Report of Children's Employment Commission*, xxxiv.

36. Bates, *Vanished World*, 14.

37. *History of National Union of Boot and Shoe Operatives 1874–1957*, 25 and 202–3.

38. *Royal Commission on Agriculture*, Reports of Investigators: Buckinghamshire, 13.

39. Sparkes, *English Country Chair*, 30; and Woods, *Rural Industries*, 105.

40. Tansley, 'On the Straw Plait Trade', 72.

41. Horn, 'Buckinghamshire Straw Plait Trade', 52.

42. *Victoria County History of Oxfordshire*, 2, Oxford 1907, 252.

43. Quoted in Palliser, *History of Lace*, 389–90.

44. *Factory and Workshops Commission*, Pt. I, Appendix D, No. 77, 173.

45. Report of the Inspectors of Factories for the Six Months Ending 30 April, 1874, 11.

46. *Factory and Workshops Commission*, 173.

47. Grey, *Cottage Life*, 81–2.

48. Eland, *In Bucks*, 98.

49. *Second Report of the Children's Employment Commission*, Evidence, 202.

50. The Log Book of Ivinghoe School is preserved at Buckinghamshire Record Office, E/LB/116/1.

51. Reproduced in Razzell and Wainwright, ed., *Victorian Working Class*, 17. See also Horn, *Victorian Country Child*, 109–11, for description of glovemaking, and 'Among the Agricultural Labourers with the "Red Vans"', *Report of the English Land Restoration League*, London 1894, 15, in Bodleian Library, Oxford, for the slop trade.

52. Jefferies, *Hodge and His Masters*, II, 43. See also *First Report of the Royal Commission on the Employment of Children, Young Persons and Women in Agriculture*, 75, 78.

Chapter 6

1. Horn, 'Agricultural Labourers' Trade Unionism', Appendix G.
2. Hasbach, *History of English Agricultural Labourer*, 224.
3. Caird, *English Agriculture 1850–51*, 511.
4. Hunt, *Regional Wage Variations*, 15.
5. Hunt, *Regional Wage Variations*, 19; and *Report on the Wages and Earnings of Agricultural Labourers*, 28.
6. Horn, 'Agricultural Labourers' Trade Unionism', Appendix G.
7. Horn, *Joseph Arch*, 28.
8. See Ditchley Estate Wages Books, at Oxfordshire Record Office, DIL/I/e/2e.
9. Fox, 'Agricultural Wages in England and Wales', 328; and Labour book of farm at Wereham, Norfolk, 1855–77, at Museum of English Rural Life, Reading, NORF.11/4/1.
10. Wages Book for Hackwood Estate at Hampshire County Record Office – entry for December 1873, 11M 49/69/1. At the same time the Estate allowed pensions of 2s a week to former employees. Wages Book for Ditchley Estate, entries for February 1872 and July 1872, at Oxfordshire Record Office, DIL/I/e/2e.
11. Dent, 'Present Condition of English Agricultural Labourer', 351.
12. Rider Haggard, *Rural England*, 1,249.
13. Samuel, 'Quarry roughs: life and labour in Headington Quarry 1860–1920' in Samuel, ed., *Village Life and Labour*, 179–81, and information from my late brother-in-law, Ian Horn.
14. Information from Mrs M. N. Dowrick of Coombe, St Austell, Cornwall, in correspondence with the author, January/February 1975.
15. Munby Diaries at Trinity College Cambridge, Vol. 22, 24 Munby described one of the girls as being 'perched… on the gate, with thick hobnailed boots, a short lindsey skirt, a tattered jacket and an old shapeless brown wideawake, under which short yellow locks fell all about her bronzed face… and she carried a stout switch, too'.
16. *First Report of the Royal Commission on the Employment of Children, Young Persons and Women in Agriculture*, Evidence, 299.
17. Selley, *Village Trade Unions*, 20; and Marlow, *Tolpuddle Martyrs*, 223.
18. *Illustrated London News* VIII (14 February 1846), 114.
19. National Archives, H.040.56.
20. Horn, *Joseph Arch*, 18–19.
21. Horn, ed., *Agricultural Trade Unionism in Oxfordshire 1872–81*, 132. Full accounts of the early movement among the labourers can be found in Horn, *Joseph Arch;* Groves, *Sharpen the Sickle!*; Dunbabin, *Rural Discontent*.
22. Horn, *Agricultural Trade Unionism in Oxfordshire 1872–81*, 28 – extract from Oxford District Minute Book for 7 May 1872.
23. Dunbabin, *Rural Discontent*, 77.
24. Horn, 'Agricultural Trade Unionism and Emigration, 1872–1881', 92–7.
25. Farm accounts of John Butler of Dorset, at Museum of English Rural Life, Reading, DOR.5.3.2; Wages Books for the Ditchley Estate at Oxfordshire Record Office, DIL.I/e/2d–e; Audley Park End Farm Accounts, at Essex Record Office, D/DBy.A.267.
26. *Labourers' Union Chronicle*, 4 October 1873.

27. Dunlop, *Farm Labourer*, 147.

28. Horn, *Agricultural Trade Unionism in Oxfordshire 1872–81*, 69.

29. Orwin and Felton, 'A Century of Wages', 246.

30. Springall' *Labouring Life*, 105.

31. *English Labourers' Chronicle*, 28 November 1885.

32. 'Among the Suffolk Labourers with the Red Van'; see also Horn, 'The Warwickshire Agricultural and General Workers' Union 1893–97'.

33. Reminiscences of Charles Slater of Barley, near Royston, Herts., at Museum of English Rural Life, D.71 /8,32.

34. Heath, 'The Rural Revolution', *passim*.

35. Ashby, *Joseph Ashby*, 186–7.

Chapter 7

1. 'William Plastow's Story', in Harman, ed., *Countryside Mood*, 151.

2. 'William Plastow's Story', 151.

3. Gibbs, *Cotswold Countryman*, 144. The book was first published in 1898 under the title of *A Cotswold Village*.

4. *Midland Free Press*, 18 April, 1885, for an account of a reading room at Great Easton in Leicestershire. For an account of the club at Combe in Oxfordshire see *Life in Our Villages by the Special Commissioner of the Daily News* (George Millin), London 1891, 90.

5. Ashby, *Changing English Village*, 374–5.

6. Arch, *Story of His Life*, 34.

7. *Reminiscences of William Clift*, 98.

8. Kilvert, *Kilvert's Diary*, ed. William Plomer, 211.

9. Morris, *British Workman*, 15.

10. *Leicester Chronicle and Leicester Mercury United*, 14 August 1869.

11. Kitchen, *Brother to the Ox*, 60–65.

12. Reminiscences of Charles Slater of Barley near Royston, Hertfordshire, at Museum of English Rural Life, Reading, D.7 1 / 8.

13. Rose, *Good Neighbours*, 94–5; and information from my late brother-in-law, Ian Horn.

14. Fuller, *West Country Friendly Societies*, 21.

15. Accounts of Swanbourne Club Feast held on 28 May 1844 in Fremantle MSS., Buckinghamshire Record Office, D/FR. 125/ 13. The society was started in November 1843 and was still in existence in the 1890s. On 14 December 1843, the incumbent, who was the treasurer, submitted the rules for Sir Thomas Fremantle's approval, 'under the fear that they may not have met with your final approval'.

16. Williams, *Wiltshire Village*, 235.

17. Fuller, in *West Country Friendly Societies*, p. 110, quotes this verse.

18. *Leicester Chronicle and Leicestershire Mercury United*, 17 August 1878. For a discussion of quarrels in the harvest field see also Morgan, 'The Place of Harvesters in Nineteenth-Century Village Life', in Samuel, ed., *Village Life and Labour*, 36.

19. Springall, *Labouring Life*, 71.

20. Ashby, 'A Harvest Home', 527. Ashby wrote under the pen-name of J. A. Benson.

21. Fuller, *West Country Friendly Societies*, 155.

22. Hardy, *Under the Greenwood Tree*, London Papermac P.62, 1968, 55, 58.

23. *Within Living Memory*, 35.

24. *Within Living Memory*, 52–3.

25. Hole, *English Custom*, 101.

26. Quoted in Green, *History of English Agricultural Labourer*, 47.

27. Hole, *English Custom*, 16. See also Horn, *Victorian Country Child*, 158–9.

28. Marshall, *Fenland Chronicle*, 200–201.

29. Material on Hiring Fairs at Museum of English Rural Life, Reading, D68/53.

30. Kitchen, *Brother to the Ox*, 98.

31. See Hiring Fair material at Museum of English Rural Life, D68/53.

32. Skinner, *Facts and Opinions Concerning Statute Hirings*, 7–8 (in British Library of Political and Economic Science at the London School of Economics).

33. Quoted in Bovill, *English Country Life 1780–1830*, 57.

34. Sanger, *Seventy Years a Showman*, Fitzroy ed., London 1966, 135–7. The book was first published in 1910.

35. Purser, *Our Ilmington*, privately published in New Zealand 1966, 4.

36. Mr Thomas in correspondence with the author, January 1975.

37. 'Bourne', *Change in the Village*, 49.

Chapter 8

1. Pugh, ed., *Letter-Books of Wilberforce*, 125.

2. Ashby, *Changing English Village*, 331.

3. Clergy Visitation Returns for Peterborough Diocese for 1875, at Northamptonshire Record Office; and Clergy Visitation Returns for Oxford Diocese for 1860, at Oxfordshire Record Office, Oxford, MS.Oxf. Dioc.Pp.d. 180.

4. 'Rebecca', 154.

5. Horn, *Victorian Country Child*, 133.

6. See, for example, school records for Souldern National School, Oxfordshire, at the National Society headquarters in London.

7. Thompson, *Lark Rise*, 191–2.

8. *Clergy Visitation Returns for the Archdeaconry of Oxford in the Year 1854*, Oxfordshire Record Society, Vol. XXV, 1954, 28 and 104.

9. Clergy Visitation Returns for the Peterborough Diocese for the year 1875, at Northamptonshire Record Office.

10. Clergy Visitation Returns for the Peterborough Diocese for the year 1875, at Northamptonshire Record Office.

11. Thompson, *Lark Rise*, 229.

12. McClatchey, *Oxfordshire Clergy 1777–1869*, 166.

13. Plomer, ed., *Kilvert's Diary*, 177, 191, 194.

14. Hillyer, *Country Boy*, 33–4.

15. Munby Diaries, Vol. 25, entry 22 May 1864 (at Trinity College, Cambridge); and Tyrell, *Countryman's Tale*, 105.

16. Clergy Visitation Returns for the Peterborough Diocese for the year 1872.

17. Jefferies, *Hodge and His Masters*, I, 165, 167.

18. Clergy Visitation Returns for the Oxford Diocese for 1860, at the Oxfordshire Record Office, Oxford, MS.Oxf.Dioc.Pp.d.180.

19. Clergy Visitation Returns for the Oxford and Peterborough Dioceses, respectively, for 1875.

20. Horn, ed., *Agricultural Trade Unionism in Oxfordshire, 1872–81*, 138.

21. *Within Living Memory*, 65.

22. Thompson, *Lark Rise*, 228.

23. Russell, *Schools and Education in Lindsey*, Part 3, 97.

24. *First Report of the Royal Commission on the Employment of Children, Young Persons and Women in Agriculture*, Evidence attached to Mr F. H. Norman's Report on Northamptonshire, 437, 446.
25. Reminiscences of Charles Slater of Barley at Museum of English Rural Life, Reading, D71/8, 10.
26. Everitt, *Pattern of Rural Dissent*, 65–6.
27. Ashby, *Joseph Ashby*, 81–2.
28. Tyrell, *Countryman's Tale*, 194–5.
29. Martin, *Shearers and Shorn*, 77.
30. *Within Living Memory*, 68.
31. Tyrrell, 'Methodist Vans: Gospel Heralds to the Villages', 170–75.
32. Martin, *Shearers and Shorn*, 77.
33. Russell, *Schools and Education in Lindsey*, Pt 4, 80.
34. Clergy Visitation Returns for the Peterborough Diocese for 1875.
35. Armstrong, ed., *Armstrong's Norfolk Diary*, 97.
36. The whole affair is discussed in Ronald Fletcher, *The Akenham Burial Case*, London 1974.
37. Armstrong, *Armstrong's Norfolk Diary*, 171.
38. Ashby, *Changing English Village*, 337; Taylor, 'Hodge and his Parsons; 361, 362.
39. Horn, *Joseph Arch*, 211.

Chapter 9

1. Chadwick, *Report on Sanitary Condition of Labouring Population*, 223–7.
2. *Supplement to the 55th Annual Report of the Registrar General of Births, Deaths and Marriages in England*, xxxii.
3. Streatfeild, ed., *Day Before Yesterday*, 251.
4. Rose, *Good Neighbours*, 137–8.
5. Springall, *Labouring Life*, 59.
6. Horn, *Victorian Country Child*, 184.
7. Jessopp, *Arcady*, 148–9.
8. The Rules of the Butleigh Friendly and Benefit Society are preserved at the Museum of English Rural Life, Reading, D69/69. The society was established in 1832 and was still in operation in 1893.
9. Fuller, *West Country Friendly Societies*, 57–8.
10. Bicester Union, Weekly Medical Returns by District Medical Officers, IVII, Oxfordshire Record Office.
11. Grey, *Cottage Life*, 164.
12. Diaries of the Reverend W. C. Risley at the Bodleian Library, Oxford, MS.D.D. Risley CI.3/39.
13. Grey, *Cottage Life*, 177–8
14. Mid-nineteenth century medical recipes and cures at Gloucestershire Record Office, D269C.F. 17
15. '*I Walked by Night*' by the King of the Norfolk Poachers, ed. H. Lilias Rider Haggard, 15–17.
16. Corbett, *History of Spelsbury*, 260, 267.
17. Cobbe, 'Workhouse Sketches', 456.
18. Swete, *Cottage Hospitals*, 170.
19. Basingstoke Village Hospital documents at Hampshire Record Office 8M.62/70.
20. Report of the Stansted Mountfitchet District Nursing Association for 1891, at Essex Record Office, T/P.68/24/1.

21. Minute Book of the Burnham District Nursing Association 1892–1935, at Buckinghamshire Record Office, DN/31 /1.
22. *Report of the Select Committee on Medical Relief*, 105.
23. *Return of Poor Relief (Expensive Medicines) for 1876*, and *Circular Letter from the Poor Law Board*, 33.
24. Hungerford District Medical Officer's Relief Book, G/H.7/1, at Berkshire Record Office. Kingsclere Union Medical Relief Book 1872–76, at Hampshire Record Office, PL/III/ 11/36.
25. Kingsclere Union Medical Relief Book.
26. For the later Hungerford cases see Hungerford District Medical Officer's Relief Book G/H.7/5.
27. Horn, *Victorian Country Child*, 182–3; see also Lambert, 'A Victorian National Health Service', 14.
28. Cornish, *Reminiscences of Country Life*, 34.
29. *Supplement to the 29th Annual Report of the Local Government Board: Report of the Medical Officer for 1899–1900*, 40.
30. *Royal Commission on Labour: The Agricultural Labourer*, 133.
31. Account Book of Thomas Parr, carpenter/wheelwright for 1847–66, at Museum of English Rural Life, Reading, D.66/21.
32. Account Book for the Bennett family, carpenters, at Gloucestershire Record Office, D/689/4. There are several volumes in this series.
33. Fuller, *Friendly Societies*, 87.
34. *Royal Commission on the Aged Poor 1893–94*, Evidence of Mr Ward, Q.15696–Q.15701, see also Appendix IX, 989–91.

Chapter 10

1. Edwards, *From Crow-Scaring to Westminster*, 22.
2. Longmate, *Workhouse*, 95.
3. *General Report of the 1871 Census of Population*, Pt II, lxix. For the census returns for the workhouses quoted see at the National Archives for Kendal RG.10.5286; Blandford R.G.10. 1978; Thame RG10.1431 and Wantage RG.10.1267.
4. Anstruther, *Scandal of Andover Workhouse*, 151–2.
5. Alresford Petty Sessional Court Minute Book at Hampshire Record Office, 22M60.A, Item XP6.
6. Digby, 'Labour Market and Continuity of Social Policy', 78.
7. Rose, 'Allowance System under New Poor Law', 614, 618.
8. CuttLe, *Legacy of Rural Guardians*, 47–8.
9. Martin, *Shearers and Shorn*, 64.
10. Minute Book of the Alcester Board of Guardians, Warwickshire Record Office.
11. The Minute Books of the Wantage and Abingdon Poor Law Unions are preserved at the Berkshire Record Office.
12. Webb, *Poor Law History*, Pt II, 351.
13. Booth, *Aged Poor*, 226.
14. *Royal Commission on the Aged Poor*, Q.6715.
15. *Royel Commission on Aged Poor*, Evidence of Mr J. H. Thomas, clerk to the Guardians of the Carnarvon Union, Q.7358.
16. Samuel, *Memoirs*, 15. For the Warwickshire details see *Select Committee on the Aged Deserving Poor*, Q.2712.
17. *Within Living Memory*, 76.
18. Entry in the Horspath Branch Minute Book at the Bodleian Library, Oxford, MS.Top.Oxon.d.533.

19. Marsh, *Changing Social Structure*, 159.

20. Booth, *Aged Poor*, 134.

21. Newdegate MSS. Pensioner's Book, probably for Arbury, 1871–1882 at Warwickshire Record Office CR.136/A.(549).

22. I am indebted to the late Mr Harrison of East Hendred for a sight of this Will.

23. *Royal Commission on Labour: The Agricultural Labourer*, Report on the Thame Union, 58–9.

24. Entry in the Horspath Branch Minute Book at the Bodleian Library, Oxford.

25. Webb, *Poor Law History*, 358.

26. Webb, *Poor Law History*, 361.

27. Cuttle, *Rural Guardians*, 42.

28. The Minute Books of the Banbury Poor Law Union are preserved at the Oxfordshire Record Office, T/G/l/i/32.

29. Cuttle, *Rural Guardians*, 40–41.

30. The Minute Books of the Wokingham Poor Law Union are preserved at Berkshire Record Office; see also Jefferies, *Hodge and His Masters*, II, 144–5.

31. *Within Living Memory*, 135–7.

32. Chamberlain, 'Old-Age Pension', 728; see also Collins, 'Introduction of Old Age Pensions', 250. For details of percentages of the old in receipt of indoor relief see Booth, *Aged Poor*, 47.

33. Bruce, *Coming of Welfare State*, 141.

34. Holwell, 'Village Baker before 1914'; 142.

Chapter 11

1. *Royal Commission on a Constabulary Force*, 136.

2. *Royal Commission on a Constabulary Force*, 131.

3. *Royal Commission on a Constabulary Force*, 145 and 180.

4. *Royal Commission on a Constabulary Force*, 63.

5. Critchley, *History of Police*, 92–4.

6. Peacock, 'Village Radicalism in East Anglia, 1800–50', in Dunbabin, *Rural Discontent*, 27.

7. Ivinghoe Petty Sessions Minute Book is preserved at Buckinghamshire Record Office, PS/I/M/1 and Henley Divisional Petty Sessions Minute Book is preserved at the Bodleian Library, Oxford, MS.D.D.Henley AXVI, 10.

8. Quoted in Dunbabin, *Rural Discontent*, 62.

9. *Second Report of Select Committee on Police*, Minutes of Evidence, Q.2751.

10. Papers on East Suffolk Police Force, at National Archives, H.O-45.7487 and *Report of the Inspectors of Constabulary for* 1863, 50. East Suffolk had one policeman to every 1,572 inhabitants; this was a rather lower proportion than in other areas – such as West Suffolk, with one to every 1,288 persons, Norfolk with one to every 1,442 and Oxfordshire with one to every 1,474 persons.

11. *Leicester Chronicle and Leicester Mercury United*, 23 July 1870.

12. Dunbabin, *Rural Discontent*, 70; and Kerr, *Bound to the Soil*, 61.

13. Peacock, 'Village Radicalism', 43.

14. Peacock, 'Village Radicalism', 44, and *Select Committee on the Police*, Q.3470.

15. Hudson, *Shepherd's Life*, 165–6.

16. *First Report of Select Committee on Police*, Minutes of Evidence, Q.795.

17. Tobias, *Crime and Industrial Society*, 219.

18. Peacock, 'Village Radicalism', 45.

19. Papers on Riots and Disturbances at National Archives, H.O-40.56.
20. *Second Report of Select Committee on Police*, Q.3579.
21. Trench, *Poacher and Squire*, 154.
22. Quoted in E. W. Bovill, *English Country Life*, 179.
23. Notice preserved at Hampshire Record Office, 8M/62/72.
24. Chester Kirby, 'The Attack on English Game Laws', 23.
25. *Select Committee on Game Laws*, Pt I, Q.6055-Q.6063.
26. Arch, *Story of His Life*, 148–50.
27. Henley Petty Sessions Minute Book, at Bodleian Library, MS.D.D.Henley AXVI, 10: entries for 12 April 1866 and 3 January 1867.
28. Swinford, 'History of Filkins', 14.
29. Ivinghoe Petty Sessions Minute Book, at Buckinghamshire Record Office.
30. Statistics on Game Law cases in *Report of Select Committee on Game Laws*, vii; and *Return of Prosecutions in England under Game Laws* 1857–62, 2.
31. *Judicial Statistics*, Parliamentary Papers 1893–94, CIII.
32. Trench, *Poacher and Squire*, 190.
33. Connell, *Truth About Game Laws*, 37–45.
34. Quoted in Horn, *Victorian Country Child*, 195–6.
35. Quoted in Kerr, *Bound to Soil*, 142–3.
36. Ivinghoe Petty Sessions Minute Book, at Buckinghamshire Record Office.
37. Moreton Petty Sessions Minute Book, at Berkshire Record Office, P/M/2/2.
38. See *First Report of the Commissioners Appointed to Inquire into the Working of the Master and Servant Act 1867 and the Criminal Law Amendment Act*, Minutes of Evidence, 106–9.
39. *Quoted in Tobias, Crime and Industrial Society*, 158.
40. Grey, *Cottage Life*, 127–8.
41. Swinford, 'History of Filkins' 58. Swinford recalled that as soon as the boys started to play cricket, 'the policeman was on our track. We arranged that each should pick up what he could, before running away.'

Chapter 12

1. Horn, *Victorian Country Child*, Kineton 1974, 92.
2. Quoted in Thirsk, *English Peasant Farming*, 323.
3. Cecil, *Life in Edwardian England*, 127.
4. Thompson, *Lark Rise*, 407; see also Orwin and Whetham, *History of British Agriculture 1846–1914*, 317.

BIBLIOGRAPHY

Manuscript Collections

Abingdon Board of Guardians Minute Books. (Berkshire Record Office.)

Alcester Board of Guardians Minute Books. (Warwickshire Record Office.)

Alresford Petty Sessions Minute Books. (Hampshire Record Office.)

George Amos, blacksmith, of Weston-sub-Edge, Accounts of. (Gloucester Record Office.)

Audley End Park Farm Labour Account Books. (Essex Record Office.)

Banbury Board of Guardians Minute Books. (Oxfordshire Record Office.)

Basingstoke Village Hospital MSS. (Hampshire Record Office.)

Bennett family, carpenters, of Wotton-under-Edge, Gloucestershire, Accounts of. (Gloucester Record Office.)

Isaac Besley, blacksmith and wheelwright, of East Hendred, Berkshire, Mortgage documents. (Consulted by kind permission of Mr Harrison of East Hendred.)

Bicester Board of Guardians Minute Books. (Oxfordshire Record Office.)

Bicester Poor Law Union weekly medical returns. (Oxfordshire Record Office.)

John Boaden of Cury, Memories of. (In the possession of Mr J. Boaden of North Harrow.)

Burnham District Nursing Association Minute Book 1892–1935. (Buckinghamshire Record Office.)

Butleigh Friendly Society Rules. (Museum of English Rural Life, Reading.)

John Butler, Farm Labour Books. (Museum of English Rural Life, Reading.)

Census Returns for 1841, 1851, 1861 and 1871. (National Archives.)

Chesterton Farm, Gloucestershire, Rules of. (Museum of English Rural Life, Reading.)

Dairy Agreements. (Dorset Record Office.)

Ditchley Estate Wages Book. (Oxfordshire Record Office.)

Mrs M. N. Dowrick of Coombe, Cornwall in correspondence with author, January/February 1975.

Edmund Esdaile in correspondence with the author, January 1975.

Fleming family, wheelwrights and carpenters, of Gaydon, Accounts of. (Warwickshire Record Office.)

Fremantle MSS. (Buckinghamshire Record Office.)

J. Gabb, blacksmith, of Falfield, Gloucestershire, Accounts of. (Gloucester Record Office.)

G. Gardner of Wellesbourne in correspondence with the author, December 1974.

Hackwood Estate Wages Books. (Hampshire Record Office.)

Hall Farm, Great Wilbraham, Cambridgeshire Harvest Agreements. (Museum of English Rural Life, Reading.)

Henley Petty Sessions Minute Books. (Bodleian Library, Oxford.)

Hertford MSS. (Warwickshire Record Office.)

Hiring Fair MSS. (Museum of English Rural Life, Reading.)

Home Office MSS. (National Archives on Police and Riots and Disturbances.)

Horspath Branch Minute Book of National Agricultural Labourers Union. (Bodleian Library, Oxford.)

Hungerford Poor Law Union Medical Officers' Relief Books. (Berkshire Record Office.)

G. Hyatt, Farm Labour Accounts. (Gloucester Record Office.)

Ivinghoe Petty Sessions Minute Books. (Buckinghamshire Record Office.)

Kingsdere Union Medical Officers' Relief Books. (Hampshire Record Office.)

Long Buckby Co-operative Society Minute Books. (Northamptonshire Record Office.)

Manning Collection on Oxfordshire Folklore, etc. (Bodleian Library, Oxford.)

Moreton Petty Sessions Minute Books. (Berkshire Record Office.)

Munby Diaries at Trinity College, Cambridge. (Quoted by kind permission of the Master and Fellows of Trinity College.)

Newdegate MSS. (Warwickshire Record Office.)

Oxford Diocese, Clergy Triennial Visitation Returns. (Bodleian Library, Oxford.)

Thomas Parr, carpenter/wheelwright, Accounts of. (Museum of English Rural Life, Reading.)

Peterborough Diocese, Clergy Triennial Visitation Returns. (Northamptonshire Record Office.)

Reminiscences of Mrs Florence Davies. (Bodleian Library, Oxford: MS.Top. Gen.c-40.)

Reminiscences of F. W. Brocklehurst. (Museum of English Rural Life, Reading.)

Reminiscences of Fred Green. (Museum of English Rural Life, Reading.)

Reminiscences of old people. (Essex Record Office.)

Reminiscences of Charles Slater of Barley. (Museum of English Rural Life, Reading.)

Reminiscences of Alec Walter, ploughwright. (Museum of English Rural Life, Reading.)

Reminiscences of Arthur Wilkinson. (Oxfordshire Record Office.)

Risley Diaries. (Bodleian Library, Oxford.)

School Log Books. (The relevant county record offices.)

Stansted Mountfitchet District Nursing Association, Report for 1891. (Essex Record Office.)

Sun Insurance Company Records. (Guildhall Library, London.)

George Swinford, 'History of Filkins'. (Bodleian Library, Oxford: MS.Top. Oxon.d-475.)

Donovan Thomas of Lambourn in correspondence with the author, January 1975.

Wantage Board of Guardians Minute Books. (Berkshire Record Office.)

Frank Wensley of Nailsea in correspondence with the author, January 1975.

Wereham, Norfolk, Farm Labour Books. (Museum of English Rural Life, Reading.)

Wokingham Board of Guardians Minute Books. (Berkshire Record Office.)

Official Publications

Aged Deserving Poor, Select Committee on, PP, 1899, VIII.
Aged Poor, Royal Commission on, *PP*, 1895, XV.
Agriculture, Reports of Special Assistant Poor Law Commissions on the Employment of Women and Children in, *PP*, 1843, XII.
Agriculture, First and Second Reports of the Royal Commission on the Employment of Children, Young Persons and Women in, *PP*, 1867–68, XVII; 1868–69, XIII.
Agriculture, Royal Commission on, *PP*, 1919, IX.
Children's Employment Commission, Second, Fourth and Sixth Reports of, *PP*, 1864, XXII; 1865, XX; and 1867, XVI.
Constabulary Force, Royal Commission on, in England and Wales, *PP*, 1839, XIX.
Education, Annual Minutes and Reports of the Committee of Council on, *PP*, 1845, XXXV.
Education, Report of Board of, for 1900–01, *PP*, 1901, XIX.
Education, First and Second Reports of the Royal Commission on the State of Popular Education in England, *PP*, 1861, XXI.
Factory and Workshops Commission, *PP*, 1876, XXIX.
Game Laws, Select Committee on, *PP*, 1846, IX.
Game Laws, Select Committee on, *PP*, 1873, XIII.
Judicial Statistics, Annual Returns of.
Labour, Royal Commission on: The Agricultural Labourer, *PP*, 1893–94, XXXV.
Local Government Board, Supplement to 29th Report of, *PP*, 1900, XXXIV.
Master and Servant Act 1867 and Criminal Law Amendment Act, Report of Commissioners Inquiring into, *PP*, 1874, XXIV.
Medical Officer of the Privy Council, Sixth Report of, *PP*, 1864, XXVIII.
Medical Relief, Report of the Select Committee on, *PP*, 1854, XII.
Police, First and Second Reports of Select Committee on, *PP*, 1852–53, XXV.
Poor Law Board, Circular Letter of (on Expensive Medicines), *PP*, 1867–68, LX.
Poor Relief (Expensive Medicines), Return of, for 1876, *PP*, 1877, LXXI.
Population, Reports of the 1871 and 1901 Censuses of, *PP*, 1873, LXXI, Pts I and II; and 1902, CXVIII and CXX.
Registrar of Births, Deaths and Marriages, Annual Reports of.
Wages and Earnings of Agricultural Labourers, Report on, *PP*, 1900, LXXXII.
(PP=Parliamentary Papers)

Newspapers, etc.
Daily News
Daily Telegraph
Dorset County Chronicle
English Labourers' Chronicle
Illustrated London News
Labourers' Union Chronicle
Leicester Chronicle and Leicester Mercury United
Midland Free Press
Oxford Times
Royal Leamington Chronicle
The Times

Periodicals

'Agricultural Gangs', *Quarterly Review* 123 (1867).

Joseph Ashby (under pen-name J. A. Benson), 'A Harvest Home', *Land Magazine* 2 (May 1898).

Joseph Chamberlain, 'Old Age Pensions', *National Review* 108 (Feb. 1892).

Frances Power Cobbe, 'Workhouse Sketches', *Macmillan's Magazine* III (Apr. 1861).

John D. Dent, 'The Present Condition of the English Agricultural Labourer', *Journal of the Royal Agricultural Society of England* Vol. 7, Second Series, Pt II, No. XIV (1871).

Anne Digby, 'The Labour Market and the Continuity of Social Policy After 1834: The Case of the Eastern Counties', *Economic History Review*, 2nd Series, XXVIII, No. I (Feb. 1975).

A. Wilson Fox, 'Agricultural Wages in England and Wales during the Last Half Century', *Journal of the Royal Statistical Society*, LXVI (1903).

Richard Heath, 'The Rural Revolution', *Contemporary Review*, (Feb. 1895).

John Holwell, 'A Village Baker before 1914', *The Countryman* 80/1 (1975).

Pamela Horn, 'Agricultural Trade Unionism and Emigration, 1872–1881', *Historical Journal* XVII (1972).

Pamela Horn, 'The Warwickshire Agricultural and General Workers' Union, 1893–97', *Midland History* 114 (Autumn 1972).

Pamela Horn, 'The Agricultural Children Act of 1873', *History of Education Journal* 3 (Jun. 1974).

Pamela Horn, 'The Buckinghamshire Straw Plait Trade in Victorian England', *Records of Bucks.* XIXII (1971).'

Pamela Horn, 'Child Workers in the Pillow Lace and Straw Plait Trades of Victorian Buckinghamshire and Bedfordshire, *Historical Journal* XVII/4 (1974).

D. W. Howell, 'The Agricultural Labourer in Nineteenth Century Wales', *Welsh Historical Review* VI (1972–73).

Chester Kirby, 'The Attack on the English Game Laws in the Forties', *Journal of Modern History* IV (1932).

R. J. Lambert, 'A Victorian National Health Service', *Historical Journal* V (1962).

C. S. Orwin and B. I. Felton, 'A Century of Wages and Earnings in Agriculture', *Journal of the Royal Agricultural Society of England* 92 (1931).

G. P. Pierce, 'Village Life in Hampshire', *Hampshire* 214, (Feb. 1962).

'Rebecca' (Anon.), *Quarterly Review* 74 (1844).

Michael E. Rose, 'The Allowance System under the new Poor Law', *Economic History Review*, 2nd Series, XIX, No. 3 (Dec. 1966).

A. J. Tansley, 'On the Straw Plait Trade', *Journal of the Society of Arts* IX (21 Dec. 1860).

Arnold D. Taylor, 'Hodge and his Parson', *Nineteenth Century* 31 (Mar. 1892).

Arthur Tweedy, 'Recollections of a Farm Worker', *Bulletin of the Cleveland and Teesside Local History Society* 21 (Summer 1973).

Charles W. Tyrrell, 'Methodist Vans: Gospel Heralds to the Villages', *Proceedings of the Wesley Historical Society* XXXIX/6 (Oct. 1974).

Printed Books and Pamphlets

Montagu C. Allwood, *The Third and Fourth Generation*, privately printed Wivelsfield Green 1940.

Ian Anstruther, *The Scandal of the Andover Workhouse*, London 1973.

Joseph Arch, *The Story of His Life told by Himself*, London 1898.

'Among the Agricultural Labourers with the Red Vans', *English Land Restoration League Report* 1894 (pamphlet in Bodleian Library, Oxford, and in British Library).

'Among the Suffolk Labourers with the Red Van', *Special Report of the English Land Restoration League for* 1891, London 1891 (pamphlet in Bodleian Library, Oxford, and in British Library).

H. B. J. Armstrong, ed., *Armstrong's Norfolk Diary*, London 1963.

M. K. Ashby, *Joseph Ashby of Tysoe*, Cambridge 1961.

M. K. Ashby, *The Changing English Village 1066–1914*, Kineton 1974.

Revd J. C. Atkinson, *Forty Years in a Moorland Parish*, London 1891.

H. E. Bates, *The Vanished World*, London 1969.

G. A. Beck, ed., *The English Catholics 1850–1950*, London 1950.

Charles Booth, *The Aged Poor in England and Wales*, London 1894.

George 'Bourne' (Sturt), *The Bettesworth Book*, London 1901.

George 'Bourne' (Sturt), *Change in the Village* (first published 1912), London 1955 ed.

E. W. Bovill, *English Country Life 1780–1830*, Oxford 1962.

Edith Brill, *Life and Tradition in the Cotswolds*, London 1973.

Maurice Bruce, *The Coming of the Welfare State*, London 1966 ed.

James Caird, *English Agriculture in 1850–51*,'2nd ed. London 1968.

Gaius Carley, *The Memoirs of*; ed. Francis W. Steer, Chichester 1964.

Edwin Chadwick, *Report on the Sanitary Condition of the Labouring Population of Great Britain* (first published London 1842), new ed. edited by M. W. Flinn, Edinburgh 1965.

Cheshire Village Memories, Cheshire Federation of Women's Institutes, 1969.

Clergy Visitation Returns for the Archdeaconry of Oxford in the Year 1854, Oxfordshire Record Society, Vol. XXV, 1954.

William Clift of Bramley, *Reminiscences of*, Basingstoke 1908.

E. J. T. Collins, *Sickle to Combine*, University of Reading pamphlet, 1969.

J. Connell, *The Truth about the Game Laws*, Humanitarian League Publications, New Series, No.2, London 1898 (in Bodleian Library, Oxford).

Elsie Corbett, *History of Spelsbury*, Oxford 1962.

James C. Cornish, *Reminiscences of Country Life*, London 1939.

T. A. Critchley, *A History of the Police in England and Wales 900–1966*, London, 1967.

George Cuttle, *The Legacy of the Rural Guardians*, Cambridge 1934.

Alice C. Day, *Glimpses of Rural Life in Sussex During the Last Hundred Years*, Kingham, Oxford 1928.

J. P. D. Dunbabin, *Rural Discontent in Nineteenth Century Britain*, London 1974.

O. Jocelyn Dunlop, *The Farm Labourer*, London 1913.

George Edwards, *From Crow-Scaring to Westminster*, London 1922.

G. Eland, *In Bucks*, Aylesbury 1923.

Frank Emery, *The Oxfordshire Landscape*, London 1974.

George Ewart Evans, *The Horse in the Furrow*, London 1960.

George Ewart Evans, *Ask the Fellows Who Cut the Hay*, paperback ed., London 1965.

George Ewart Evans, *The Farm and the Village*, London 1969.

George Ewart Evans, *Where Beards Wag All*, London 1970.

George Ewart Evans, *The Days That We Have Seen*, London 1975.

Alan Everitt, *The Pattern of Rural Dissent: The Nineteenth Century*, Leicester University Department of English Local History Occasional Papers, 2nd Series, NO.4, 1972.

Ronald Fletcher, *The Akenham Burial Case*, London 1974.

Alan Fox, *A History of the National Union of Boot and Shoe Operatives 1874–1957*, Oxford 1958.

Margaret Fuller, *West Country Friendly Societies*, Reading 1964.

Frank W. Galton, ed., *Workers in their Industries*, London 1895.

J. Arthur Gibbs, *Cotswold Countryman* (first published as *A Cotswold Village*, in 1898), Fitzroy ed., London 1967.

F. E. Green, *A History of the English Agricultural Labourer*, London 1920.

Edwin Grey, *Cottage Life in a Hertfordshire Village*, St Albans 1934.

Reg Groves, *Sharpen the Sickle!*, London 1949.

Lilias Rider Haggard, ed., *'I Walked By Night, by the King of the Norfolk Poachers*, 2nd ed., London 1951.

Rider Haggard, *Rural England*, I and II, London 1902.

Thomas Hardy, *Under the Greenwood Tree*, London Papermac, 1968.

R. Harman, ed., *Countryside Mood*, London 1943.

W. Hasbach, *A History of the English Agricultural Labourer*, London 1908.

M. A. Havinden, *Estate Villages*, Reading 1966.

P. Head, 'Boots and Shoes', *The Development of British Industry and Foreign Competition 1875–1914*, ed. D. Aldcroft, London 1968.

Francis G. Heath, *The English Peasantry*, London 1874.

Richard Hillyer, *Country Boy*, London 1966.

E. J. Hobsbawm and G. Rudé, *Captain Swing*, London 1969.

Christina Hole, *English Custom and Usage*, 3rd ed., London 1950.

Pamela Horn, *Joseph Arch*, Kineton 1971.

Pamela Horn, *The Victorian Country Child*, Kineton 1974.

Pamela Horn, ed., *Agricultural Trade Unionism in Oxfordshire 1872–81*, Oxfordshire Record Society, Vol. XLVIII, 1974.

William Howitt, *The Rural Life of England*, I and II, London 1838.

W. H. Hudson, *A Shepherd's Life*, London 1954 ed.

E. H. Hunt, *Regional Wage Variations in Britain 1850–1914*, Oxford 1973.

Richard Jefferies, *The Toilers of the Field*, London 1892.

Richard Jefferies, *Hodge and His Masters* (first published 1880), Fitzroy ed. (Vols. I and II), London 1966.

Augustus Jessopp, *Arcady: For Better for Worse*, London 1887.

Marion Johnson, *Derbyshire Village Schools in the Nineteenth Century*, Newton Abbot 1970.

Barbara Kerr, *Bound to the Soil*, London 1968.

Francis Kilvert, *Kilvert's Diary*, ed. William Plomer, London paperback 1964.

Fred Kitchen, *Brother to the Ox*, London 1963 ed.

Mary Lewis, ed., *Old Days in the Kent Hop Gardens*, West Kent Federation of Women's Institutes, 1962.

Life in Our Villages by the Special Commissioner of the 'Daily News' (George Millin), London 1891.

Norman Longmate, *The Workhouse*, London 1974.

Joyce Marlow, *The Tolpuddle Martyrs*, London 1971.

David C. Marsh, *The Changing Social Structure of England and Wales 1871–1951*, London 1958.

Sybil Marshall, *Fenland Chronicle*, Cambridge 1967.

E. W. Martin, *The Shearers and the Shorn*, London 1965.

D. McClatchey, *Oxfordshire Clergy 1777–1869*, Oxford 1960.

Isaac Mead, *The Life Story of An Essex Lad*, Chelmsford 1923.

R. E. Moreau, *The Departed Village*, Oxford 1968.

Revd M. C. F. Morris, *The British Workman Past and Present*, Oxford 1928.

C. S. Orwin and E. H. Whetham, *History of British Agriculture 1846–1914*, London 1964.

Mrs B. Palliser, *History of Lace*, 2nd ed. London 1902.

A Pattern of Hundreds compiled by members of the Buckinghamshire Federation of Women's Institutes, 1975.

Pershore: A Short History (Anon.), Pershore 1972.

E. H. Phelps Brown, *The Growth of British Industrial Relations*, London 1959.

R. K. Pugh, ed., *The Letter-Books of Samuel Wilberforce 1843–68*, Oxfordshire Record Society Vol. XLVII, 1970.

John Purser, *Our Ilmington*, privately printed Wellington, New Zealand 1966.

Arthur Randell, *Sixty Years a Fenman*, ed. Enid Porter, London 1966.

P. E. Razzell and R. W. Wainwright, ed., *The Victorian Working Class*, London 1973.

Oliver Ready, *Countryman on the Broads* (first published in complete form as *Life and Sport on the Norfolk Broads*, in 1910), ed. I. Niall. Fitzroy ed., London 1967.

Walter Rose, *Good Neighbours*, Country Club ed., London 1969.

Walter Rose, *The Village Carpenter*, Cambridge 1937.

Revd C. Russell, *A History of Schools and Education in Lindsey, Lincolnshire, 1800–1902*, Pt 3 and Pt 4, Lindsey County Council Education Committee 1966.

Viscount (H.) Samuel, *Memoirs*, London 1945.

R. Samuel, ed., *Village Life and Labour*, London 1975.

'Lord' George Sanger, *Seventy Years a Showman*, Fitzroy ed., London 1966.

William G. Savage, *Rural Housing*, London 1915.

John Saville, *Rural Depopulation in England and Wales 1851–1951*, London 1957.

J. W. Robertson Scott, *The Land Problem*, London n.d., *c.* 1914.

Roger R. Sellman, *Devon Village Schools in the Nineteenth Century*, Newton Abbot 1967.

Ernest Selley, *Village Trade Unions in Two Centuries*, London 1919.

Brian Simon, *Education and the Labour Movement 1870–1920*, London 1965.

Revd J. Skinner, *Facts and Opinions Concerning Statute Hirings*, London 1861 (pamphlet at British Library of Political and Economic Science at London School of Economics).

E. M. Sneyd-Kynnersley, *HMI – Passages in the Life of an Inspector of Schools*, London 1908.

Ivan Sparkes, *The English Country Chair*, Bourne End 1973.

L. Marion Springall, *Labouring Life in Norfolk Villages 1834–1914*, London 1936.

Noel Streatfeild, ed., *The Day Before Yesterday*, London 1956.

George Sturt, *The Wheelwright's Shop*, Cambridge paperback ed. 1963 *(see also* George 'Bourne').

Horace Swete, *Handy Book of Cottage Hospitals*, London 1870.

Joan Thirsk, *English Peasant Farming*, London 1957.

Flora Thompson, *Lark Rise to Candleford*, Oxford 1963 ed.

J. C. Thresh, *Housing of the Working Classes in Chelmsford and Maldon Rural Sanitary Districts*, Chelmsford 1891 (pamphlet at Essex Record Office).

J. J. Tobias, *Crime and Industrial Society in the Nineteenth Century*, London 1967.

Charles Chenevix Trench, *The Poacher and the Squire*, London 1967.
S. J. Tyrell, *A Countryman's Tale*, London 1973.
S. and B. Webb, *English Poor Law History* (Pt II), London 1929.
Alfred Williams, *A Wiltshire Village*, London 1912.
Within Living Memory, Norfolk Federation of Women's Institutes 1971.
K. S. Woods, *The Rural Industries Round Oxford*, Oxford 1921.
David Wray, *Pitstone Windmill*, National Trust pamphlet n.d.
Thomas Wright, *The Romance of the Shoe*, London 1922.

Thesis

P. L. R. Horn, 'Agricultural Labourers' Trade Unionism in Four Midland
   Counties, 1860–1900' (Leicester University Ph.D. thesis, 1968).

INDEX

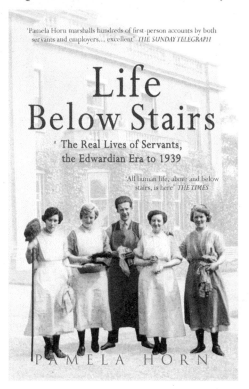